£ 19.99

DS

LETTERS FROM MONGOLIA

LETTERS FROM MONGOLIA

Reginald and Ann Hibbert

The Radcliffe Press

LONDON • NEW YORK

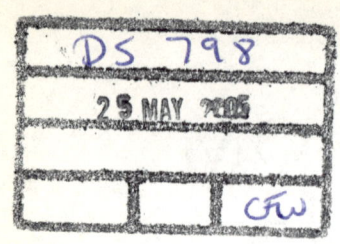
Published in 2005 by The Radcliffe Press
6 Salem Road, London W2 4BU

In the United States and in Canada
distributed by Palgrave Macmillan, a division of St Martin's Press
175 Fifth Avenue, New York NY 10010

ISBN 1 85043 578 2
EAN 978 1 85043 578 5

A full CIP record for this book is available from the British Library
A full CIP record for this book is available from the Library of Congress

Library of Congress Catalog card: available

Typeset in Sabon by Oxford Publishing Services, Oxford
Printed and bound in Great Britain by MPG Books Ltd, Bodmin

Contents

List of Illustrations   vi
Acronyms and Abbreviations   viii
Glossary   x
Map of Mongolian People's Republic   xii
Note on Transliteration and Pronunciation of Mongolian   xiv
Preface   xv

1. A New Posting   1
2. Progress on the Domestic Front   33
3. Ann Settles In   69
4. Trip to the North   112
5. Family Separation   128
6. Yak Hair for the Cavalry   139
7. A Spell in England and Back to Ulan Bator   161
8. Upgrading the Mission   171
9. Party Congress and General Election   195
10. And the Rains Came Down   204
11. Going Home   211

Notes   217
Appendix: Economic Planning and Development   225
Index   247

List of Illustrations

1. The authors on the steps of Ulan Bator Hotel.   6
2. My first call on the foreign minister, Mr M. Dügersüren (right), who was accompanied by the chief of protocol and the head of the second department, responsible *inter alia* for relations with Western countries.   19
3. View from our hotel windows showing Foreign Ministry (with spire) and next to it the Yugoslav embassy. Next to that was the Bulgarian embassy, but it is not in the picture. These buildings are all on Peace Street, the main street of Ulan Bator.   22
4. Sükhbaatar Square with the mausoleum of Sükhbaatar and Choibalsan in front of the government of the Great People's Khural.   29
5. Sükhbaatar.   30
6. In full winter kit in January near Lun Somon, west of Ulan Bator. The cairn of stones is a minor *ovo* at a highpoint in the track. The stones are added by travellers to show respect for the spirits of the place.   31
7. Camels in their full winter coats.   39
8. Milking a mare, with her foal held beside her to help induce the flow of milk.   51
9. A Mongolian family in their *ger*.   79
10. Jane, William and George beside a stone tortoise or turtle that survives with two or three other such remnants on the otherwise desolate site of Kharkhorin, once the principal seat and encampment of the great khans. In the background is the wall of stupas enclosing what remains of the old monastery of Erdeni Dzu.   81
11. Mid-morning break by the Kerulen River.   127
12. Raising water from a well in the Gobi.   147
13. An excursion for the heads of diplomatic missions and their families organized by the Foreign Ministry at Terelj, a holiday camp for senior cadres and meritorious workers in the foothills of the Khentey mountains. The

scene is of a shooting competition, which, to the general
astonishment, was won by Ann.   167
14. Arrival at Ulan Bator station of the once weekly trans-
Mongolia 'express' from Moscow to Peking. Douglas
McAdam is holding the bags and a Queen's messenger is
winding his camera.   172
15. Gandantegchinlen monastery, at that time the one
surviving 'show' monastery in Ulan Bator.   190
16. *Arat* family outside *ger*.   212

Acronyms and Abbreviations

AN-2	round-engine Russian biplane
ATS	Auxiliary Territorial Service
BEA	British European Airways
BOAC	British Overseas Airways Corporation
CC	central committee
CMEA	Council for Mutual Economic Assistance
CMG	Companion of the Order of St Michael and St George
CO	commanding officer
CPR	Chinese People's Republic
CPSU	Communist Party of the Soviet Union
CSCE	Commission on Security and Cooperation in Europe
ENSA	Entertainments National Service Association
ETA	estimated time of arrival
FCO	Foreign and Commonwealth Office
FO	Foreign Office
G	Gwyneth (Ann's sister)
GDR	German Democratic Republic
GPO	General Post Office
GUM	*Gosudarstvenny Universalny Magazine* (State Department Store)
HK	Hong Kong
HM	Her Majesty
HMG	Her Majesty's Government
ICI	Imperial Chemical Industries
Il-14	Short-range transport and passenger aircraft
KLM	*Koninklijke Luchtvaartmaatschappij* (Royal Dutch Airline)
MBFR	mutual and balanced force reductions
MFA	Ministry of Foreign Affairs
MPR	Mongolian People's Republic

MPRP	Mongolian People's Revolutionary Party
OCTU	Officer Cadet Training Unit
PM	prime minister
PRO	Public Record Office
QM	Queen's Messenger
SAS	Scandinavian Airlines System
UB	Ulan Bator
USSR	Union of Soviet Socialist Republics
VIP	very important person
WC	water closet (lavatory)

Glossary

aaruul	dried curd
aimag	province
airag	mild beverage made of fermented mare's milk
arat	shepherd who wanders with his herd
argal	dried dung used as fuel
arkhi	local vodka
ayag	bowl
baatar	warrior or hero
baikhgui	there is nothing
Bogdo Gegen	living Buddha
buudz	steamed dumplings
byaslag	cheese
del	Mongolian gown
dezhurnaya	receptionist
gazik	Russian jeep
ger	tent
gospodin	Mr
gulya	goulash
hainag	cow and yak crossbreed
khadag	ceremonial scarf
khoroo	trading post
khural	legislative or representative body (parliament)
koumiss	an intoxicating fermented or distilled liquor originally made by the Tartars from mare's or camel's milk
lenok	Manchurian trout (*Brachymystax lenok*)
morin hur	horse-headed two-string fiddle
Naadam	national sports' festival
ochir	mace-like object used as symbol of elemental force
ovis ammon	giant wild sheep or argali
ovo	votive pile of stones carrying various adornments
place d'armes	place where a city's defenders assemble

réchaud	camping stove
smetana	sour cream
somon	administrative district
subbotnik	day of voluntary work to clean the country
suutei tsai	milky tea
tadcu	grandfather (Welsh)
taiga	Subarctic coniferous forest
taimen	large Mongolian freshwater fish
tovarich	comrade
tugrik	Mongolian currency
Unen	Truth (leading Mongolian newspaper)
urum	dried cream
uyan	post to which horses are tied
valenki	felt boots
yurt	portable, round, tent-like structure first used by the nomads of Mongolia
zakuski	appetizer course in a Russian meal

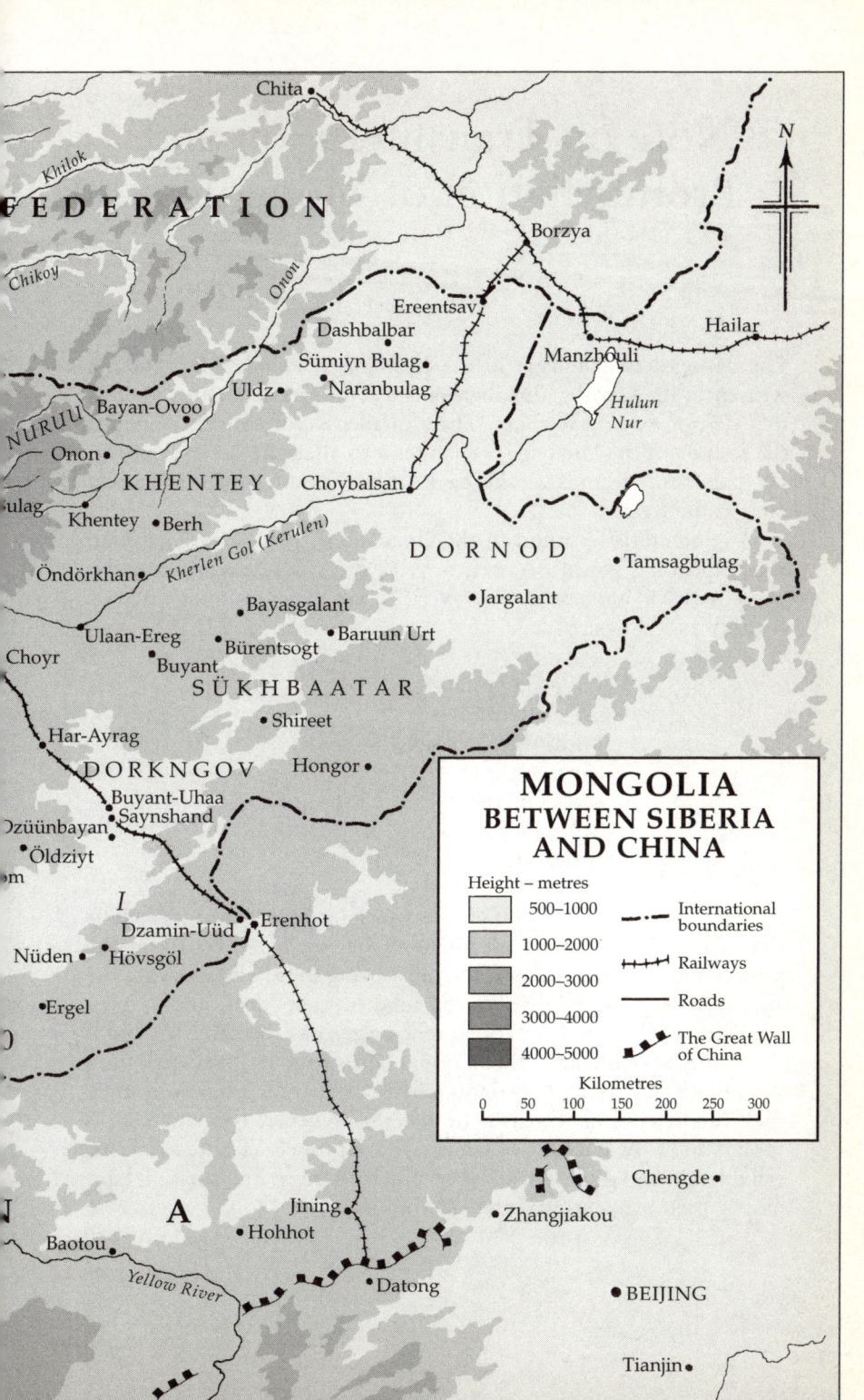

Note on Transliteration and Pronunciation of Mongolian

The Mongolian language in the Mongolian People's Republic is written in the Cyrillic alphabet, plus a few extra letters for sounds that do not exist in Russian. The alphabet is not entirely suited to the sounds of the language, which tend to alternate between somewhat guttural sounds at the back of the mouth and open labial ones at the front.

A characteristic sound of the language is the contrast between short and long vowels. A, e, i, o, y, Y, ø can all be lengthened by being written aa, ee, ii, oo, yy, YY, øø. The pronunciation is roughly as follows:

> a as in bath.
> e as in egg.
> i as the e in scene.
> o as in stop.
> y as in awl.
> Y as in soon.
> ø as in burn.

The name of the capital city has usually been transliterated as Ulan Bator. In fact it is spelt in Mongolian as Ylaan Baatar and is pronounced Awlahn Bahter, the 'ah's being long, and carrying the accentuation. The Mongols' silk robe is spelt 'deel' and is pronounced 'dehl'. The Mongolian tent or *ger* has the same 'e', but a short one. Sookhbaatar, the national hero from 1924, is spelt with the double YY (and is pronounced Sookhbahter), but is usually spelt Sukhebator in English. In general however, the language is spoken in fairly staccato syllables, without much accentuation, the syllables being pronounced very much as they are spelt. I have mostly used conventional transliterations.

Preface

This book is a collection of letters, the letters my wife Ann and I wrote to our parents from Ulan Bator in the years 1964, 1965 and 1966. We were there as the first Western representative to take up permanent residence at the capital of the Mongolian People's Republic. We became members of a diplomatic corps that otherwise consisted entirely of representatives of communist countries from eastern Europe and Asia.

We did not know that our letters were being preserved. During our years of retirement they found their way back to us, with other family relics, from the attics and cupboards of our parents. We have now read them ourselves and find that they make a convincing narrative, undistorted by memory, of a strange experience, perhaps the strangest experience of our diplomatic service career.

The letters have three aspects. They tell the tale of getting to know Mongolia more or less from nothing. They illustrate some of the difficulties for wives and children and family life of overseas service in remote places. They show something of the ingenuity required at both ends to gear the grand and complex machinery of the diplomatic service to the small and simple clockwork by which so miniscule a post as Ulan Bator has to function.

In editing the letters we have naturally omitted a mass of personal and family material. One of the peculiarities of our situation was that the timing of our letters, once a fortnight, was dictated by the Queen's messengers' schedule. As a result, Ann and I were sometimes writing by the same bag about the same events. This has made it expedient here and there to include a sentence or two from one of Ann's letters in one of mine, and vice versa, and sometimes to alter the order of our paragraphs. But such adjustments have been very few. The letters have not been touched up. They give exactly the feel of events as we experienced them at the time.

In a sense the book is written back to front. It does not start with an introduction about Mongolia. It ends with one. Readers will find that it leads them into Mongolia, as we were led, knowing nothing much about it. We hope this will give them a feel for the adventurous nature of our assignment. Towards the end some weightier material is included from a few Ulan Bator dispatches and letters now held at the Public Record Office at Kew. Their PRO reference numbers are given. For those who have a real taste for weight there is a paper in the Appendix giving a short account of the Mongolian People's Republic as a country, a state and an economy. This paper was written in 1967 when I was attached for a sabbatical year to the Chinese Studies Department of Leeds University. Mongolia has changed politically since then, but in the essentials of geography, history, demography and economic resources it cannot have changed. The paper can still serve as a starting point for anyone who wants to think about Mongolia.

When Ann and I went to Mongolia we had been abroad for over six years in Guatemala, Turkey and Belgium. Earlier we had had two spells in London, with two years in Austria in between. Even earlier, in the postwar 1940s, before we were married, I had served for two years in Romania. In London I had first been in the Southeast Asia department of the Foreign Office and later in the Soviet section of the Northern department. There seemed to be nothing in that apprenticeship that marked me out for so odd a posting as Ulan Bator. But I had read Russian at Oxford. The Foreign Office is sometimes like the army if you belong to a minority faith you can be dismissed from church parade and sent on an obscure fatigue. I think that is how we happened on Mongolia.

Reginald Hibbert
Pennal, Gwynedd

1

A New Posting

Our leave in the UK passed pleasantly. In July Ann and I spent ten days getting to know Scotland from the border country to John o'Groats and from east coast to west coast. When we returned to London David Muirhead,[1] the head of the personnel department, invited us to lunchtime drinks on a Saturday. He took me aside and told me that he wanted to nominate me to establish a new resident mission at Ulan Bator, the capital of the Mongolian People's Republic. Would this be acceptable to me? He took care to say that promotion was still very slow: if I took the post I would be promoted to Counsellor straight away. It was not possible to predict when I might be promoted if I did not take it.

I learnt that the Mongolian People's Republic was the old Outer Mongolia, which had been part of the Chinese empire. In the aftermath of the First World War it had broken away from China with the help of the Soviet Red Army and had been set up as a separate state, a people's republic, under Soviet tutelage amounting to control. It had been recognized by China when the communists came to power there. It had been admitted to the United Nations in 1961 as a Soviet-sponsored candidate when an East–West deal was done over new members. The Mongolian government had subsequently expressed a desire to have relationships with countries outside the communist bloc. I wondered why the USA had not stepped forward, given its leading role in east Asia. I was told that Washington was inhibited by its relationship with Chiang Kai-shek, who regarded Outer Mongolia as still belonging to China. Britain had decided to respond to the Mongolian approach and to explore the possibilities of a bilateral relationship with Ulan Bator. Terence Garvey,[2] who had been Chargé d'Affaires at Peking since 1962 (in Chinese jargon he was head of the office for negotiating diplomatic relations), had been nominated as non-resident ambassador to Mongolia in 1963. It had now been decided to go a step further and set up a permanent mission at Ulan Bator. I was being asked to go there and set myself up as resident Chargé d'Affaires. It was obviously going to be a demanding, pioneering assignment. At that time, being completely ignorant about Mongolia, I had no way of knowing what the demands would be.

When David Muirhead and I rejoined our wives, I told Ann briefly what had been proposed. Her reaction was, 'I suppose you refused' (Ann had been hoping for a spell at home). I had to confess that I had not done so. Muirhead told us to think it over and let him have an answer on Monday. It was clear to me that, as I had not already said no, we were going to say yes. I have never asked for a particular posting and never refused one. I think it is best to trust to fate.

The family's life was going to be transformed. William, aged seven, would have to be sent to be a boarder with George. We would see even less of the children than in Turkey. Ann would have to divide her time between the children and me, between England and Mongolia. I would be largely out of touch at the end of a very long and slow communication line.

Nevertheless, we were asked not to tell anyone what was in prospect. The senior board in the FO had yet to give its approval, and the Mongolian government had to be asked to give its consent and to provide accommodation for me. Sir Roderick Barclay[3] at Brussels had already been consulted and had agreed to release me, but no one else was supposed to know. Against this background we returned to Brussels at the end of July.

西藏西藏

Ann to her parents

Brussels, 3 August 1964

The ambassador does not want Reg to go at the beginning of September. This suits us too because it would really be a great nuisance to have to pack up before the end of the children's holidays. The arrangement is therefore that as Jane goes back on 16 September, we shall leave here on 15 September. We shall stay in London until 15 October, when Reg is due to leave. The boys will be with us for a week after Jane goes to school, which I hope will be long enough for me to get William equipped. We are looking round for a small flat: for that month we must be quite self-contained, as we shall have a great number of arrangements to make and things to buy. As regards my coming to housekeep for you, I cannot be free until after 15 October. Until that date I must be free to do what I can to help Reg get off.

After that I shall probably have to find somewhere to live where I can stay with the children through the Christmas holidays. There will be so much packing and repacking that I don't think it will be possible to stay with you all the time. Besides, I am sure it would be much too disturbing for you.

16 August 1964

Jane left yesterday for Spain, in a Caravelle from Brussels to Malaga, a three-hour flight. She comes back on Saturday week.

Our news is not yet official. It is gradually seeping out, and most people in the embassy know about it, but quite unofficially. I think they are still waiting in London to get the approval of the Mongols.

Reg is working very hard to revive his Russian. I have glanced at the Russian alphabet and put it on one side for the time being! I imagine I shall manage to pick up something.

Reginald to Ann's father

Brussels, 2 September 1964

You and Mo will like to know that the news of our destination is no longer confidential. The senior promotions board has approved it. All we need now is a Mongolian visa. We can say that we are going to Ulan Bator if the Mongols will let us in. So far the only reaction from their side has been for the Mongolian ambassador at Peking to say that accommodation is very difficult. Terence Garvey has been told to press hard for a definite answer as soon as possible.

My successor arrives here on the 6th and we are booked to leave on the 15th. On that night we shall all stay at the St Ermin's Hotel near Caxton Hall. Jane goes to school on the 16th and the rest of us move into a flat in the Paragon at Blackheath. So you see, everything has suddenly become very definite.

Ann to her parents

Brussels, 10 September 1964

The business of getting away from here is proving quite a job. Not only all the ordinary problems of clearing up a really very well-established household, but all the business of deciding what one doesn't need for two years and what one could possibly do with in Mongolia. Anyway, somehow we shall be leaving Brussels at eight o'clock on Tuesday morning by train, reaching Victoria at about three if all goes well. We found the flat at Blackheath from an advertisement in *The Times*. I am enclosing a change of address notice so that you can see what we are telling everyone.

I have been hopelessly interrupted in this letter. It is now Friday morning and the packers are here already.

William is in a frightful state of nerves and is driving us all round the bend. I think that George is rather disturbed too but keeps it much more to himself, which is less tiring for the rest of us. Jane being so much more mature is quite capable of coping with this particular emergency. I hope that people will be kind and visit and write to them all while we are away.

西藏西藏

Back in London we had only one month in which to prepare for Ulan Bator. Fortunately we had an adequate base in the Paragon at Blackheath. The children were back at school. We could concentrate on preparations.

We were going to be faced with big difficulties of communication, supply and accommodation. Two Queen's Messengers would arrive from Peking once a fortnight after a meandering journey dropping off diplomatic bags in south and east Asia, and they would return to London in the same way. There would therefore be about a month or more between writing a letter and receiving a reply to it. It would not be possible to rely on the open post service. I would have no radio communication and ciphers, but would be able to receive and send *en clair* cables through the Mongolian post office, should this ever be necessary. There was only one train a week from Peking to Moscow across Mongolia, and one train a week in the opposite direction. There was no air service between Peking and Mongolia. There was a direct flight once a week by Aeroflot from Moscow, via Omak and Irkutsk.

On two or three other days there were flights by Mongolian air-craft between Irkutsk and Ulan Bator. Telephone communication between London and Ulan Bator was reckoned to be impossible and between Ulan Bator and Peking or Moscow uncertain.

As regards accommodation, the Mongolian government had indicated that we would be housed in a hotel. This turned out to be the Ulan Bator Hotel, the only recognizable hotel in the city, built fairly recently by the Chinese and furnished by the Czechs. The aim on the British side was to obtain a separate and adequate house for the mission; but we would obviously have to do time in the hotel while trying to persuade the Mongols to earmark some-thing for us from their exiguous housing stock.

As regards food and drink and other personal supplies we could obtain no clear picture of what awaited us. We put in an order to Ostermann-Petersen at Copenhagen for a few luxury foods, cases of liquor, cigarettes and some toilet articles, Ostermann-Petersen being said to be experienced in dispatching goods on the Trans-Siberian Railway. No one could forecast when the con-signment might arrive.

The FO was having a steel cupboard and other simple items of office equipment, including most importantly a paper shredder, sent from Peking. I was also going to have a Land Rover with a good set of tools and a supply of spares, and I was given a morning of instruction in Land Rover maintenance, which served to brush up my memories of keeping army vehicles running.

The FO was able to provide a report by my old Worcester College friend Brian Stewart[4] who had made a journey home from Peking to London via Ulan Bator, and some reports on his one or two visits there by Terence Garvey, the non-resident ambassador. In the short time available it was difficult to obtain, and even more difficult to find time to read, the few books that give a useful impression of the Mongols. I soon came to understand that there was very little between the present day and the Mongol narrations[5] written in the thirteenth century by the two Franciscan friars, John of Plano Carpini and William of Rubruck, first generation disciples of St Francis of Assisi, who had been sent, the former by Pope Innocent IV and the latter a few years later by St Louis of France, to reconnoitre the Mongol menace, which had already reached Hungary and seemed to threaten western Europe. These friars had reached and resided for short periods at the tented

1. The authors on the steps of Ulan Bator Hotel.

capital of the great Khan, at Karakoram, now Kharkhorin to the west of Ulan Bator (formerly Urga). It seemed to me that I was to be the first representative of a Western monarch and government to reside at the capital of the Mongols since the thirteenth century (not counting the Russians, of course).

I was drawn to the early twentieth-century books of the Scandinavians Sven Hedin and Henning Haslund, the former writing mostly about Inner Mongolia and the latter about the north of Khalkha Mongolia (the present-day Mongolian republic), and one or two books by nineteenth-century missionaries. Then there were the books on modern Mongolia by Charles Bawden of London University and Owen Lattimore, then at Leeds University, both of whom I was able to meet briefly. But the books that had the greatest resonance for me when I grew to know Mongolia a little were the thirteenth-century narrations. There was much in them that, in attenuated form, characterized for me the Mongols of today. I became acquainted with scholarly French, German and American writing on Mongolia only after I had left the country.

I met in Cambridge Dr Lindgren-Utsi who had made extensive ethnographical studies of the Mongols, more particularly in Buratiya in the Lake Baikal region of the Soviet Union, and especially about Shamanism. Her Finnish husband, Utsi, introduced reindeer at Aviemore. She was full of all sorts of fascinating information, but not in a joined-up way as far as my interests were concerned.

Cambridge, in the shape of the Scott Polar Research Institute also provided me with valuable advice about clothing and kit for winter conditions. As a result, Ann and I arrived at Ulan Bator excellently equipped for the winter.

Ann stayed on in London for three months in order to visit the children at school and look after them at half term and in the Christmas holidays. She had no fixed base but stayed mostly with her parents, with excursions to Brighton, Seaford, Cliveden and my parents. It was a very unsettled time.

I left to take up my post with one assistant, Eric Cheyne, a bachelor, who was going to provide my office 'staff'.

西藏西藏

Reginald to Ann

Moscow, 22 October 1964

I do not know whether you knew yesterday that the aircraft left for Copenhagen over an hour late. We missed the connection at Copenhagen. I was put on a KLM aircraft to Stockholm and there caught an SAS Caravelle to Moscow. There was no car to meet me at Sheremetyevo airport, so I took a taxi. The taxi driver lost his way in Moscow and did not know where the embassy was. I remembered it was on the bank of the Moskva River opposite the Kremlin, but my version of the street name was wrong, as it had just been renamed after Maurice Thorez. I finally arrived at 11.00 p.m. Tom Brimelow[6] was out at another airport, meeting his wife and daughter and Violet Conolly,[7] who were arriving from Tashkent after failing to get to Ashkhabad. We finally sat down to borsch and cold chicken and Uzbekistan grapes after midnight and got to bed at half past one.

The best features of the trip were two excellent SAS meals, a marvellous sunset at Stockholm and a brilliant view from the air of Moscow at night. Otherwise it was cloudy all the way.

Today I have been paying calls on ambassadors accredited at Ulan Bator but not resident there and on the Mongolian ambassador in Moscow. I had had five cognacs by lunchtime – fortunately out of little vodka glasses.

This evening Violet Conolly and I went to the Bolshoi to see *Giselle*. It was beautifully danced and badly mimed (too much ham) with a typically Russian mixture of corniness and high drama.

Moscow is much vaster than in 1947 and much improved in outward appearance, though still shabby by Western standards. It is much more human, but it still gives the sharp sensation of being a different world with no obvious common ground with the West and powerful inner forces of its own. The shock of the sensation is increased when you see and hear coloured people (diplomats and students) speaking Russian between themselves.

The weather is very mild: Tom Brimelow has lent me a light coat. I am going to have a look at the Kremlin churches – now restored as museum pieces – tomorrow afternoon. Perhaps I shall be able to buy some postcards, for which I have so far had no time or change. No one in Moscow seems to have any change, a phenomenon that no one can explain.

I hope you have transferred yourself successfully to Pilgrims Lane [Ann's parents' house] and have not been in difficulties over the things I left behind.

26 October 1964

Eric Cheyne and I arrived at Peking dead on time after a good flight. We left Moscow at 10.20 p.m., were given quite a good supper, had 'lights-out' at about midnight and landed at Omsk to refuel at about 1.40 a.m. A blizzard was blowing and there was nothing to be seen in the air terminal. I had had a glimpse of the Urals as we flew over the Sverdlovsk region at 30,000 feet. As we flew on from Omsk the cloud began to clear and we flew into a beautiful dawn at about 3.15 a.m. (Moscow time). We came down at Irkutsk at about 5.30 a.m. (Moscow time) for refuelling and frontier controls, only to find it was 11.30 a.m. on the ground.

They gave us breakfast in the airport restaurant and then flew on over Lake Baikal. Our departure was delayed by the disappearance of a girl belonging to a party of French students. You should have seen the flap among the Russians when they found themselves with an unclaimed passport. Police and Intourist girls scattered to look for her. She was finally spotted sitting on a bench in front of the airport building talking to a Soviet soldier, not 100 yards from the aircraft. The harpies of Intourist descended on her and the soldier literally ran away. She was given a tremendous wigging.

Itkutsk looked like all the worst parts of the Black Country huddled together. From there on it was clear and sunny, white with frost and snow all the way to the Gobi desert. We flew directly over Ulan Bator. It looked like Adapazari with the major part of Ulus put down in the middle, and with miles and miles of open range all round.

The Great Wall of China is very near Peking – only 70 miles or so away – so we were well down as we passed it. China begins in a real sense immediately inside it, with innumerable villages, close set and bushy and surrounded by huge stripy fields, dotted over an immense cultivated plain stretching indefinitely southwards. The contrast between China and the Mongolian lands (Inner and ours) is most striking, as also is the difference between the Mongolian mountains and steppe and the undistinguished scrubby hills of Siberia.

Peking's winter has not yet started and the garden here is still full of flowers – chrysanthemums and poinsettia – which shows how mixed the climate is.

The Garveys are most attentive – too attentive – hosts; but I am very comfortable, and the inscrutable servants press and clean and polish things every time I throw them down. Michael Wilford[8] and his wife are all right once one has disagreed with them forcefully over some minor point in one's arrangements. I told Mrs Garvey I thought Owen Lattimore was shifty, and she turned a pale purple. She is going to take me round the Forbidden City tomorrow.

Two samples of Chinese conversation: (a) *Me*: 'Thank you'; *Chinese official*: 'No thanks'. (b) *Wilford*: 'Hibbert has one, and Cheyne has one too'; *Chinese official*: 'Mr Cheyne is not a diplomat and should not have two' – angry outburst from Wilford!

Could you possibly send Jean Brimelow a box of chocolates via the Moscow parcel bag? I enclose a card to go with it. The

Brimelows were embarrassingly generous hosts. They did not leave me a minute to myself.

You can buy an excellent fur hat at the Ukraine Hotel in Moscow, but only for sterling. They are quite cheap: the trademark is Beriozka. Being with the Brimelows, I had to go to an ordinary Soviet shop and pay in roubles, so I did not get a good one. Eric Cheyne did better.

I do not think the air journey would be too difficult for the children. The Soviet airhostesses are very attentive, and the weariness of the journey can be slept off. But in my case I had to have tea on arrival and talk Mongolian. I slipped into bed at 5.45 p.m., but had to be up again at 7.00 to change for dinner, and I finally got to bed at half past midnight. I am a dutiful houseguest!

Peking, 29 October 1964

I am off to Ulan Bator in an hour and a half. It has been busy here, but not entirely with business. Yesterday Joan Wilford took us to see the Great Wall and the Ming tombs, and I have been eating and drinking fairly continuously. Today I had to eat two lunches, one with the French and one beforehand, arranged at the last moment, with the Mongolian ambassador. At the latter I found myself obliged to make a speech in Russian with no notice whatsoever. Eric Cheyne and I promise ourselves a rest at UB, but we may find ourselves involved in the same sort of thing there.

I look forward to hearing from you in a week or so.

British Embassy, Ulan Bator
31 October 1964
(sent through the open post)

We arrived this morning and are now more or less installed. We have our entire air luggage, our basic office equipment and some commissary stores.

The weather is like the best winter weather in Turkey – frost, a brilliant sun, a bright blue sky and sharp, clear air. If we can soon manage to take over the Land Rover we should be able to begin enjoying it.

Today being Saturday, I shall not be able to begin doing anything until Monday. It is pleasant to have some time to put one's thoughts in order. The only trouble is that after being busy in such a random way for so long, I find myself uneasy when faced with a day of leisure in a place that at this initial moment means nothing to me.

We are eight hours ahead of you here, which means that I get up when you go to bed and have tea when you have breakfast and have coffee after dinner when you have lunch.

I think you are at Brighton or Seaford this weekend; I forget which. When you see them, please give my love to the children and tell them I am having an extraordinary series of dislocated experiences. I shall write to them about it next week.

Our little hotel suite is not too bad. You and I would enjoy it. I think it will be all right here for the children too.

You must let me know when this letter reaches you.

3 November 1964

If I write this letter tonight, mostly about the experiences of getting here, I shall be able to write another letter to you at the weekend when we have the bag for the first time.

Eric Cheyne and I finished our short stay in China by visiting the Great Wall and the Ming tombs. The short stretch of the former, which foreigners are allowed to visit, extends about a quarter mile on both sides of the main road some 80 miles north of Peking. It has been made up like Rumeli Hisar on the Bosporus. You are on the mountains that circle Peking to the north. Looking northwards you see a plain with a lake, which is the beginning of the road to Inner Mongolia (or, to give it its official name, Mongolian Autonomous Region of the Chinese People's Republic). In the grey distance you can see the mountains that are the beginning of the Mongolian plateau.

The Ming tombs, forming a sort of Valley of the Kings for the Ming emperors, are nearer to Peking. They are in various stages of preservation or decay, depending on the whim of the authorities that decide where to have museums. The tumble-down tombs are the most picturesque, reminding me a little of overgrown Maya ruins, but the restored and museumized ones are the most interesting, with displays of superb grave furniture and one completely excavated burial chamber like the inside of a pyramid. The valley was full of persimmon trees loaded with bright orange fruit, and here and there one could catch a glimpse of the peasants gathering the fruit in great piles in the middle of their villages, or flailing the corn, or working in 'brigades' in the fields.

We passed one handsome old archway (a Chinese version of an arc de triomphe) carrying an inscription in 12 different scripts, of which six vertical and four horizontal were unidentifiable to me. Asia has a curious way of making a European seem very ignorant.

The embassy people at Peking are allowed only three 'lungs', the wall, the tombs and a beach at Tientsin. No wonder they like to visit Mongolia! Joan Wilford took us on our little tour. She is much the best value in Peking. Everyone else takes too much tone from the Garveys, that is they are keen, busy and not very humanly responsive. I found Stewart Ross amiable and amusing, although not my sort of person. He told me that when he saw Sir John Nicholls[9] recently, Sir J commented that the Garveys no doubt liked the Mongols because they were easy to patronize! Ross has much in common with Henry Carr.

We left Peking just after nightfall in a plush train of modern build but Soviet antimacassar style, with an impressive Chinese crew who seemed determined that people should stick to their routine drill for passengers and not enjoy themselves. Most of the train was full of young Chinese in a huge delegation going to Poland and east Germany. They naturally toed the line, leaving the crew free to attend to the rest of us. We rapidly became acquainted with two Polish geologists, a young Dutchman from a shipping company in Hong Kong, a Soviet diplomatic courier, the Mongolian vice-minister of communications and the stationmaster of Ulan Bator station. Whenever any of us got together for a drink, the Chinese would decide to spring-clean that particular compartment or part of the corridor. We used to stay put, but the Chinese did not give up. I think they found the Mongols incorrigible. The stationmaster seemed to spend a good deal of time ringing the bell for the Chinese to come and remove his empties, and when they did not come quickly enough he called the guard (also Chinese but very urbane).

By morning we were well into Inner Mongolia, with the huge plain all round us, occasional hills and sparse groups of horses, cattle and men. At breakfast time we changed wheels at Tsining, that is the train was run onto a series of jacks, the standard-gauge bogies were run off and broad-gauge bogies were run in. It was already frosty and has stayed more or less frosty ever since. In the afternoon we reached the frontier at Erlien on the Chinese side (all inscriptions and notices in Chinese and the old vertical Mongolian script). Chinese officials examined everything and everybody that or who did not have diplomatic status, and we bought the last kilo of apples we are likely to buy for a long time.

We pulled across to Mongolia and stopped at Dzamyn Ude where the Mongolian officials took over. A young woman who looked like an ungroomed ATS private said, in Russian, 'I am the health officer. Are you well?' 'Yes, very, thank you.' She looked nonplussed and after a pause said 'Thank you' and moved on. I asked if I could go for a walk. 'No', she said, 'This is a quarantine station.' 'He is the English Chargé d'Affaires', shouted the Ulan Bator stationmaster. 'Then of course he can go for a walk', she said. Once I was out, all the other members of our group followed. There was a guard on the station and each soldier came to attention and saluted as we walked past. Meanwhile, all the Mongolian officials, including the health person, crammed themselves into the compartments of the vice-minister and stationmaster to spend a happy hour drinking. All the notices and inscriptions here were in the Cyrillic Mongolian script and Russian. The pamphlets in these scripts in the waiting room were critical of the Chinese leadership. On the Chinese side I gathered that the pamphlets had been critical of the Soviet leadership.

It was dark by the time we left, pulled by a beautiful diesel-electric locomotive built at Kharkov (in China everything was steam and bit old-fashioned). The Mongolian restaurant car was a revelation. I had a mouthful of Mongolian beer and have not touched it since. The soup was mutton stew and the second course was stewed mutton. A cheese with a Parmesan-type texture but without a Parmesan taste followed it. The vodka was good.

I forgot to mention that there was an odious woman from Oxford (town not gown) on the train. She had been visiting her daughter and son-in-law in Peking. The son-in-law is an Oxford graduate in Chinese working in the Foreign Languages Publishing House in Peking, namely for the 'new' China. The whole family were evidently pro-China cranks. I blotted my copybook by saying that it might be better to live in the Soviet Union rather than China. Thereafter I was spoken to only when the menu needed translating. I think she thought it was a mean FO (and gown) trick when she got mutton twice.

We arrived at Ulan Bator shortly after dawn, I with my face splitting with appreciative smiles as the stationmaster pointed out every feature of a fine landscape and reassured himself every few minutes that I was not cold ('There you are! What did I tell you? You must drink plenty in Mongolia').

We were met at Ulan Bator station (it was Saturday morning) by an official called Purev from the Mongolian FO. He took us to the hotel, fixed up a lorry to bring our heavy baggage and then disappeared until I managed to track him down on Monday morning. The lorry was an open coal truck, but all went well because we had with it three incredibly tough Mongols who solved all problems and overcame all obstacles by brute force. I think it can safely be said that Ulan Bator passenger station has no facilities for handling anything other than hand luggage – and even for that they mostly use the passengers.

Once our baggage was back at the hotel our men tore the crates to pieces, broke the hotel lift (which in any case is used only on state occasions such as the arrival of a chargé d'affaires), dumped everything in our rooms and said goodbye by swallowing between them, neat and without a pause for breath, a half bottle or more of whisky divided into three tumblers.

A telegram had arrived from Peking, in Russian but trans-literated into the Latin alphabet, telling us that Eric Cheyne's trunk should be at the airport. It finally reached us after most of the hotel staff had had a go at reading it. We were offered a Zhuulchin (Mongolian Intourist) taxi and driven to the airport, where several dozen grizzled Mongols (grizzled women as well as grizzled men) were waiting about in *del*s [Mongolian gowns] and sheepskins and long boots for something to fly somewhere. We were told that the customs house was shut, but after much arguing by our taxi driver who was obviously playing up the chargé d'affaires line, they gave us the key to the customs shed, which was about the size of a small cottage, and told us to take what we wanted. There was nothing inside except Eric Cheyne's trunk.

We spent Saturday afternoon and most of Sunday unpacking, getting ourselves straight, accustoming ourselves to wait for things that do not happen, and learning to be on our toes for unexpected things and sometimes unwanted ones that happen now and then. It does not take long to get the hang of it. You just have to stay firmly in the present. It has much in common, especially the food, with being in the army, in the ranks, in the old days.

More of Mongolia next time: the splendid feature of the place at present is the superb weather – sparkling, frosty sunshine in great brilliance all day long. Our Land Rover is here but has no antifreeze and the temperature outside is steadily at or below freezing, with a dozen or so degrees of frost at night.

Reginald to Jane

4 November 1964

I have experienced so much since leaving London that I cannot possibly tell you all about it in one letter. I have written a long letter to Mother about my journey. I expect she will show it to you. I hope one or two postcards have reached you.

In Moscow, as well as seeing *Giselle* at the Bolshoi, I went to the Arts Theatre to see Chekhov's *Three Sisters*. The weather on the flight was clear from Irkutsk onwards and we had a wonderful view of Lake Baikal, of Siberia's endless tufty low hills to the north, of the Sayan Mountains to the south and of the vast empty plains and valleys of the Mongolian plateau beyond the peaks of the mountains. We flew over Ulan Bator, and it looked tiny and miles from anywhere.

In Peking we came back into unseasonable warmth and humidity. China is full of people and every possible inch seems to be cultivated. The Great Wall really does divide two completely different geographical zones and ways of life. You certainly know when you are in China that you are in a big and disciplined country that has completely non-Western ideas and traditions. Peking is difficult to see. It is very flat and mostly one-storey, and the main streets are enormously wide while the side streets are much too narrow. There are no concessions to foreign devils like us: all writing everywhere is in Chinese. The chrysanthemums are unworthily straggly. It is only now, in Mongolia, that I appreciate retrospectively how good the food was.

The courtyards and groups of pavilions and halls in the Forbidden City are very fine in a highly stylized way: they left me with a strong impression of China's traditional isolation and introspection. There are beautiful things in the museum halls, but none that touched a human passion.

I have left little space to write about Mongolia. When you see it you think – what a marvellous place for all the Davey Crocketts at heart! But then you encounter layers of communist bosses, or at any rate bosses who toe the Party line. It is perhaps easier to say what there isn't than what there is. By Mongolian standards I am living at the highest possible standard and indeed, except for the food, it is not too bad. But when you suddenly think of something you want, say a screwdriver or a passport photograph, or a piece of blotting paper or a bottle of something drinkable, you know that it is nowhere to be found.

Reginald to Ann

8 November 1964

Thank you for your letter, which arrived by our first bag. I am glad you are thinking of booking on the Moscow–UB aircraft on 26 January. The aircraft is an Ilyushin 18, a turbo-prop aircraft, not a TU jet. They do not fly jets into Ulan Bator airport because of the surrounding mountains and hills. The Ilyushin 11–18 is said to be very comfortable. If you send your passport by the next bag I will get a Mongolian visa put in it.

I hope you are managing to find somewhere for Christmas. It is not going to be easy for you. I have heard from Jane – a lively letter. Thank you for sending me George's and William's letters.

It came as a surprise when the Queen's Messengers arrived yesterday to find that I was already accepting UB as a normal place to be, and that the curiosity and concern of people outside Mongolia seemed unexpected. Life here is a bit unorthodox, but it is assuming an acceptable pattern of its own. At any rate the dawns and sunsets and the sunshine are superb.

Our suite in the hotel is reasonably comfortable, although the beds are hard, or at any rate firm, and the bathroom is cockroachy (I have asked the FO for some insecticide powder). It will be a great improvement when I can hive Eric Cheyne off into a room of his own. The hotel staff keep out of our way.

The food is difficult and uninteresting. You have to be ingenious to get any variety out of the menu. It could be bad to be fussy. Rye bread and glasses of black tea play a big part in the diet, and so do soups full of bits of vegetables and meat. There is always some sort of a choice of meat dish, but you cannot always tell what part of the chosen animal you are eating. There are a few limited so-called salad dishes (shredded cabbage, potato, pickled cucumbers, occasionally tomatoes). Round that sort of core you have to give a meal individuality by grasping whatever offers, for example yoghurt or cheese or one or two other products the

Mongols manage to conjure out of various sorts of milk (sheep and goat as well as cow), or sometimes some sort of cake, or now and then an apple, or Georgian Borjomi mineral water, or a sort of pickled herring, or *suutei tsai*, milky tea, which is really milk with an outsize tea leaf in it. If you want a drink you have it in your room, and you make your own cup of coffee. And if you want anything else you open a tin. In this way, and if you are neither a gourmand nor a gourmet, you can work out a form of coexistence with the food. I find *airag* or *koumiss*, fermented mare's milk, unattractive as it has an aroma of ammonia, or at any rate the *airag* offered in the hotel has. But it can serve as a device to make a meal different. I am feeling very well on all this.

The Mongolian staff are acceptable only if you make up your mind to let yourself drift a bit. For example, if you want your rooms tidied, you must get hold of the first woman you see in the corridor with a vacuum cleaner or duster and ask her to come at once. She will do so; but you have to decamp and leave the suite to her, dropping whatever you thought of doing and sitting in the lounge-landing with a book or paper until she finishes. Generally speaking, if you want something to happen you let your wishes be known and you accept a 'no' or two from members of the staff you approach; but the word seems to go round, especially if you let yourself be seen occasionally in the company of important people like the Zhuulchin (Intourist) manager, and someone eventually appears and does what you want. In the last resort I can always put in a written note to the Protocol Department of the Ministry of Foreign Affairs or the Bureau for Servicing the Diplomatic Corps. But one obviously does not waste such thunder and lightning on little things. Even so, I put in seven Notes last week.

On Saturday we had great celebrations of the October Revolution of 1917. I found myself at the Soviet Ambassador's[10] reception sitting at the high table with the Politburo (the leaders of party and state) and the ambassadors (all communist), and drinking outrageous toasts to such things as international communist solidarity, the rapid building of socialism in Mongolia, and the mighty strength of the Soviet Union, which protects us all from the imperialist exploiters. Everyone enjoyed it hugely and received me in the friendliest fashion, and the Soviet Ambassador did me the honour of conducting me to the front door when I left, which was a most helpful gesture in front of the bosses of Mongolia.

This week I shall start paying calls, starting with the Foreign Minister, Mr Dügersüren,[11] for whom I have a very nice letter from Mr Gordon Walker. The days are not going to be dull as there are plenty of people whom I must get to know.

We have a chauffeur called Batsukh, who appeared like magic from nowhere as soon as I said I wanted one. For a chauffeur he shows a remarkable familiarity with the army officers whom we meet. My dossier has evidently been passed round. When I wrote to the Soviet Ambassador to announce my arrival I signed as usual R. A. Hibbert. He addressed his reply to Mr Reginald Hibbert.

We drove into the steppe on Friday afternoon. It was windy and the cold sharp, much sharper than in UB. Our arctic kit will not be wasted. I am increasingly convinced that the children can come out here for Easter without much difficulty and we shall be able to keep them amused. Do you think Jane could leave school two days early in order to fly to Moscow in time to catch the Tuesday night plane, as there is only one a week?

西藏西藏

When I asked for a chauffeur, I asked also for garaging for the Land Rover. After a delay I was told that there was room for it in a garage at some distance from the hotel. This was a hangar-like building, and it turned out that the big black limousines of the government and Party chiefs were kept there. The building was bare and without any facilities except two inspection pits. Its floor was thick with dust in dry weather and with mud in wet weather.

As there was no one else to look after our vehicle, I had to maintain it myself. Every three or four weeks I would put on my overalls and spend a morning checking the Land Rover and doing any little jobs that needed doing to prevent it being shaken to pieces on the roadless tracks outside the city. I became aware on these occasions that some of the Mongolian chauffeurs were choosing to do a little work on their cars at the same time as I. The incentive for them was that when I was there they could borrow from my excellent tool kit, which they much admired. I found myself treated as a sort of colleague by the chauffeurs as well as, on diplomatic occasions, by their bosses. It was a curious case of being both upstairs and downstairs simultaneously. Batsukh enjoyed the prestige our advanced technology brought him, but he

2. My first call on the Foreign Minister, Mr M. Dügersüren (right), who was accompanied by the Chief of Protocol and the head of the second department, responsible *inter alia* for relations with Western countries.

was not himself mechanically minded, which tended to confirm my belief that he belonged to the officer class.

西藏西藏

Reginald to Ann

9 November 1964

I am giving this to the QM to post in Hong Kong. It may reach you a day or two earlier than the letters in the bag. Colonel Murray, the top QM came on this first run. He will telephone you to tell you what he thought of us and of this place.

I have been thinking about next year. What do you think of the following? The children come out for Easter and go back. They come out again at the end of July and stay until the beginning of September. You then go back with them, with us paying the fare, and I would then reclaim your fare from the FO when I return on leave in, say, November. I think the FO would probably agree to this. We could give our tenants notice at Broad Lane but let them stay an extra month until you arrive home. If you think the general scheme is feasible I will try it on the FO.

I wish you were here. I think you would find it amusing and even in a sort of a way enjoyable. It is quite the most casual way of life I have ever known, apart from Oxford. It suits me well enough. I feel as though I am a character in *Waiting for Godot*.

Reginald to his parents

9 November 1964

Ulan Bator is very small and not beautiful, but it has a wonderful setting and at present a fine, frosty climate. The really cold weather has not started yet.

Tomorrow morning we have to see the Queen's Messengers off on the train at 7.00 a.m. The temperature then will be about 10° Fahrenheit – about 22 degrees of frost. We shall have to wear our long underpants and fur hats. But by 9.00 a.m., with the sun up, the temperature will have risen to about 30° F. By midday it will be warm enough in the sun to take one's hat off, but not for long, and one's feet will feel cold if one stands still. From 4.00 p.m. onwards the temperature will drop rapidly again.

Our hotel is very much overheated by steam from the UB power station. One of our problems had been to find ways of cooling it down. We now have a more English regime in our suite. It is possible slowly to get most things adjusted to our needs, but not the food. Fortunately, I am not much concerned about what I eat and am prepared to have a go at anything. In any case I have lived on a much duller diet than this in the past. But I have to encourage my assistant a little. He tends to cut off fat and eat no breakfast if he cannot have eggs, and refuse all forms of offal and not like rye bread. I expect he will soon find out that you go hungry if you are fussy in Mongolia. I have probably lost some weight: I feel very fit here.

The dryness is a bit of a problem. Shoes curl up and my face is tender for shaving, and one needs to drink plenty. Everyone here drinks lots of tea in the Turkish style, namely glasses of tea with sugar. The Mongols drink their 'tea with milk', which is really milk with dashes of tea and salt and butter, all stewed up together.

As I sit and write, overlooking Peace Street, the main street of the town, I can see the beginning of the steppe about a mile away, with wooded hills white with frost rising beyond. It is already ceasing to feel strange. By the time Ann comes in January I shall be a hardened Mongol.

Reginald to Jane

16 November 1964

I hope my postcards and letters loaded with Mongolian stamps are reaching you through the open post. Here is another one.

It grows slowly colder here. Emerging from the hotel in the early morning is like taking a cold bath. You feel it at once pinching your face and hands. It would be painful to go out without having put a hat on.

On Sunday I drove out in to the country just outside UB. It was absolutely silent and empty except for a rustling from dozens of mouse-like animals, which rushed to their holes as we approached. In the distance, near the airport, we could see a great herd of animals, over a hundred, and when we came near they turned out to be Bactrian camels. A few big hawks were circling round. We seemed to be miles from any human habitation. In fact we were only 20 miles from Ulan Bator.

There is a very interesting museum here, full of all sorts of bits and pieces from Mongol history. The trouble is that all the labels are in Mongolian. I had my first formal Mongol lesson this evening from the head of the UB Pedagogical Institute, no less. It made me feel that it would be a long time before I would be able to read the labels.

Reginald to Ann's father

16 November 1964

The purpose of this letter is to send you the pretty stamps through the post. You would be amused to see how one buys stamps here. A woman at the newspaper stall in the hall of the hotel puts a cardboard box of the latest issues on the counter and anyone interested rummages through the box until satisfied. She then tots up a sum on her abacus and often finds that she cannot give the right change. She lets me have a revolving credit, but many people have to take extra stamps to make up. The divorce between philately and postage seems to be complete.

3. View from our hotel windows showing Foreign Ministry (with spire) and next to it the Yugoslav embassy. Next to that was the Bulgarian embassy, but it is not in the picture. These buildings are all on Peace Street, the main street of Ulan Bator.

Reginald to Ann

Wednesday 18 November 1964

I think our first QM reaches London today. So you should be reading my first letters from here in a day or two. Our second QM arrives on Saturday with letters from you. Meanwhile, you are probably waiting for the outward bag, which closes on Monday. So we both read and write at the same time, but a fortnight apart. I have been away for a month. I certainly feel out of touch.

Here we make progress in a curious sort of way, a bit crablike. All sorts of strange things happen and some very funny ones. It is hard to know where to start.

Last week I called on the other heads of mission, all communists of course. This involved so much drinking that I could not manage more than two a day, one before lunch and one at teatime. They serve their national cognac at any time, and they see you drink it by proposing toasts – a deplorable habit. If you flinch, out comes the vodka. Then there is wine and finally coffee or tea and all sorts of *zakuski*. Of course we all become close buddies very quickly, but it is a wonderful way of avoiding the heart of the matter – of any matter. At the end of the visit you have no idea what or where the heart might be. The colleagues are not very interesting but they are all amiable. The Chinese Ambassador is in many ways the most civilized. He received me with cognac and pale tea in covered pots at 10.00 a.m. There were some blue/black halves of eggs on the table, ancient eggs I suppose, but I did not get round to having one.

This week I have started calling on Mongolian ministers and high officials, which is much more like hard work. They know so little about the world that they do not know what to say and mostly seem to enjoy sitting and gazing at the extraordinary phenomenon of a resident representative from a distant, capitalist state.

One of the difficulties of life here is that I have to get the phone 'repaired' nearly every time I want to make a call. I would willingly take potluck and call on people on the chance of seeing them, but of course they would not like that. So life resolves itself into days when I make no phone calls at all, and days when I get the phone switched on and make several calls all at once. You can imagine that my programme is inconsequential but the system no doubt economizes the energy of the official eavesdropper.

Last week was full of cultural events. On one night the Soviet Embassy gave a showing of a Soviet film of *Hamlet*, screenplay by Pasternak. It was a good film, but more Pasternak than Shakespeare. The satellites all crept and said it was marvellous – the best Hamlet ever. I said it was excellent Pasternak and was promptly examined for ten minutes by the Soviet minister to make sure that I was not a discontented customer or potential bell-wether for black sheep.

The next night there was a concert by Soviet singers at the opera house. I had become friendly with the bass at the hotel on the strength of a visit he is going to pay to London next March for a *Daily Worker* anniversary concert. He is a charming man and was a bit upset when I warned him that his performance in London would be a small political event rather than a big musical one. At the concert the heads of mission were placed in three boxes – big ambassadors, little ambassadors and chargés d'affaires, or so it looked to me. Suddenly, the Cuban chargé walked out, dragging his wife with him. I thought he was unwell, but next day he called (he lives immediately below us) to say that I was not to think he had walked out because of me! It was simply that he was insulted by being segregated from the ambassadors. I said that I was sorry that my arrival had depreciated the chargé d'affaire's currency, but this was beyond his English and my rusty Spanish. To make up, as he evidently thought he should, he sent his wife out to shop for us. She came back with two dozen eggs (unobtainable), a four-kilo ham (unheard of) and 24 apples. The bill was about £7. We have been unable to obtain a knife to cut the ham, so we are eating our way through it with my penknife.

Our Land Rover is running well. Eric C and I have passed our driving tests, which is not bad when you think that the only text available of the local rules was in Mongol. In fact Eric C gave hopelessly wrong answers, but as I was translating them into Russian he received full marks. We had one awkward moment. My UK driving licence is in a red cover. Eric's is in one of the old buff covers. The militia captain was very suspicious. Why did we have different sorts of licences? Which of us was second-class? I told him that Eric, as a Scotsman, belonged to one of our national minorities and therefore had different coloured documents. This seemed a reasonable explanation and was accepted.

Sometimes I go for a drive and/or walk in the morning or afternoon. Our driver, Batsukh, perks up at the sight of the open country. He lives in a *ger* on the opposite side of the town from our garage, about four or five kilometres away. He walks to and from the garage. It is wonderfully quiet and solitary as soon as you leave the immediate area of Ulan Bator. You can wander where you like, but the distances are so huge that it is difficult to wander effectively. I think one has to pick a hill and walk up it in order to have a finite element to grasp. There seem to be great herds of Bactrian camels wintering round the city. Can you imagine me in any other post going for a stroll in the afternoon in an unbalanced sort of open-air zoo?

The minimum night temperature readings outside my window have been (Fahrenheit) 8°, 4°, 11°, 13°, 12°, 9½°, 14°, 11°, 21°, 4½°, 4½°, 7°, 8° and, this morning, 1°. The QMs arrive and depart at the coldest time of the day. I find that I am comfortable in the sun outside UB in the middle of the day wearing my mountain boots, two pairs of socks, long pants, string vest, viyella shirt, two sweaters and windproof anorak with the wolverine trimming. I think our kit will be just right. Warm headgear seems particularly important. The cold strikes one's head very quickly.

In spite of our temperatures we have no antifreeze for the Land Rover. Oh, Peking! I hope to have some flown out from London. I want to make a trip to Tsetserleg and Karakorum before the winter sets in really hard, in order to see what travelling conditions are really like; but the distance is more than 400 kilometres and I cannot risk getting stuck somewhere without antifreeze. I could drain off, but there would be no water with which to refill!

They do the washing and ironing beautifully. And the hairdresser is better than the one at the Reform Club. And they do nice things like open the State Bank after closing hours so that I can cash a cheque. It is not to be missed. I wish you were here already!

Reginald to Jane

19 November 1964

I write this just as you are receiving my first letter, which has been wandering through Peking and Hong Kong and the Orient in general for many days. I cannot reply to a letter from you because if I wait until the QM comes at the weekend I shall be too busy to write to you at all. So you have to have a letter out of nowhere, so to speak.

I have got to know some of the people in the hotel here. There is a curious Hungarian who is here as part of a technical assistance programme. His particular job is to teach the Mongols to play decent dance music. He used to be the conductor of the band of the Hungarian State Circus. He is in despair about the hotel's dance band, which has a Stone Age Victor Sylvester style. He came up to my room last night and played Hungarian gypsy music on the piano (yes, I have a piano in my suite, so you can enjoy strumming on it when you are here). On Saturday night he is organizing a party with a Dutch businessman who is here to buy sausage casings and who sails very close to the wind with a marvellous takeoff of the Mongolian language. Then there is a young man from Leningrad who is organizing an exhibition of Russian art here, and an old lady from Bulgaria with bright, blonde hair who is teaching singers at the opera house. Last week there was a charming Russian singer and his accompanist who obviously regarded me as a cultural type and wanted advice on which Russian music would be most appreciated at a *Daily Worker* anniversary concert in London next March. There are many others, of whom the Poles and Czechs are the friendliest and the east Germans the most difficult. There is plenty of variety provided you speak Russian.

A Russian who had been out on an expedition told me yesterday that his vehicle had broken down and he had had to walk 30 kilometres before he came to a small cluster of *gers*. The vastness and emptiness of the place have to be seen to be believed. The Mongols say they are stamping out nomadism, but it is difficult to believe that they can get rid of it completely until they are rich enough to build a few roads. There are little camps of nomads in the hills round Ulan Bator, each with its herd of camels. I imagine that they have brought goods of some sort to the city and are waiting for something to turn up before they move on.

Reginald to Ann

22 November 1964

The bags made up in London on 9 November arrived yesterday, and there was no letter from you. But thanks for the packet of paperbacks.

You must not cut it too fine in waiting to catch the bag. As it is I cannot have a reply to this letter until Christmas. I shall no doubt hear something from you in a fortnight. Jane, George and William all wrote to me, no doubt stimulated by you, for which many thanks. William asks if I know when he will be taken out next!

I enclose a cheque in case you need more cash. I have no idea what the FO has been paying into my account. I have received no pay chits so far.

Could you order and have sent through the bag some really modern pop music, Beatles and later or earlier. If the packages are not too large they stand a chance of being sent by airfreight. Informal parties tend to start up here in the hotel on Saturday nights and the Cubans and Hungarians set a fairly hot pace in music. It would be amusing to throw in some up-to-date British stuff. Last night there were Hungarians, Bulgarians, Poles, Czechs, a Swiss, a Dutchman from Spain and me. The drinks are equally international. It was a pity that I had to be up early this morning to parade at the railway station with the other heads of mission

and the government to welcome back Tsedenbal,[12] the PM and
First Secretary of the Party, from Moscow.

I do not think Eric Cheyne is enjoying Mongolia as much as I
am. The language barrier is total for him and he finds the food
hard to bear. I might have guessed that he belongs to a milieu
where steak is central to meat eating. Not in Mongolia! He is
away today on an excursion for embassy secretaries organized by
the MFA. Tonight he moves into his own room, next to this one,
so I shall at last have our suite to myself.

23 November 1964 (airletter posted in Hong Kong)

The QM has brought us some of these, so I inaugurate them by
writing to you.

We have just finished the usual sort of bag rush. The QMs tend
to be a bit in the way, as they have to be looked after. Naturally,
they cannot read a word of Russian and cannot even order a meal
successfully. And of course they want to know where everything is
in UB and to see the sights.

The hotel is full of the Soviet Aleksandrov song and dance
ensemble at present (170 of them). Noises of accordions, drums,
balalaikas and voices come from behind doors along the corridors
as performers practise their twiddly bits. Fat managerial men in
fur coats march up and down the stairs enquiring kindly after the
pulled muscles of the people they meet.

We have a busy week ahead – Aleksandrov ensemble, fortieth
anniversary of the 1924 declaration of the Mongolian Republic,
national wrestling championships, Yugoslav National Day, and a
turnout at the airport tomorrow to say goodbye to the foreign
minister who is leaving for the UN General Assembly at New
York. I shall fall behind with my flute playing.

2 December 1964

I have been paying the bills for our first month. I find that once I
have paid all the fixed charges on government account, the amount
of money I can spend personally is strictly limited. It is almost
impossible to spend more that 20 tugriks a day on food (11.15
tugriks to the pound). There simply is not any luxury food to buy.
Eric and I buy eggs and apples and *smetana* (Russian for a sour
cream rather like creamy yoghurt) from the diplomatic shop,

bread and butter from the hotel and oranges from Hong Kong (via the QMs) and make breakfast in our rooms. Apart from that we eat in the hotel restaurant at about six or seven tugriks a time. We have a little store of caviar for special occasions – it is sold to heads of mission only and is inexpensive. We have the usual range of drinks sent up from Peking. Laundry costs me about 23 tugriks a week. Of course I do not know what the costs will be when a large order reaches us from outside, if a large order ever arrives.

My current problem is to decide where to put our little electric stove (two rings and a little oven). I am trying to persuade the hotel to rig up the WC by our front door as a little kitchen, but they may want us to take another room across the corridor. It is difficult to say which solution would be better.

The thermometer took a downward plunge at the end of November. The night temperatures for the past week have all been below 0°F, reaching down to –10°F. The cold is beginning to bite. Yesterday I drove out about 30 kilometres on the road northwards and walked up a hill in the middle of nowhere. The light wind was behind me as I walked up, but when I turned round and walked down it was against me and it stung hard before I could lower my earflaps and shut myself in. Even the 200 yards walk across Peace Street to the Foreign Ministry becomes uncomfortable unless one is fully and carefully dressed for being outside. Before going out you have to look at the thermometer and not at the lovely sunshine.

Last weekend I climbed to the top of the Bogdo Ula, the former holy mountain overlooking UB to the south. The snow was about a foot deep on top and completely powdery. I suddenly found myself about 20 yards from a small herd of a dozen deer, very fat and healthy looking. We exchanged stares and then they slowly wandered away, apparently conscious of being in a game reserve or perhaps on a holy mountain. Here and there among the rocks I came upon patches where deer had been lying and snow had melted under them. On the way down I met two gnarled and creased old woodcutters who put on a pantomime to convey to me all the different sorts of wild animals on Bogdo Ula. They seemed delighted to meet another human being.

Last week we had the fortieth anniversary of the 1924 declaration of the republican constitution, after the death of the last *Bogdo Gegen* (the highest lama of the Khalkha Mongols and their

4. Sükhbaatar Square with the mausoleum of Sükhbaatar and Choibalsan in front of the government of the Great People's Khural.

living Buddha). The day started for the diplomatic corps with a somewhat incongruous tour of the central museum (meteorites, minerals, plants, birds, beasts, fish, dinosaurs complete with eggs and footprints from the Gobi, Manchu atrocities and ancient Mongol relics). As the Mongol labels had previously baffled me, it was interesting to hear some explanations in Russian.

We all solemnly shook hands at the end, and we shook hands again half an hour later when we paraded on Sükhbaatar Square[13] (pronounced Sookhbahter) to lay a diplomatic corps wreath on Sükhbaatar's tomb. Wreaths were laid by the government and party leaders, a little group of 1921 partisans covered with medals and badges and with old wooden faces with what a furniture man would call a distressed finish, by us, by a group of children and by a group of trade unionists.

We filed into the mausoleum (like Lenin's on Red Square) to the sound of a funeral march played by a military band. The government leaders and ambassadors continued to chat with one another and wave to friends in the crowd right up to the door, but the Soviet ambassador did his best to set an example of dignified and meditative deliberation. Inside, I was glad to see that they do

5. Sükhbaatar.

not have a mummified corpse as in Moscow but a tomb not unlike those of Seljuk sultans in Turkey, or those of the Russian grand dukes in the Arkhangelski Sobor in the Kremlin. Next to Sükh–baatar's is the similar tomb of Choibalsan. Both had some very Seljuk-looking carving on them and the names were written down the top in the handsome old vertical script, but funerary busts above the tombs in con–ventional Soviet superman style spoiled the effect.

Again we shook hands, rushed off to lunch and shook hands again at the theatre at 3.00 p.m. for a solemn meeting. Old President Sambu[14] (pronounced Sambaw) read a long report – he was a member for the first Great People's Khural in 1924, which proclaimed the constitution. And that was followed by a concert by the national orchestra of traditional Mongol instruments, which was fascinating. There was a 10- or 12-foot horn, the *morin hur*, or horse-headed two-string fiddle, and all sorts of other curiosities. We also heard the famous long song and some short songs (long means long-drawn-out notes capable of carrying great distances across the steppes, and short means sprightly tunes). We saw some traditional dances (danced by Mongolian ATS, who seemed more shapely than most Mongolian women, unless it is simply that I have been here a month already), and heard some modern Mongol pop music, which was encored again and again by the audience in general but not by the top people and ambassadors.

More handshaking and a quick change and there we were shaking hands again at a government reception in the local 'Kremlin'. The system here is that there are two halls for sheep and goats, the goats having to make do with a broadcast of the goings-

6. In full winter kit in January near Lün Suma, west of Ulan Bator. The cairn of stones is a minor *ovo* at a highpoint in the track. The stones are added by travellers to show respect for the spirits of the place.

on in the upper house. As a head of mission I was on the central table in the top house, next to the high table where Tsedenbal and the Party bosses stood. One does not sit at the table – it is a sort of cocktail party not a dinner – but one is not expected to wander far from one's proper station.

Tsedenbal proposed various toasts (no one else seems to have much to say when he is around) and on each occasion we performed a sort of Strip-the-Willow round our table and the president's table clinking glasses with all the colleagues and top Mongols. The food was indifferent (it would probably be better if they let it be more Mongol) and the drink was mostly vodka and cognac – they have a tiresome habit of pretending that it is cissy for men to drink toasts in anything else, but women are allowed to drink them in wine. After a while Tsedenbal went to show himself to the lower house. Eric Cheyne was there and told me that Tsedenbal was followed by an attendant with a couple of bottles so that his glass could be refilled when it had been emptied onto the floor by over enthusiastic glass clinkers. Could it be that these special bottles contained water and not vodka? I had a liquid

conversation with an ancient partisan who addressed me in Mongolian as if presenting credentials. I made a suitable ceremonial
reply in English that seemed to please him and his cronies – then a
final handshake and out into a fall of snow.

This afternoon I came across the surviving lama temple[15] in
Ulan Bator and I have asked if I can go to the monks' ceremonies
on Sunday. There were quite a few people going through the attitudes of prayer on the prayer-boards before the shrine. The monks
in their red and saffron robes looked sleek and fat though not very
clean. An official in the protocol department said, 'Oh yes, that
monastery is still working.' The high lama is in India at present at
a world Buddhist conference. He drives round UB in a big blue
Zis, which is an ambassadorial type of car.

I hope everyone finds these little chronicles interesting.

2

Progress on the Domestic Front

The hotel management finally agreed to let us rig up our little electric cooking stove in the WC by the front door, with the hand washbasin being taken into service as a kitchen sink. The three single rooms opposite us in our corridor were taken by the Soviet embassy, which presumably made it easier to keep an eye and an ear on us.

西藏西藏

Reginald to his parents

4 December 1964

We are progressing satisfactorily here, that is my attaché and I, although I think I might enjoy it more if I were completely by myself. He speaks no foreign languages to any worthwhile extent: I find myself having to 'carry' him everywhere and in everything. He is called an Attaché instead of a clerical assistant only because this is a communist country. I use Russian, German and French here and even a little Spanish with the Cubans. But it is not always easy to strike up acquaintances with foreigners if one has a silent partner hanging around. I am sure he finds his enforced silences trying too. Perhaps it will become easier when Ann is here, as he will then have to accept being on his own more often. At any rate I now have my three-room suite to myself. Eric has a two-room suite next door. We pay the equivalent of £8 a day for the rooms.

The winter slowly deepens here. The whole landscape slowly whitens like a head of hair. There is no real snow cover, but the occasional flurries of fine powder snow do not melt and slowly accumulate, and the frost gradually whitens the hillsides as it gets more intense. The scene is very beautiful but is spoiled in town by the smoke billowing out of the chimneys in every building and every *yurt* (the Mongol word for tent is not *yurt* but *ger*). It is not easy to enjoy the winter weather spontaneously because one has to dress up so carefully to go out. But it is usually worthwhile to make the effort.

The street scenes in Ulan Bator are always colourful because so many people wear the long Mongolian gowns, *dels*, mostly in brilliant colours and the smarter ones in Chinese silk. Here and there one sees old herdsmen in from the country in huge fur bonnets made of marmot or fox skins and old fashioned Mongolian boots with pointed, turned up toes and no heels (for riding). Everyone walks great distances here. There is hardly any public transport and in the mornings, at lunchtime and in the evenings the town is full of people moving to and fro. They all walk fast because of the cold, so that the impression is of a vigorous and hardy people. The place is full of children, the smaller ones dwarfed by their fur hats and collars, and the babies completely invisible in rolled parcels of blankets. The little children behave like English children, and it is interesting to watch the change as they grow older and begin to behave in the characteristic ways of grown-up Mongols.

A happy Christmas! For once, I have no preparations to make at all, which is very relaxing.

Reginald to Ann

6 December 1964

This time I had five or six letters from you – such abundance! The bag room put your letter of 1 November in the wrong bag and your letter of 9 November missed the bag. Your latest letter was dated 22 November and so is nearly up-to-date. [Some detailed advice on clothing for Ann and the children then follows.]

I am getting on quite well here, but Garvey is being very possessive. He has sent a letter inviting Cheyne and me to pack up and go to Peking for Christmas, returning in the New Year. How would we pack up? What would we leave behind, and in whose care? I cannot think that the FO would welcome such a move. I have refused for what I hope sound like good reasons. Besides, Eric and I have no desire for a fresh brainwashing by Rosemary Garvey. Fortunately, they cannot get at us here, as they will slowly find out.

Reginald to Ann's father

7 December 1964

The Queen's Messengers have been shivering here this weekend. They did not have quite the right kit and were not acclimatized. When they arrived the temperature was −10°F and even the midday temperatures have been well down. I took one of them to see the Museum of the Living Buddha today and I thought he was going to freeze up completely. The thought crossed my mind that I should have to fold him up into a lotus position and leave him there for the rest of the winter.

The museum is full of many fine things. It is the old winter palace of the *Bogdo Gegen*, the living Buddha who was the leading prince of the Khalkha Mongols until 1924. Some old drawings of Urga in 1912, almost entirely a tented city, were fascinating. The clothes and jewels and hats of the *Bogdo Gegen* and his wife were splendid. Of course, it is strange to think of a living Buddha being conventionally married, but the vices depicted in much of the art bequeathed to him by his previous incarnations suggest that we should applaud his apparent normality. I am afraid lamaism in Mongolia was much debased by its mixture with Shamanism, and the results were fairly earthy. There is not much difficulty here in equipping an orthodox communist anti-God museum.

Reginald to Ann

7 December 1964

I have sent your passport to travel section at the FO with an entry visa valid until 15 February. You do not need anti-cholera injections.

I have heard from Cox's and King's that our heavy baggage has reached Leningrad.

We are just about halfway to seeing each other again. ... I have suggested that Eric Cheyne might have a week or so of leave to go to Hong Kong in February, soon after you arrive. You and I would then be entirely free for a short while. I have also suggested that you and I might go to Peking for a few days in March. I do not know if any of this will be agreed. If Garvey had his way I should go to Peking much sooner, but I am stalling in order not to be too 'possessed'. It seems to me that there is no hurry, but of course Garvey is anxious that I should not be independent. I think that all we have to do is sit here and in the end people are bound to agree to what we want.

You ought to aim to spend a night in Moscow *en route*. It would be impossible to count on making the connection to the once-weekly flight from Moscow on the same day as you leave London. I have written to Moscow to see if someone will confirm the general offer they have already made to put you up.

14 December 1964

Last Friday Eric and I made a trip to a collective farm. I asked the MFA to arrange it in order to get an idea of arrangements for travel outside UB. They arranged for us to go to Sükhbaatar Way Farm close to Ulan Bator because of the wintry conditions. This was very convenient.

A member of the MFA came with us. We set out at 8.30 a.m. just as the sun was rising. We were heavily wrapped up, but I could have done with another layer in the Land Rover.

In no time at all the Land Rover was iced up over every window. The heater is inadequate to clear more than squares of about eight inches each way for the driver and front seat passenger, and there is then no heat left over for the interior. It is possible to postpone the frosting up for a little by opening a window, but breath freezes the moment it touches the glass whether the window is open or not. So if we wanted to see the landscape we had to open a window, which was an antisocial act. I am writing to London to ask for supplementary heating if any can be supplied.

We drove to Nalaikh, which is a little coal-mining village about 45 kilometres east of Ulan Bator. The collective farm headquarters was about three miles from Nalaikh. There we were received by the managing committee ranging from a very friendly chairman (aged 34 and very capable) to the oldest member aged 67, with a face like a withered, rotten windfall and with such loud breathing that he kept on stopping the meeting. We drank *airag* (*koumiss*) and ate lumps of dried milk and dried cream slices and Russian chocolates and were given an introductory talk (400,000 hectares, 110 kilometres from north to south, 4600 people, 73,000 animals, of which 17,000 horses, 950 camels, 35,000 sheep and so on). They were keen to have questions, so I asked plenty. They also asked many questions, some of which were fairly technical, about British farming, which I could not answer.

We then climbed into the Land Rover and a Russian Gaz and set out for the sheep. We drove 40 kilometres or a little more to the south, all the way through about six inches of crunchy powder snow. The Gaz was better on the level but we were better at climbing. The chairman took a poor view of our heating and said he would have brought his office stove complete with dried dung fuel if he had known that the British were so Spartan. We passed a small herd of horses and a herd of sheep on our way. Otherwise we saw no living beings. We found the flock we were looking for in a lovely wide valley – some 650 sheep with a shepherd on horseback, the horse's coat white with rime. A little way further on were three *ger*s (*yurt*s with the three families responsible for this flock). They were tucked in below the rising ground at the end of the valley. We admired the new wooden shelters half open to the sky that had been put up for the sheep and the store of hay behind them (these are main points in current propaganda after 1.3 million animals were lost in the severe winter of last year).

Then we entered the head shepherd's *ger* and he and his wife went through their guest ceremonies. First we were given large bowls of *airag* and various forms of dried milk and cream to nibble with it. Then Mongolian food bowls of *arkhi*, the local vodka – I mean the little wood bowls lined with silver that Professor Lattimore and Dr Lindgren-Utsi showed us. Then we had some tea, that is the Mongolian tea soup, in china bowls, and finally a weaker sort of *arkhi* distilled at home from *airag*. The old shepherd made a great speech of welcome and I made a reply (Mongol–Russian interpretation by the MFA man). The children and neighbours stood staring at us from just inside the door (they all have crimson cheeks from the cold), and one of the wives from next door turned out to be a Kazakh in a form of Kazakh costume. The old man showed us his family photos and various other treasures, and his wife told us all about her other children (away at boarding school at the farm headquarters), and the children quarrelled about who could ride best. After a while we rose and the family posed for photographs, looking splendid in their best *del*s. I may add that at one point Eric had to be commanded to down his drinks and not flinch.

We drove back to HQ by a different 40-kilometre stretch of emptiness and had a very good lunch in the farm dining room, much better than we have at the hotel, but of course in Mongolian style – more drinks, toasts and semi-speeches.

After lunch we drove off northwards into the mountains to look at cows. We went about 50 kilometres this time and, on the way, we stopped an ancient Mongol on his camel so that I could have a ride. The camel screamed and did not like it, but the old Mongol made it scream harder by giving us a remarkably agile demonstration of how to vault into the saddle with only one hand on the front hump. Seven families in seven *gers* looked after the cows, 130 of them in a 'farm', not a herd. We were entertained in two different *gers*, songs by some of the girls being added to the programme. The cows came in from the mountainside as we left and we saw them being put into shelters in groups of 20, one woman caring for each group with the help of her small children.

We returned to the HQ and visited the hospital, school, community centre, kindergarten and crèche. Then final drinks, speeches, thanks and off home.

These little groups of herdsmen live five or six kilometres from the next group, a dozen kilometres or so from their brigade HQ, and 40 kilometres or 50 kilometres or more from the farm centre. They have no transport except horses and camels, and the temperature was –10°C at midday and –20°C by 16.30 hours. Of course they live in the middle of a superb landscape and it is dry and sparkling and blue and sunny. Their *gers* are cosy when the stove is burning hard (provided the women have collected plenty of dried dung from the steppe), but their lives are tough and solitary and almost timeless, in the sense that the past goes back to the last lambing season and the future stretches to the next lambing season and there is little or nothing beyond. It is fine to spend a day with them, but it feels hard to leave them behind to live out a lifetime so unchanging and bare and at the mercy of the elements.

I now have a very vivid impression of the difficulties of winter travel in Mongolia. The Foreign Ministry are right to say that it is not to be undertaken lightly. Certainly our Land Rover is inadequate as at present equipped.

But we can still do a good deal with it round Ulan Bator.

Reginald to Jane, George and William

16 December 1964

As you are all together, there is a good excuse for writing to you

7. Camels in their full winter coats.

all together. I hope you will have had a good Christmas and New Year by the time you read this. The letter itself will spend Christmas in Hong Kong. Here we shall have a holiday from Christmas instead of a Christmas holiday.

Winter has really come and I have had the woman who looks after our rooms – Zogsood, a Hero of Labour – seal the windows, except one little top one in each room, which can be opened if we feel too hot. She seals them with a sort of adhesive tape after stuffing the frames of the outside windows with cotton wool. All sorts of people now appear in fur- or fleece-lined *del*s who used to appear in Western clothes. In the distance people look very stout, with matchstick legs. People who have no long, leather boots wear *valenki* or felt boots and look as though they have swollen legs and blunt feet. The old men walk with a forward stoop and their hands clasped behind their backs. Apparently this is the old Mongol way of walking. Of course, they used not to walk much – they always rode.

When I went for a climb this afternoon I found myself being followed by a lot of cows. They came running from all the surrounding hills to join me. I suppose they see human beings only when it is time to go home and they thought I had come to fetch them. When I got back to the Land Rover, Batsukh shot off at high speed and we left the cows behind. I saw a yak for the first time last Saturday.

What is it like living at Hampton again? And how was Christmas at Cliveden? I look forward to hearing about your festivities.

Reginald to Ann

18 December 1964

[Letter requesting innumerable little items – ink, boot polish, scarves to give as presents, address labels and bills to be paid.] Our order from Ostermann-Petersen is stuck at Tallinn. We are obtaining supplies from firms in Hong Kong, by sea to Tientsin and then by train via Peking. It looks as though HK will be much the best supply point. I hope our baggage will soon be on its way eastward from Moscow, with the help of the embassy spurring on the Russian railways.

Your letter through the open post took ten days to reach Ulan Bator and another three to reach me. Not bad. On behalf of the GPO I am taking up with the Mongols the question of postal communications. By the way, we have a Post Box number, 703, and our telegraphic address, Prodrome, Ulan Bator, is working satisfactorily. Telegrams in English from the FO reach me within the day. I can ring Peking without too much delay. I have not yet had cause to ring Moscow. Ringing London seems out of the question.

20 December 1964

Thank you for your letters about visiting G and Ron at Chidding-fold, and about Cliveden and meeting various people, including Van Oss.[1] The bag room seems to have been thrown off balance by the Christmas rush. Eric received no letters from home by our bag this weekend, which is a bit upsetting for him as his mother is in hospital at Brora and a sister is in hospital somewhere else with a difficult pregnancy. They are a family that sticks together, but Mongolia has an unsticking effect.

Thank you very much for the gramophone records. We gave a little party last night and the records were tremendously popular with the guests. The Czech ambassador is borrowing the Beatles next week to record them on his tape recorder.

The fishermen here (chiefly the Soviet ambassador) say that, apart from the *taimen* or arctic char, which can be caught in very large sizes (15 kilograms or more) and which is the real game fish here, there are plenty of pike and apart from that something the Russians call *lenok*, a word that does not figure in my dictionaries. There are said to be grayling, perch and roach in Mongolian waters too. My rod is on its way with our baggage. It would be a good idea if you bring one too.

Shoes wear out and break down very quickly here. You must get a pair of vibram-soled climbing boots and/or shoes from Mrs Lawrie. You cannot get any worthwhile exercise outside UB without them.

Here the Christmas question simply does not arise. Please thank the children for their cards and tell George that his attracts special attention and is much admired as an English joke. I am lunching on the 25th with the Yugoslavs. I do not know if they realize that it is Christmas Day. For the Mongols the New Year is the time of celebration.

21 December 1964

Two more requirements – one or two all-sizes washbasin plugs, and some ice trays for the two refrigerators we now have.

The hotel is crowded to the doors at present with men and women from the backwoods who are here for the session of the Great National Khural, which opens tomorrow and to which I am invited. They look a pretty leathery-skinned crowd. They bring the whiff of the backwoods with them. I can see that the remote parts of this country must be very rough indeed.

I am having a visitation from Terence Garvey from 9 to 12 January. It will help to while away a few days before you come.

We are having a heat wave – last night's temperature was only 0°F. The Queen's Messengers are here and feel that their improved cold-weather kit is wasted.

29 December 1964

Thank you for your Christmas telegram. And thank you for the 'fruits confits', which we are still eating, and for the candied pineapple, which I pressed into service as a present for Mme Yugoslavia who had us to lunch on Christmas Day. Apart from that we had no Christmas, but I enjoyed having a quiet day with plenty of reading, flute playing and listening to carols and Christmas music on the radio from Singapore, Ceylon and Australia. Some of the eastern European communities had a holiday on the afternoon of the 24th and the 25th, but only as a sort of official drinking time.

On Boxing Day we did the right thing and went to the theatre to see a Mongolian opera – *The Three Kings of Sharingol*. They were nothing to do with Epiphany, although they were white, black and yellow. We bought tickets at the box office, which is not the best way to do it if you belong to the diplomatic corps; the sour old woman in the ticket-selling hole offered us two seats in the front of an approved diplomatic corps box, so that seemed all right. When we arrived the theatre was crowded from top to bottom with country bumpkins in *del*s and boots and shaved heads and their wives in their usual bright colours. The whole place smelled of animals and milk and *argal* (the dried dung they burn in their *ger*s). A tough woman attendant hurled herself into our box, threw out two peasants, shook the rest up, beamed at us and put us into two front seats that had been cleared in the Mongol sea. We became quite a conversation piece for all our neighbours, and ripples of sensation spread outwards when I addressed a word or two in Mongol to those seated next to us (do you remember the Austrian exclamation when one said 'Guten Morgen?' – 'Aber Sie sprechen perfekt Deutsch!'). The opera turned out to be a modern creation on an old fairy-tale theme, with much talking, some pastiche modern harmonies and some indifferent singing. Lord Furness[2] cannot be serious about bringing the company to London. It must be that they look after him very well while he is here – he has some wrestler friends, I am told. The real fun was with the audience. At one point an actor on the stage scanned the heavens for a bird that was supposed to be flying around. An old chap in the box next to us lurched to his feet and started gazing up into the roof of the theatre until his neighbours shouted to him to sit down – 'baikhgui' they called, which means 'there is nothing', like 'yok' in Turkish. They all knew the story and a rustle of approval went through the house when the plot took exactly the turn they had expected. They repeated words and phrases to one another and roared with laughter at anything remotely comic. Some of them had terrible coughs and the din from the audience was greater than the din from the stage. The only comparatively silent period was when six slave girls did an oriental dance in what looked like Maiden Form bras. I had a scarred, stubble-headed old Mongol leaning against me and scratching himself for most of the time. His wife was behind me and poked me in the back whenever she got excited. A man at the back of the box kept on grumbling because he could not turn a light on to read his newspaper. At the end no one clapped and a most desperate struggle ensued in the cloakroom. We were spotted as foreigners and everything came to a standstill while all available attendants concentrated on getting us properly dressed to withstand the terrible frost (the theatre is 50 yards from the hotel). It was a unique Boxing Night.

A few days before I had been to a party at the Polish embassy: the Polish Ambassador is Dean of the Corps and he gave two parties for heads of mission, men only. I was bidden with the Chinese Ambassador, the Hungarian Ambassador, the North Vietnamese (whom we do not recognize), the North Korean (whom we do not recognize) and the Cuban. The Chinese, the Vietnamese and the Hungarian brought their interpreters in order to be able to converse in Russian. The Cuban's interpreter failed to turn up, so I had to feed him with occasional scraps of conversation in English or Spanish. The Pole is deaf and conducts all conversations in a loud and penetrating shout. We started at a circular table on which were arranged in a circle the exact number of glasses required, the glasses for the interpreters being slightly smaller. I soon envied the interpreters because we had to drink salvo after salvo of Polish vodka, sometimes with wine sandwiched between. The Orientals cheated as usual, namely they proposed toasts and only pretended to drink, but the Pole and the Hungarian swallowed glass after glass and insisted on having a British drinking partner. After a while we staggered to the dining room where the Pole put a tape of modern jazz on his tape recorder. The Chinese and his satellites looked disapproving and the Cuban denounced it as American. The old Hungarian was in fighting mood by now and said he liked it and anyway it sounded to him like Polish folk music. The Pole drowned it with his shouting and kept up a rapid fire of toasts, but in a lull the Chinese formally requested some Polish music and the Pole had to comply. The food was not bad but was quite spoiled by the drink. Happily I was opposite the

Hungarian and his interpreter whom I like and next to the Korean who speaks good Russian. After dinner we moved to another room, also set out for our exact number with suitable discrimination against the interpreters, and there we drank coffee and brandy and beer. By this time the Chinese consented to understand English (he was in Ceylon before this) – so it must have been a good party! We started at 6.30 and were away by 9.00, suffering from diminished responsibility. The things I do for England!

There are ominous signs that everyone here is preparing to see the New Year in in similar style. I think there may be a big government reception with Strip the Willow toasts round the top table.

I expect your Christmas was more normal than mine. I hope you enjoyed it and stored up some normalcy to see you through Mongolia.

Reginald to William

1 January 1965

This is the first letter I am writing in 1965. Today in Mongolia is rather like Christmas Day in England. There is a big tree with coloured lights and paper chains in the middle of Sükhbaatar Square, and next to it stands a huge figure of Grandfather Frost. He wears Mongolian clothes, that is to say a fleece-lined *del* and long boots and a fur hat with a pointed crown and ribbons hanging down his back. His costume is light blue, not red, and he carries a leather satchel, which is supposed to contain letters and presents. Today is a holiday and all the families in Ulan Bator seem to have a New Year tree and to give one another presents and to have family parties. This morning I saw many Mongolian boys and girls wearing new things that had obviously been given to them as useful presents. There are very few toys on sale here.

It snowed a little two days ago. In some parts of the town ice has slowly formed on the pavements, and boys put on ice skates and skate up and down the pavements. Everywhere the children run and slide rather than walk. They often go about in threes, taking it in turns to be the middle one who sits on his heels and is pulled along by the other two. They enjoy the winter and are very hardy.

Last week I passed a caravan of seven camels outside Ulan Bator. One of them was being ridden by a boy about George's size and one by a girl about your size. Country children soon learn their parents' work here, but usually they are given young animals to look after, not fully grown working ones. But still, the camels did not seem to mind being told what to do by children.

In the market, which is held in Ulan Bator on Sundays, it is possible to buy a camel for about 700 tugriks, which is just under £70. The camels look very healthy at present because they all have thick winter coats – of camel hair of course. Camels are used mostly in the winter. In the summer they fatten up and grow good humps on the pastures. This makes it possible for them to work with little food in the winter, when horses and oxen become too thin and weak to work properly.

Enjoy your Easter term. I shall look forward to seeing you at the end of it.

Reginald to Jane

1 January 1965

We have found to our astonishment here that the New Year is celebrated like Christmas. On the 29th there were taps on my door all day as messengers left cards from all sorts of official people. I had no cards at all and could not find any good ones to buy. What was worse, presents started to arrive from the ambassadors, Minister of Foreign Trade and the head of the tourist organiz-ation. In most cases they sent bottles of national drink or books or cigarettes (or cigars and rum from the Cuban). The Minister of Foreign Trade sent me three of the porcelain figures they sell to tourists, and the Soviet Ambassador sent me *And Quiet Flows the Don* in four volumes. I hastily packed up some bottles of whisky and sent them off and wrote letters of thanks and sent out visiting cards with New Year greetings. On the 30th it got worse – cards arrived from all the members of the higher ranks of the govern-ment – the PM and all six Deputy PMs and the President, all the cards being signed personally by them and their wives; and more came from all the principal members of the Ministry of Foreign Affairs and their wives. So I sat down and inscribed a little pile of visiting cards with a new year's greeting in Mongolian (which I thought would make up by personal effort and attention for not having a proper greetings card) and sent them all out for delivery by our driver, Batsukh. Of course, cards continued to trickle in from unexpected people, but I think I have managed to field the lot. At any rate, I now have a collection of autographs of the top Mongolian leadership. Next year we shall have to have a properly printed greetings card from London. Some of the Mongolian cards are very attractive – I think each ministry prints its own – they were far better than anything on sale to the public.

We have the Cuban national ballet here at the moment. They all speak English and only one or two can speak Russian. Their conductor has a Fidel Castro beard but is really a very mild man. They have been dancing *Coppélia* and doing it very well. The prima ballerina is called Alicia and the leading male dancer is called Alonso. Alicia's daughter is also in the company, and she has a son of six who is going to be given a child's part when they get back to Cuba so that they can claim three generations on a single stage. The casual clothes the members of the company wear about the hotel must be an eye-opener for the Mongols, who are not used to anything stylish at all. And Mongolia is undoubtedly an eye-opener for the Cubans. They are all shivering, although in fact it is very warm for the time of year – only between $-5°F$ and $-15°F$.

It will not be long now before I see you again.

Reginald to Ann's mother

3 January 1965

I am sorry to hear that you have fallen and hurt yourself. The Reform Club stairs are steep and hard I am afraid. I hope you are feeling better and recovering the use of your arm.

The local pundits say that the winter progresses in periods of about nine days from the New Year onwards, each period beginning with a sharp fall in temperature. So far nothing has happened and we continue to fluctuate between $-5°F$ and $-15°F$. When you know the form, these are quite comfortable.

We have just had some exciting political events here – a rumpus in the Central Committee, calls on Tsedenbal and company to resign, and a victory for T with various expulsions from the party. This has given me plenty to read and write about. It is most obliging of the Mongols to stage this sort of thing for me so soon after my arrival.

We have the Queen's Messengers here at present. This team is not a nice one. One of them is horrid. He seems to think that Eric and I are here to provide him with entertainment and look after him. He has a daughter who rides horses and he simply cannot go home without some photographs of Mongolian ponies. You can imagine how happy I was to help him spend an afternoon not looking at Mongolia, but simply driving around and freezing and looking for a group of horses to photograph! And I have the bag contents to deal with.

The hotel staff are used to our ways now and do not disturb us much. My little 'flat' is comfortable. We have a dear elderly woman who is in charge of cleaning our rooms and dealing with laundry, but I am afraid she looks after me better than Eric Cheyne, which is a bit hard on him.

The hotel restaurant remains the least comfortable part of the place. This is largely due to the hopelessly slack ways of the staff. It is like having a lot of children playing at being waitresses. They are very charming about it. The way to win them over is to speak Mongolian, but of course that takes time. Meanwhile the best course is to keep in well with the management, flatter and flirt with the pleasant ones and be fierce with the really useless ones.

I shall be very relieved to see Ann on the 27th. I hope she will not find it too chilly. I don't think she will, and we know how to cope with it.

Reginald to Ann

4 January 1965

I had four letters from you this weekend and enjoyed them all. This is the last bag by which I can write to you. You cannot reply except by coming here. We are nearly back together again. Your two letters by open mail took about a fortnight to reach me, no better than the bag. The Moscow telephone link seems inoperable. I am going to speak to the Soviet ambassador about it. Moscow needs to learn to be more helpful.

Do bring *Beasts, Men and Gods*[3] with you. We are gathering quite a good little library of books on Mongolia. It does not matter what they contain. No one can complain about books on my shelves as long as the less acceptable ones are not pressed on outsiders.

I advise against buying a fur hat with earflaps. Smart women do not wear them. They wear various creations that pull down over the ears and are entirely satisfactory.

Terence Garvey is coming here on Saturday and staying until Tuesday. I shall give a cocktail party on Saturday and a lunch on

Monday. They will keep me very busy for a few days. It takes an inordinate amount of time and energy to lay on that sort of thing in this hotel.

It will be interesting to see how Garvey behaves towards me. After he had seen my first dispatch he instructed me to report to him and not to the FO. I protested and quoted Foreign Service Regulations and sent a copy of my letter to London. Garvey wrote me a rude reply, which I ignored. Now, by the last bag, he has had the uncomfortable experience of forwarding to me, on instructions, a letter from the Chief Clerk, no less, giving me the full right to report to the Secretary of State and correspond freely with London (of course with copies to Peking). His invitation to go down to Peking for Christmas was, I think, all part of his possessiveness in relation to Mongolia. When I refused on all sorts of good grounds, he announced that in that case he was coming to Ulan Bator. But that was before he received the Chief Clerk's letter. Of course, I can now write and say, quite sincerely, how much I am looking forward to seeing him and why doesn't Rosemary come too. What foolishness! I shall show you the correspondence when you are here.

London has agreed that Eric Cheyne can go off to Hong Kong for a fortnight in mid-February. I am going to tell Garvey that you and I could go to Peking for a week at the beginning of March.

Tucked away here behind barriers of space and time, I find myself in a relatively strong position for dealing with this sort of thing. The only trouble is that I have no one to consult and try out ideas on. Thank goodness you will be here soon. Eric Cheyne is a superb workhorse but in no way a kindred spirit. Perhaps Garvey thought I would not have the nerve to call his bluff all by myself. I doubt if he will try again.

You will probably say I am too inclined to find someone higher up to cross swords with. It really is not so. You will see that it is only legitimate self-defence – as all warring nations say. However, it tends to be a competitive life and one sometimes has to compete with zest or go under. Besides, I was not going to put up with the drawbacks of isolation without also having its privileges.

Could you please order and pay for a copy of *Mongolian–English Dictionary*, edited by Ferdinand D. Lessing, University of California, Berkeley, 1960. The Cambridge University Press handles it in the UK. This is for a Hungarian professor of Mongol and Tibetan who lives in the hotel here and has been much attracted by Beatles music. But that is for your information only. The book should come by bag addressed to me, of course.

I am glad you like Russian. I must work harder at Mongolian.

You have already written your last letters to me, and I shall receive them on Saturday week, and a week and a half after that you will be here. It has been a very long time without you. I hope you like it here. The visitations of the Queen's Messengers (arrive Saturday depart Tuesday) increase pressure once a fortnight, and I have plenty to do, but there is rarely any need to rush and we can arrange a good deal of most days to suit ourselves.

This will reach you just before the children go back to school. I suppose you will return to Pilgrims Lane after that? I hope that you as well as they have enjoyed the holidays. I imagine you will put all surplus kit and equipment into store at Cox & Kings.

12 January 1965

This is a very hasty note written in Garvey's compartment in the Peking train at 7.10 a.m. We have had a frantic but harmless three days. It will be a relief to spend a day or two doing innocent things like cleaning my shoes.

I hope your journey will be relaxed and comfortable. The FO say they are sending a typewriter with you, but do not bother yourself about that – it will arrive by freight in the fullness of time.

Reginald to his parents

17 January 1965

I hope the children are not going to feel that we are too out of touch. I am much impressed by my out-of-touchness. It is very difficult to get anything done from here. For example, the hotel laundry has boiled one of my pairs of long underpants and shrunk them to half-size. I write to Thresher & Glenny for a new pair and tell them to put them in the bag on such and such a date. After a month I receive a reply that the suppliers did not send them the right pair in time, that they are sorry and will await my further instructions! I have sent them an angry rebuke but of course it does no good – the underpants will reach me in the spring. Perhaps it is good to be reminded that the Mongols are not alone in inefficiency.

As the winter draws on, the variety of food available here

grows smaller. Of course the Mongols themselves, even town Mongols, are at present living almost entirely on boiled or some-times stewed mutton and tea. Their tea is a sort of soup, much boiled (tea and milk together) and tasting a bit burnt, with a film of fat on the surface. They drink this in the morning and all day long. In the evening they have their big mutton meal, which is a cross between mutton soup and mutton stew; if there is any left over they eat it for breakfast in the morning in addition to their milky tea. Only the more sophisticated town-dwellers eat bread. Fruit, vegetables and eggs are almost unknown to them. I am told that in summer they switch almost completely from meat to milk, drinking perhaps as much as ten litres of milk a day, preferably in the form of *airag*, that is *koumiss*, fermented mare's milk; but *airag* is often hard to obtain in town.

Against this background it is hardly surprising if the only vegetable available in the hotel at present is pickled cabbage and occasionally potatoes. Our diet at the moment consists of meat (mutton or beef, hacked off in fairly crude lumps and mostly stewed, and sometimes hare or duck), bread (good, strong bread, halfway to black bread), butter, rice, pickled cabbage, yoghurt, cheese and black tea (that is tea without milk, with sugar). For the last three days there have been some fresh tomatoes and also some eggs. We buy eggs from the diplomatic shop when there are some. We, that is to say I as a head of mission, can also buy a small amount of caviar there. Until a month ago we could buy sour cream, but that is 'off' for the rest of the winter. Every now and then there are apples for sale, but the last consignment was not worth eating. The Queen's Messengers bring us oranges, lemons and apples from Hong Kong, and usually a white loaf as well. The Ambassador sent us a Chinese ham last week and we are still eating our way through it. We make our own breakfast and this is always a very good meal. We have tinned things of various sorts with which we could make other meals at odd times, but Eric and I do not have time for that sort of thing and it is horrid living in closed rooms with the smell of cooking. Besides, the local hotel diet eked out with Hong Kong fruit is a healthy one even if it is unexciting. And it is, as you see, a good deal better than anything the Mongols aspire to. Curiously, one essential requirement here is good, strong teeth. My assistant has some false ones, which is a serious disadvantage.

8. Milking a mare, with her foal held beside her to help induce the flow of milk.

Reginald to Ann's father

18 January 1965

I hope the opening ceremony at your new court[4] was a happy one. It sounds as though the Cliveden Christmas was a great success. Bron and Bill seem to have been extraordinarily generous to Ann and the children, from what I gather from their letters.

By the time you read this Ann will be here with me and I shall once again be able to have a bipolar or stereoscopic view of life. I must confess that I have been growing a bit bored in the company of my clerk/assistant. He is a fairly dour Scot and does not have a gay or lively mind. Fortunately, he works very hard. I expect he finds the pressure of my constant presence burdensome.

Ann and I together shall have to take care not to weigh too heavily on him. Our ambassador, Terence Garvey, paid us a visit from Peking last weekend. Having been told from London to refrain from trying to remote control me, he was very amiable and helpful. I hope that Ann and I shall find, when we visit Peking in March, that the message has been passed to his wife, whose main aim last October was to put right thoughts into my unwilling head. Once she can be persuaded to accept one as an equal human being she is probably a nice person to know.

We are having a mild winter here. The temperature has so far failed to plunge to –40°C. When the Ambassador was here we had one really cold day and we made a trip into the country on that day. I think he suffered a bit – at any rate he has now at last admitted that Ulan Bator is not a bed of roses or a fun post. My only problem as regards kit is that I have not yet mastered a way of keeping my feet warm in the Land Rover. It has no insulation underfoot. Perhaps a foot muff would be the answer, but it is too late to try it this year. I wish you and Mo could have my sunshine and dryness instead of the English winter.

Ann to her parents

British Embassy, Ulan Bator, 29 January 1965

Well, here I am sitting in Outer Mongolia all the world as though it were Golders Green or Manchester, except that the sky is a cloudless blue and the sunshine is brilliant.

First of all I will tell you about my journey, which was loaded with near disaster but in fact went off quite easily. The flight to Moscow was delayed but uneventful, with nothing but cloud all the way. I found the long descent very painful on the ears: BEA gave us nothing to chew or suck. When we arrived in Moscow we climbed off the plane and I promptly sat down on my behind! The ground was covered with solid ice.

The Brimelows were there to meet me, which was just as well as I found that the FO travel section had not provided me with a transit visa for the Soviet Union. I had absolutely no piece of paper to show that I was entitled to land in Moscow. This was very awkward. However, Tom Brimelow talked very hard to a nice young officer who said that I must leave my passport at the airport and could go away for the night. By this time it was about 8.30 Moscow time. The airport is about an hour's drive out of the town, but as it was pitch dark I couldn't see anything much except a dead straight road with a border of snow and trees on either side, just the sort of road one can imagine galloping along in a troika chased by a pack of wolves!

I spent a comfortable night with the Brimelows and the next day was taken round Moscow a bit and visited the Kremlin. Moscow struck me as being a very grey and gloomy place. An overcast sky, which I gathered persists for most of the winter, has a very depressing effect on everyone, and this combines with the drabness of the people in the streets and the covering of dirty snow. The only bright spots are the little golden dome, on the churches in the Kremlin, and here and there inside the big store called GUM, which is really a huge covered market and still is slightly reminiscent of the colourfulness of an Eastern bazaar, although all the goods are fairly shoddy and the people seem pretty glum, even the ones tossing back their glasses in the champagne bars – they don't serve beer, only Soviet champagne.

In the evening I was driven out to the airport and without any difficulty was handed back my passport. The aircraft was big like a Britannia, all one class and quite full. There was a group of Poles (I think) who seemed very gay and had brought fishing rods with them, and a whole lot of East Germans, about four families with children. Apparently they were coming out to build houses and factories and were due to stay for about two years. I don't think they had much idea what they were coming to.

We were kept waiting a few minutes while what I discovered later was a group of very important Russians got on the plane and sat at the back after everyone else was settled. We took off soon after 8.00 (Moscow time) and at 9.30 the little airhostess came round with drinks, vodka and a sort of fizzy drink, which I think was non-alcoholic and quite refreshing. Around 10.15 we were given dinner, which consisted of a little dish of crab mayonnaise – very good; a piece of chicken and some boiled rice and about eight tinned peas; an apple; some black bread and butter and a white roll; a chocolate éclair; and tea with lemon and/or sugar. It wasn't at all bad. The only drawback was that in the morning (by my watch 4.45 a.m.) we got exactly the same meal with garlic sausage instead of crab mayonnaise and no butter. In the meanwhile we had come down at Novosibirsk. I had expected to come down in Omsk and apparently so had all my fellow passengers. I understood later that this change was due to our having important passengers on board – a security measure according to Reg. Anyway, it is difficult to imagine a more desolate spot. It was pitch dark and just as one had always imagined Siberia to be – so cold that coming out of the 'plane with all one's furs on (I had bought a fur hat in Moscow) it was like jumping into a cold bath. A bleak wind was blowing the powdery snow along and the place was lit by brilliant arc lights that only seemed to make the spaces beyond darker. Inside the airport there were row upon row of

chairs in which sprawled hundreds of people who looked as
though they had long ago given up any hope of getting away,
some of them might even have been dead, it was difficult to say.
We waited there about half an hour and then climbed thankfully
back into the plane. About 3.15 the sky began to lighten and
before 4.00 a.m. it was bright sunlight. Below us was a moon
landscape of endless angular hills covered with a thin powdering
of snow, obviously eternally windswept – I have never seen anything so bleak or giving so much the impression of vast distances
of absolutely uninhabitable land, though here and there we could
see minute signs of cultivation. And then abruptly we came to the
rim of the lake, huge cliffs falling quite suddenly into an immense
white sea. There was no sign of Irkutsk: we were obviously not
going to land there as scheduled, and we quickly passed over the
southern tip of Lake Baikal. Almost immediately we were over
Mongolia and the contours of the hills became much softer and
rounder though still white and bare as far as the eye could see.

We landed in Ulan Bator an hour before time and our important passengers got down first and were greeted by a group of
distinguished Mongols. Reg was not there to meet me as no one
had told him that the plane was arriving early. I got out into the
brilliant sunshine wrapped up to the ears and found the air like
Switzerland; but round the corner of the airport building the wind
was very sharp. After I had waited a good half hour Reg turned up
looking very distinguished in his smart, long, fur-collared and -
cuffed sheepskin coat and astrakhan hat. I was glad to see him, as
I couldn't understand a word of what was going on around me.
We collected my luggage and climbed into the Land Rover, driven
by our Mongolian driver, who also seemed very smart in Western
clothes and fur hat, and were driven to the town about three or
four miles away down a dead straight road with nothing but bare
snowy slopes on either side. The town is dominated by a power
station belching huge clouds of filthy smoke, and one approaches
over a very Chinese looking bridge, which crosses the Tuul River,
now frozen absolutely solid. UB is a tiny place with one or two big
buildings sticking out of it, very reminiscent of one or two smaller
towns in Turkey. There is a huge colony of workers' flats, very
ugly blocks about six or seven storeys high, built by Chinese
labour. At the moment they look bright and clean, but judging by
everything else they will soon look shabby and dirty. In the older,

outer parts of the town the people all live in *yurts* (in Mongolian *gers*) and these are gathered in groups behind wooden palisades and all look absolutely filthy. Once one is inside the hotel one is surprised by the apparent comfort, that is to say it is solidly built and is very warm indeed, and the furniture is quite comfortable.

We have a suite of rooms that is almost like a little flat. You come in through the door from the wide impersonal landing and the corridor and find yourself in a small lobby with a coat rack on the wall (and cases of drink stacked below it) and a mirror with a light over it, and off it is a little lavatory (WC and hand washbasin) in which Reg has rigged up our little electric stove – two rings and a small oven. Straight ahead you go into a small sitting room with a comfortable settee and two armchairs, a desk on one side, a bookcase on the other and a low table in the middle. The window looks out from the front of the hotel, across a small square with young trees in it, to the main road through the town with a few buildings on the far side of it – the Yugoslav embassy, the Bulgarian embassy and the Foreign Ministry – and beyond that are the white hills. Facing the window and turning right you come into a larger room with a table and chairs and a couple of easy chairs where we can eat meals. If you turn left from the little central sitting room you come into the bedroom, which has a dressing table, a wardrobe and a double bed, which is made up of what are called 'biscuits' in the army – three hard square pieces of mattress per person, six in all. They are quite the most uncomfortable things to sleep on that anyone has yet invented. To cover us we have an eiderdown each, and that is all. So you are either boiled, or your toes are sticking out and growing cold, or you turn over and take the whole thing with you and your back freezes. So far I haven't slept well. Turning left from the bedroom, there is a small space with a wardrobe in it and from that, turning left again, you enter a very adequate bathroom with, so far, reliable plumbing. A final touch – we have Reg's tall and narrow steel security cupboard in our bedroom.

This is the general programme of the day as it is at the moment. The first morning Reg brought me breakfast in bed as I really was exhausted by the journey. But this morning I got up at about eight and heated some coffee (made the night before) and milk (powdered milk as in wartime and quite disgusting), poured out some orange juice from a tin and boiled three eggs (Eric joins us for breakfast). There is also local black bread and butter, and we have some marmalade. Reg and Eric then go off to do some work in Eric's room next door. The elderly Mongolian chambermaid comes and cleans the rooms very vaguely. I wash up, do some washing, write this letter, and make a cup of tea at about eleven. Meanwhile, Reg has returned to do some work in our larger reception room. At about twelve thirty we go down to the hotel restaurant for lunch. This is a vast hall with a stage at one end and lots of tables with fairly dirty tablecloths on them. These slowly fill up with eastern European and Soviet aid workers and advisers who live in the hotel alongside us. Reg is the only one of us who can read the menu, which is in Mongolian and Russian. We have some sort of soup, which is not bad, but very greasy, then some probably tasteless meat with boiled rice. Sometimes there is cabbage salad, sometimes a very few tiny tomatoes. Afterwards we have some yoghurt or a milk product halfway between yoghurt and cream cheese, and that's it. It certainly isn't very nice. Our stores from Denmark have not arrived yet. We have a few things (for example the fruit juice and marmalade) brought by the QMs from Peking, and we can buy some things sometimes from the 'diplomatic shop' – eggs for example, or fresh milk, or today some apples – but you never know if there is going to be anything there and it is terribly expensive.

After lunch, Reg and I go out for either a little drive or a walk, but it is too cold to be out for long. Yesterday afternoon there was the opening of a picture show by local painters and the diplomatic corps were invited. I met the Hungarians, Yugoslavs, Czechs, Poles, and so forth, and their wives. They are a dowdy lot. We saw one Mongolian painting we would like to buy if we can find out how.

We go down for supper at about seven and the food is just like lunch, except that there is no soup. So it is worse. And so to a hard night's sleep.

We have just heard that our heavy luggage from London has arrived. This should make quite a difference to our comfort. So far, for example, Reg and Eric have been holding their boiled eggs in their hands to eat them. Now we shall have some household equipment of our own. Tomorrow Reg and Eric have to go to the station at 7.30 a.m. to meet the Queen's Messengers and to collect our luggage. On Sunday we are going to the theatre.

I am still very tired. The change from being too hot in the hotel to too cold outside is exhausting, but I shall get used to it. Reg is better than I have seen him for ages.

西藏西藏

The important Russians on Ann's aircraft were A. N. Shelepin, a secretary of the Central Committee and member of the Politburo of the Communist Party of the Soviet Union, and his entourage. The aircraft was diverted from its scheduled itinerary, as advertised on the flight departure board at the airport in Moscow, for reasons of security without any notice given to anyone but the bosses in Ulan Bator. The other heads of mission in UB, being communists, were summoned to be present at his arrival. I was not invited because it was a Party and not a state occasion. His visit was presumably connected with the dissension that had been occurring in the Mongolian Politburo. From my hotel window I became aware that ambassadorial cars were driving along Peace Street at an unusually early hour, and I wondered what I was missing. Batsukh, my driver, picked up the news of the early arrival of the aircraft on the chauffeur's grapevine and came and alerted me. Otherwise, I would have been even later in meeting Ann.

西藏西藏

Ann to Reginald's parents

30 January 1965

I found Reg in good form here. He is very well and quite cheerful. After all this time the charm of novelty has worn off a bit for him, but on the other hand he has managed to find ways of coping with all the practical difficulties of the situation.

The small consignment of luggage we sent off from London in October arrived yesterday. We can now drink tea out of cups instead of glasses. We have two or three pictures to put up and also our record player and some records and our radio with three short-wave bands for picking up the BBC world service. I think Reg has very much missed having any decent music.

The snow here is very fine and powdery because of the dryness and cold. It is more like salt or icing sugar than the snow we know in the UK. We appear to be living on the southern limit of the tree line. We can see conifers on the tops of the hills to the south, but

Reg says that they are only on the northern slopes. On the southern slopes they dwindle away into the Gobi.

So far I don't seem to have had much free time, but it is difficult to judge as this weekend we have the Queen's Messengers here and they drop in for drinks and tend to hang around and talk. Last night I went to the circus with them. It was great fun and I think the children will enjoy it enormously. It is always the same programme – good old-fashioned stuff, jugglers, acrobats, strong men and some very simple clowning.

I have a splendid golden coloured fox fur hat, which I bought in Moscow. It is just a sort of basin that you can pull down over your ears, and when I turn up the big collar of my fur coat I don't feel the wind at all, especially if I wear a polo-necked sweater.

Reginald to Ann's father

1 February 1965

Ann is beginning to get used to the strange physical conditions here – very hot in, very cold out, excessively dry, irregular hours and restricted diet. It makes a great difference having her about the place. Our baggage from London has also arrived. A narrow way of living that had seemed inseparable from Mongolia has been superseded in a weekend.

Tomorrow is New Year's Day in the old Mongolian calendar. It is the first of the first or major month of spring in the year of the blue snake in the sixteenth sestenary (the sestenaries started in the year AD 1027). Today is the last of the last or major month of winter in the year of the blue dragon. The month that starts tomorrow is commonly called the white month. It is, so to speak, the Mongolian harvest time. Between now and March some 8,000,000 young animals will be born in the Mongolian People's Republic and milk, the main food of the Mongols, will again become abundant (hence the adjective 'white'). It is the time of hardest work and most treacherous weather. Tomorrow all the herdsmen will ride round to their friends and neighbours and drink themselves into a stupor in the saddle to prepare for their great season.

Ann to her mother

1 February 1965

This aerogramme posted by a QM in Hong Kong will reach you

before my letters in the bag do. It is just to assure you that we are really quite comfortably established here. The life of the hotel is rather like life in a hospital. One tends to forget that people in the world outside are living completely different lives. We hear this afternoon that our stores from Copenhagen are here. With that and our heavy baggage, we are not too badly off. We can have minor needs, for example coat hangers and shoetrees, sent up from Hong Kong. One of the QMs will probably ring you up and tell you that they had an amusing weekend here. They were jolly people and threw themselves into the informality of it all. The trouble is one sometimes gets the feeling that it is all one way-out holiday and forgets that Reg is here to do some work.

We are just now going to a party in another room of the hotel given by a Hungarian who is leaving. He has been trying to train *the* Mongolian jazz band under a technical assistance scheme. He has had quite a difficult time.

We went last night to the opera, which was great fun. Written in couplets and with a general musical theme that sounded like *Coming Through the Rye* and dressed in old traditional Mongol costumes, it was a splendid spectacle but had a hackneyed story about a wicked khan who captures a beautiful village maiden.

Ann to her parents

9 February 1965

At the moment Reg is unfortunately in bed with a sore throat. I think he caught a cold from an American who was staying in the hotel when I arrived. On Tuesday he had to get up as usual in the cold and dark to see the QMs off at 7.00 a.m. The train was late and they had to hang around a good deal. The cold is frightfully penetrating. On Friday the same sort of thing happened. A new Romanian ambassador was arriving at the airport and it is the custom in this God-forsaken nest of communism for all the heads of mission to turn out whenever one of their number arrives or departs, unless of course one happens not to be on speaking terms with them (as in this case the Chinese with the Romanians), in which case one is conspicuous by one's absence. To say one is not well is usually taken as a euphemism, so it is a little difficult to plead ill health without giving offence. Anyway, Reg went along to the airport and had to wait an hour getting very cold indeed as it was after four o'clock, and from four on the cold gets much more intense. Going out from 70° in the hotel to −10° outside is bad for anyone with the beginnings of a cold, and the very hot central heating makes the dryness worse and aggravates the discomforts if you are suffering at all from catarrh. Fortunately, Terence Garvey has sent us a humidifier from Peking, which certainly helps to keep the atmosphere a little more normal.

I have now visited the diplomatic shop three times and each time I have come away with about a quart of milk in our little milk can. The shop is an extraordinary place as there is really nothing in it that in the normal way one would wish to buy. One presumes, however, that if there is anything in UB at all, it will appear in the shop. Yesterday, for instance, there was a queue of patient diplomats' wives or their cooks or chauffeurs buying the most miserable looking specimens of dried-up frozen chickens. There was also long fish of some sort, frozen stiff as logs. Apart from these things, which are very rare, one can buy ghastly looking meat, which seems to be all fat and bone and quite unrecognizable. Sometimes there are apples at five tugriks a kilo (1 tugrik = 1/10d). There are usually potatoes and always cow cabbage. Then there are various tins of fruit, jam and so forth at astronomical prices – mostly from Bulgaria and quite good I think, but not worth the money. At other counters there are a few bales of very poor quality material, some souvenirs of the poorest sort and a few saucepans and teapots. It's really pathetic. I haven't yet been in their one 'department store'. The only things I have seen here that I like are fox furs, red or black, which would make up into attractive collars or hats and are cheap at two dollars each.

Eric Cheyne is going off to Hong Kong next Tuesday for about ten days. Reg and I go to Peking when he gets back. We shall stay with the Garveys for ten days. Reg will be very ready for a break by then. His throat infection has pulled him down. This is a trying place to live in and I think he found my arrival and the arrival of our luggage and our stores all at once thoroughly disturbing. It put him quite out of his rather clockwork regime and his bachelor existence. I am not at all sure that he does not secretly blame me for his being smitten by this germ!

This letter is a bit disjointed. I have just come back from a very pleasant walk. I usually go out every day between 2.30 and 3.30. This is the best time of day, rather like a bright day somewhere high up in Switzerland. Outside the town it is really beautiful and it seems to be true that the sun shines for 300 days out of 365. There has been only one dull day since I have been here. The town itself has a permanent pall of smoke over it, mostly from the power station, but also from the hundreds of tiny chimneys poking out of the centres of the roofs of the *gers* where the majority of these people still live. The brilliance is five minutes drive away, outside the town.

Today there have been mass demonstrations about Vietnam. This means that columns of soldiers and factory workers have been marched in orderly fashion to the square. There someone harangues them and then they are marched away.

Ann to her mother

15 February 1965

Thank you so much for your letter with the description of Sir W. Churchill's lying in state. How very satisfactory that father was able to go to the funeral. It must have been a great experience.

Reg's throat is much better. In the end he took some Aureomycin tablets we have in our medicine chest and they seemed to do the trick. Anyway he was fit enough to ski yesterday when we were invited with the rest of the diplomatic corps to visit the Mongolian 'winter sports centre'.

I keep worrying about the children's journey and wondering whether I have thought of everything. They must have their travel pills in plenty of time, especially George, and plenty to read and sweets and chewing gum (to help relieve ear pressures). William is asking whether we shall have Easter eggs. I was wondering whether you could possibly order five chocolate eggs from the Army & Navy – not big ones. They would have to be rather carefully packed. Perhaps one big one would be more sensible. Have it put on our account. Reg thinks this an awful nuisance, but it would give a lot of pleasure.

Reginald to Jane

15 February 1965

It is a month since I last wrote to you. I have been made lazy by seeing Mother writing so much. Today I am sending your passports back to the FO complete with Mongolian visas. Everything is more or less ready for your coming here.

I was on the sick list last week but I am better now. The

trouble is that when I am out of action there is no one to talk
Russian and get things done for us. I can report that this is a most
uncomfortable place to have a cold. The atmosphere is so dry that
the cold cannot develop properly and so drags on for days and
days.

Yesterday we went for a little outing organized by the Ministry
of Foreign Affairs. They took us (heads of mission that is) to a
skiing ground about 40 kilometres north of Ulan Bator, where a
Soviet team was competing in cross-country skiing with a Mongolian team. We did not see much of the teams. In fact they were
not worth seeing. Their equipment is very poor and their style
non-existent. I managed to do a little bit of skiing myself, and
Mother had a ride on a horse-drawn sledge. It was sunny and
frosty and very pleasant in the open. The diplomatic corps was
allocated to various little wooden huts among the trees. We were
put in with the Chinese, namely the two odd-men-out together. Of
course we did not stay there, but it was comfortable to know that
there was a place with a hot stove to which one could return when
cold. We had lunch in a big hut, the men at one table and the
women at another, and of course there was all the usual drinking
of crude spirits and inane toastings.

I have not yet been out with Mother by ourselves. In the first
week we were busy with the arrival of our luggage and consign-
ments of food. In the second week I was confined to my room.
Eric Cheyne goes off for leave in Hong Kong tomorrow and we
shall be alone for a fortnight. I hope we shall be able to go out a
fair amount. The weather at present is beautifully spring-like
(Mongolian style) and by our reckoning almost warm (last night's
minimum was only –2°F). Everyone says it will be colder again but
we have had a mild winter by Mongolian standards and with luck
we shall have a mild spring.

We look forward very much to seeing you in about six weeks'
time.

Reginald to Ann's father
                    15 February 1965 (a Hong Kong aerogramme)
I think one of Ann's strongest first impressions was that I had
become a confirmed bachelor. Mongolia, or rather Ulan Bator, is a
confined space and it is habit-forming. It is only since Ann has
been here that I have realized what long hours we work. It seems

to be bad to live and work in the same place. One gets into the bad habit of never being off duty.

Reginald to his parents

15 February 1965

Our position as regards food has now changed radically. In the last few days we have received a consignment from Copenhagen via Moscow and a consignment from Hong Kong via Peking. We now have plenty to supplement the hotel food for many weeks. The consignment from Copenhagen was frozen solid except for the hard liquor in it, which was cloudy and a bit viscous. Two cases of canned beer took over 24 hours in a temperature of 70° before they became liquid again.

Our 'mild' weather, with night temperatures not much below 0°F, is splendid for the herdsmen because it is the lambing and calving season and their losses are much reduced when the temperature is not too low.

Ann to Reginald's parents

15 February 1965

I am enjoying the weather here. Of course we wear a great many clothes to go outside. I wear a string vest and a woollen vest, two sweaters, long woollen underpants, woollen knickers, woollen socks, trousers, a scarf, lined gloves, fur coat and hat and thick shoes. With all this on I am comfortable standing about in the sunshine if there isn't much wind. In the shade or in the wind one doesn't want to stand still even with all that on.

We have a nice pair of Queen's Messengers here this time. They don't hang around expecting to have drinks with us at all times of the day, which annoys Reg. He is determined to live as strictly regular a life as possible here and finds being put out of his routine disturbing. My arrival I think really rather put him out, especially as I pinched the most comfortable side of the bed.

I find it difficult to sleep really peacefully in this bed. It has very little give in it and one has only an eiderdown as covering and this keeps slipping off. It also gets very hot in the night and the central heating hisses and gurgles all night long, which is a bit disturbing and makes one wonder if it is going to blow up.

One thing that is very well done here is the laundry. They take it away for two or three days and it comes back very nicely ironed

– even the socks. But there is absolutely no form of dry cleaning here, so I imagine we shall just have to let things get dirtier and dirtier until we leave. I gather that even in Moscow the dry-cleaning is no good and the embassy staff have special permission to send things to England. One certainly learns to do without things here, especially food, which seems to be getting worse instead of better. We have found that we can order things from a firm in Hong Kong and they will arrive here in about a month, which is really quite quick. If you want to send us something now and again, perhaps you could see if you can find us some of those packets of dried food. I found some packets of *boeuf jardinière* at Selfridges, for example, and they are quite good and make a welcome change. The other day I got some ham from the diplomatic shop – to me it seems to be more like boiled pork. We had some of it for breakfast today. Rosemary Garvey has sent us a brown loaf from Peking, which is much nicer than the local bread, which has a sour taste and is rather damp. So at the moment we are doing quite well – except yesterday when there was nothing on the hotel menu except eggs – three fried eggs each. I couldn't face them and had a cup of tea and a cake.

Ann to Jane

19 February 1965

Today is our wedding anniversary, but it seems a far cry from Hampstead parish church 16 years ago. When we went on our honeymoon in Devon there were daffodils out on the riverbanks and almond and peach blossom in gardens. Probably they are there this year too. Here everything is white. Yesterday morning it snowed, but not heavily, just fine dry snow that blows about in the wind and lies in light drifts in the gutters. Today it has been snowing on the mountaintops, but it cleared in the afternoon and the sky was blue again.

Yesterday we went a little way up the Holy Mountain that looks over the town. Father did a bit of skiing. I walked up a spur through a larch wood where snow was lying quite thickly and then out from the trees along a bare ridge where the wind had blown the snow almost completely away. From the ridge there is a fine view over the town. Perhaps we shall be able to picnic there in the summer. At the moment it is much too cold. I was very glad to have my arctic anorak on, with wolverine fur round the face.

This morning we were taken round the factory 'combine' in Ulan Bator. We saw them making coats, shoes, gloves and hats from sheepskin leather, and then in another part of the factory spinning and weaving textiles from local wool. They make woollen materials and blankets. Some of the blankets had very attractive Mongolian designs.

This afternoon we are being taken to see the national archives, whatever they are. All of a sudden, you see, we are quite busy.

Yesterday I washed my hair and a Hungarian friend set it for me. I can't think what it will look like in six months time. The hairdresser in the hotel cuts Father's hair quite nicely, so perhaps she will be able to do something for mine. Perhaps you will have to go back to school with a Mongolian haircut, which would be a novelty!

On Sunday it is Father's birthday. Your card and drawing have arrived. I have no idea what we shall do to celebrate – perhaps go to a wrestling match if we can get tickets. Unfortunately, it always seems too difficult to find out what is on in advance. I expect we shall have an amusing day somehow.

Undated (a postcard)

This is a picture of the monument to the Mongolian hero (*baatar*) that is in the middle of the town square. It is difficult to imagine that there will ever be flowers there or people sitting about on seats.

Father and I are off tomorrow on a 400-kilometre trip to visit a state farm. On Tuesday we go to Peking for a week. So our life is not dull! Hope yours isn't either.

Reginald to his parents

Peking, 4 March 1965

Ann and I are living a muddled and confusing existence at present. Last week we were on tour in Mongolia for four days, arriving back in Ulan Bator on Saturday evening. There I read the contents of the bag and sent off answers, and on Tuesday morning we caught the train for Peking, arriving on Wednesday evening. In Peking I spend a certain amount of time in the office and the rest of the time meeting people at meals and looking at Peking. Ann is taken about by various people. We would prefer to be free to explore for ourselves, but shortage of time and helpfulness of kind colleagues make that impossible. There are many beautiful things to be seen here and we cannot hope to see more than a few of them.

It is much warmer here than in UB. The ice is melting and some of the trees already have buds swelling. Most of all we are enjoying the excellent Chinese food. I expect we shall do a little shopping next week, before returning to UB on Thursday.

Ann to Jane

Office of the British chargé d'affaires
Peking, 5 March 1965

I am sitting in a Chinese hairdresser – incredible! We arrived here the evening of the day before yesterday by train from Mongolia. It took us two days and a night and it was a most fascinating journey. For the whole of the first day we travelled over flat Gobi country, where you could see scarcely anything in any direction, occasional distant flocks and herds and scarcely any human beings. In the evening we got to the Chinese border and then, after running through Chinese Mongolia in the night, we gradually came down into China proper where scarcely a square yard of ground was uncultivated. It was amazing to see what the people had achieved on the bare hills, carving the land into fields and terraces and carrying topsoil in baskets from places where it was richer and laying it on their enclosures. Scarcely a mile went by without the sight of a crowd of people somewhere busily working.

We are very comfortably housed here in the Garveys' residence, with a separate suite of bedroom, sitting room and bathroom. A busy programme of sightseeing and entertainment has been laid on for us.

Yesterday I was taken for a quick look at the Forbidden City. This is a huge area in the middle of the town, which is surrounded by a great thick wall coloured a deep, rich terracotta with four gates – north, south, east and west – surmounted by great big Chinese roofs. Inside are palaces and temples and great paved courtyards and smaller courtyards where fir trees grow. Here the emperors lived with their court completely cut off from the rest of the world. Everything has been preserved and it has been turned into a museum. There are the most beautiful jade and porcelain things in glass cases, but also some of the rooms kept as they were when they were occupied, the box beds with silk hangings and the hard square thrones where they must have sat cross-legged. In the living quarters the place is a labyrinth of narrow passages, steps up and down into little courtyards which are very pretty in an austere sort of way, with these fir trees growing out of the hard, dry ground and fantastic arrangements of some sort of stone that looks like pumice and is piled into grotesque shapes in the niches and corners – pagodas and little figures of men and beasts looking sometimes like fairy-tale landscapes. In the afternoon we were taken out west of the city to the hills that form a horseshoe on that side of the town and visited the Temple of the Sleeping Buddha, also very lovely in a Chinese way.

Reginald to Jane

Peking, 9 March 1965

This letter is going to Hong Kong with the Scandinavian courier and will then be put in the bag from Tokyo. Everyone says this is the quickest route.

In the past two weeks we have seen so many new sights and had so many new impressions that it is difficult to keep my thoughts in order. Our hostess here likes to see that every moment of every day is packed full of approved activities. We have had to put up some serious passive resistance to obtain a free morning for letter writing.

西藏西藏

[Omitted from this letter is much advice about the flight from Moscow to Ulan Bator. Wear warm outside clothes if you get out at Omsk in the middle of the night. Expect breakfast at Irkutsk in the middle of the morning. Keep with the crowd from the aircraft and wait patiently for things to happen. Do not worry if the aircraft is diverted or held up. Just wait and be bored. The Russians will not lose you and the Aeroflot sausage machine will turn you out at UB in due course. We shall be waiting for you at the airport. It continues as follows.]

西藏西藏

We have bought two Chinese scrolls of Mongolian horse scenes. Peking seems like Paris after Ulan Bator, but everyone who lives here seems to find it limited and constricting. It is funny to come from UB and to be told that Peking is isolated. Of course there is a frantic round of diplomatic parties here, and the embassy staffs of every country are all housed in an enclosed and guarded diplomatic quarter, which cuts them off from the Chinese population. They can be excused for regarding Peking as a remote Asian internment camp for diplomats.

3

Ann Settles In

Ann to her mother

Peking, 9 March 1965

We are very much enjoying our stay here except that we are so completely in the hands of our hosts that we sometimes feel terribly rebellious. It is really the most fascinating place. We went on Sunday to visit the Ming tombs. The Ming emperors chose a special valley west of Peking which had been designated by the oracles. Each emperor had a tomb to himself, a long mound under which he was laid in his coffin in a big chamber with all his treasures round him and dressed in his best. Outside the mound is a tower called the spirit tower in which is a tablet with his official name, his private name and his death name inscribed on it. There is an eerie atmosphere about the place. One tomb has been opened and you can go down and look at the sarcophagus. The treasures have been taken out and put in museums, but it is still very impressive. You feel that the Chinese will have a disaster fall on their heads for desecrating their ancestral tombs.

There is so much to see here that I get impatient with people who complain of being bored. We shall be back in the ice of Ulan Bator on Saturday the 13th. Here it is almost spring.

Reginald to his parents

British Embassy, Ulan Bator, 14 March 1965

I am sorry to learn that Father's injuries were so severe. I hope that by now he is more mobile and comfortable. The last bag also brought us news of Lady Pugh's stroke, which seems to have occurred shortly after she and Sir Alun visited the children – I hope not cause and effect. We have the impression that this was more serious than the minor strokes she has had before. I am

afraid Sir Alun is going to have his hands full seeing the children
off at the end of the month. Perhaps he will ask Gwyneth to help.
We can do nothing from here.

We are glad to be back in UB for a week or two of relatively
quiet normalcy. Peking was almost spring-like in temperature.
Here spring is clearly on the way in the middle of the day, but
there is still a sharp frost in the mornings and evenings. No one is
yet leaving off their furs or fleeces. The biggest difference between
the two countries for us is the food. In Peking you can eat anything you like. We became quite good at eating with chopsticks. In
fact Chinese food is not so enjoyable unless you use chopsticks, so
that you take a little of each dish separately and do not get it too
mixed up.

Peking is a sort of Rome or Athens in the number of fine things
it has to offer. We wandered through the Forbidden City and the
Summer Palace and the Pei-hai where the centre of the Mongol
capital used to be and where the empress dowager planned the
attack on the legations in the Boxer Rising, and the Western Hills,
and the Temple of Heaven, and the Ming tombs and the remnants
of the antique shops and jade market. Ann visited the Great Wall
and went to tea in one of two old Chinese houses while I was busy
in the office.

I had a very interesting experience in going with the Chargé
d'Affaires to the airport to see Marshal Ayub Khan leaving at the
end of his state visit.[1] The Chinese lay these ceremonies on with
impressive precision and with an overwhelming display of the
strength and vigour of modern China. It has menacing overtones,
but the top leaders stand modestly among the crowd looking very
simple and patting little children on the head. I stood a yard or
two from Liu Shaoqi while he did this for the benefit of the
photographers. I shook hands with Chou En-lai as I happened to
be standing around when he came along. It sounds casual, but of
course the crowd was handpicked and except for the diplomatic
corps most of it was young. On the whole, foreigners are relegated
to the sidelines in China, and millions of people in blue clothes
bicycle to and fro building a new country by sheer manual toil and
ruthless organization. Seeing China is an experience that doubles
the size of one's world.

The return journey Ulan Bator–Peking is conveniently phased.
In each direction one sees by day the parts one did not see in the

other direction. The north–south journey takes you through a cross section of the old Mongolian lands (both Outer and Inner Mongolia), travelling from mountain to hill to plain to flat emptiness, and then the train turns east just inside the Great Wall of China and runs along beside it for many miles before plunging down through the mountains into the great green Chinese plain. The Chinese allow no foreigners into Inner Mongolia but one can gaze at it from the train and what one sees is an object lesson in historical geography.

Reginald to Ann's father

15 March 1965

I am very sorry about Mo's illness. You will have been very anxious. I am afraid the business of receiving the children from school and seeing them off to Moscow is going to add to your worries. Do not hesitate to call on my family or Universal Aunts for any relief you think they could give you.

We enjoyed our week in Peking but it is a relief to be back in our own place again. Spring dust clouds have started to envelop this city. This weekend has been unmanageable, with two Queen's Messengers and a First Secretary from Peking and his wife who replaced us while we were away adding to our numbers. Tomorrow we shall be able, we hope, to resume our normal lives until Jane, George and William arrive.

It was very good of you to take such care delivering the three of them to and fro when you visited them at Brighton and Seaford. I hope the exertion was not responsible for over-straining Mo. We know from their letters how much the children enjoyed being taken out.

Reginald to his parents

27 March 1965

The children are due here next Wednesday. We had a bit of a telegraphic tussle with the FO last week, when we were suddenly told that the children could not have student fare rebates (which would save the FO money) if they spent the night in Moscow. Student fare journeys must not include 'avoidable' stops. I pointed out that if they flew to Moscow on the Tuesday instead of the Monday they would have only one and a half hours in which to catch their onward flight, and that if they missed it they would be

stranded in Moscow for a week. After a bit of argument, and with
support from Tom Brimelow in Moscow, I won. We spent nearly
as much on telegrams as was involved in the possible extra fares
the FO did not want to pay. The government machine finds it
difficult to cope with exceptional cases.

The children are due back in London on Friday 30 April. Sir
Alun Pugh has said he will drive Jane to Brighton on Saturday 1
May. Do you think you could accommodate George and William
from Saturday until they return to school on Tuesday? I ask this
because I think the Hibberts should give some relief to the Pughs
in view of Lady Pugh's illness. Father's injury will probably prevent him from doing much, but perhaps Alan or Margaret could
see the children off to school. If you can take the boys, they should
have as quiet a time as possible with you after their very tiring
journey, so that their nervous tension unwinds.

We are having a busy week. The assistant head of Far Eastern
Department of the Foreign Office[2] is spending a weekend here. In
a few days the ambassador comes up from Peking to pay farewell
calls. We also have the QMs here at the moment, and there are
more official letters to answer than usual.

The daytime temperatures are now quite mild, but it is still
very cold at night and when the wind blows. Another month and
things will start to sprout. The winter is really very long here.

Ann to her parents

27 March 1965

I presume that long before you get this, the children will have
safely arrived here. I am still very much 'touching wood' about
this as it really does seem such an immensely long way for them to
come, and we have to hope that all formalities will be gone
through without a hitch and all documents correctly completed.
You can imagine how remorseful I have felt for you, 'Nhad, with
all these jobs in connection with the children while you have had
Mo's illness to cope with.

A crisis in this matter of the children's journey arose last week.
… It was BEA who were refusing to grant student fares and saying
that the children must fly from London by Aeroflot on Tuesday,
that there was no reason to think that there would be any delay in
the aircraft's arrival in Moscow (!), and that if they did after all
miss the Tuesday night direct flight to Ulan Bator they could take

a Friday flight to Irkutsk and change there to a Mongolian Airlines flight. Reg kept calm and batted telegrams back steadily, and Moscow came up with the helpful news that Aeroflot did not accept unaccompanied children on a route that required a change of planes at Irkutsk. That was the end of it. The extra cost of full fares for Jane and George would be £180. Reg suggested that the FO should pay it if they could not make BEA give way, and we would then argue afterwards whether the FO or we were liable to defray it. The whole contretemps was quite unreasonable.

Thank you very much indeed, 'Nhad, for all your letters giving us news of Mo's progress. I was particularly pleased to get your airletter of 10 March, which arrived long before your letters in the bag.

You will be amused to hear that one of the QMs this week is an ex-adjutant of your regiment,[3] and claims to know you from regimental reunions. No doubt he will have phoned you by the time you get this letter. He is feeling rather wretched at the moment as he developed a form of flu on the day he left London and has not been feeling well ever since (a matter of about a fortnight).

Please thank G very much for all the efforts she has made to help with the children. And thank you for the Easter egg, which has arrived safely and quite intact. I think it will please the children, as I can't make a birthday cake for George or anything like that.

Last Sunday Reg and I climbed to the top of Bogdo Ula, which means Holy Mountain. In the old days no one was allowed to kill anything, namely spill blood, within sight of the mountain and the dead were all disposed of on the other side of the town. This still goes on, but the mountain is now a nature reserve, which is a nice way of bringing ancient superstition up to date.

In the evening tomorrow there will be a visit to the theatre, but I don't know yet if I shall be included as I would be the only woman in the party. However, Reg may get them to stretch a point. Then on Monday there is a visit to a factory, and some men from the Mongolian Foreign Ministry are coming to lunch. When we have a lunch party, which we do about once a week, we have it in our rooms – not more than two or three guests. We supply an hors d'oeuvre consisting mainly of things out of tins – like ham, prawns, sardines, olives or hard-boiled eggs, then the hotel sends up some of their soup followed by some sort of meat dish, and then we supply fruit salad or jelly or something like that to finish with. It gives the impression of being quite a good meal, though in fact the central features are often quite unattractive.

On Tuesday evening we have been invited to a film show at the Hungarian embassy. Our visitor from London will have left on the train for Peking at 7.30 a.m. that morning. Then on Wednesday the children should arrive: and on Saturday the Garveys come. We shall visit a state farm on Sunday I think, and there will be a cocktail party and so on. Reg doesn't see how he is going to get any work done in between all these things.

Before I leave off I must just tell you about the visit here of the non-resident Burmese Ambassador. He came up in the train with us from Peking to present his credentials. He couldn't speak a word of anything except Burmese, which is not much use here; but he brought with him a young third secretary brought up in Rangoon who could speak English – also not much use here, although a few Mongols speak a little. On his final evening the Ambassador gave a dinner party to which he invited various officials of the Foreign Ministry, various ambassadors and ourselves. The Burmese idea of a speech was as follows:

I greet the Deputy Under-Secretary and other officials of the Foreign Ministry, the Hungarian Ambassador, the Chinese Ambassador and the other ambassadors and their ladies and the British Chargé d'Affaires and Mrs Hibbert. I would like, but am quite unable to tell the Deputy Under-Secretary and [so on and so forth] and Mrs Hibbert how much I love and honour them. But I would like to assure the Deputy Under-Secretary and [so on and so forth] and Mrs Hibbert that love for them is coursing through my veins. I would therefore ask you to join me in drinking a toast to the Mongolian people and to the Deputy Under-Secretary and [so on and so forth] and Mrs Hibbert.

All this was read very solemnly through a pair of spectacles from a large sheet of paper and was laboriously translated first into English and then very painfully into Mongolian. After the Mongolian Deputy Under-Secretary had given an equally vacuous reply and this had been translated into English and then into Burmese, the Hungarian Ambassador who is the Dean of the Diplomatic Corps and can't speak a word of anything but Hungarian stood up and mumbled a few empty phrases which his interpreter translated into Mongolian and then into English and finally into Burmese. Reg and I were sitting opposite each other and, keeping our eyes down, showed every sign of listening with rapt attention. This is the high level of social entertainment here! I will finish this letter later.

28 March 1965

We have just come back from a really lovely picnic on the banks of the Tuul River (the river that runs through UB). The ice is at last beginning to break up and in places you can see the clear mountain water running swiftly under a shelf of blue-green ice. It is very beautiful. On our way we came across a group of about a dozen Russians lying on their tummies on the ice catching fish through holes they had made. They seemed to be using twigs and bent pins, but they were hauling fish out by the dozen. We also saw a huge herd of Bactrian camels including babies, and all over the steppe the hamsters scuttled into their holes as we approached. We are now off to the ballet – the same programme as before – I doubt if they know another.

29 March 1965

As I write, the children should be arriving in Moscow. It is strange being so out of touch with them. We have been thinking so much about all of you who have been helping to get them off.

It has just begun to snow here. After a week or so of rather cold sunny weather, the clouds began to gather yesterday after-noon and last night the temperature rose to the warmest it has been at night since I arrived, –4°F; and now it is snowing. I hope it will have cleared by Wednesday morning when the children arrive.

5 April 1965

Mr and Mrs Garvey have been here to say goodbye to the Mongolian government and leave tomorrow morning at 7.30 to return to Peking. They will take this airletter with them to post in Peking, so beating the Bag.

The children arrived quite safely right on time. George unfor-tunately had been sick a couple of times, just before landing in

Irkutsk and just before landing here, but he seemed none the worse for it. The other two were perfectly all right, especially William who had been able to curl up in his seat and sleep quite a lot. Jane seemed to have been slightly harassed by having to keep the boys in order, such as preventing William from disembarking at Omsk in the middle of the night with no coat or shoes on – being half asleep. I think they were all three extremely tired, but they were able to sleep it off in 24 hours. I think that if possible Jane should have a day to recover from the journey before going back to school. I cannot see that it can make any difference to Roedean if she arrives on Sunday instead of Saturday, for they already know that she will be late by two days. I am sending an airmail letter to Mrs Fort[4] to warn her of this. I hope Reg's parents are agreeing to George and William staying for three nights with them. You have no idea how sorry Reg and I are to have involved you in all this business with the children when Mo is ill. It is most unfortunate that we are so far away.

Jane (aged 15) to her Hibbert grandparents

11 April 1965

Well, here we are in Ulan Bator. And I must say it's marvellous. I love it here. Last weekend we had the Ambassador from Peking staying here to say goodbye and this weekend we have two Queen's Messengers. So you can see that we have no lack of visitors!

With the Garveys we went to a state farm. But this Sunday with the QMs we went to the market. All the Mongols from miles around come to this and sell anything – shoes, sweets, spoons, horses, blouses, chests, sheepskins – everything in fact. Everybody pushes like mad, and one old man whose cart was bogged down to the axles in mud was selling a *yurt*. They had to unload that before the cart would move. Everybody had brought their horses with them and the horses stood quietly and patiently completely unperturbed by the crowd. They are stocky little beasts with hairy ankles. At the moment they are still rather shaggy from the winter.

After that we went to a Lamaist temple that is still in use. The monks wear really lovely costumes that, unfortunately, are begrimed and filthy. The monks themselves are a hard-faced, dirty, squalid, unshaven, bleary crowd. Some of them are appallingly fat. Some are very surly. Many are diseased looking. Fortunately there are one or two with a kind word for everybody. They were holding a service which consisted of a muttered chanting (some men had good bass singing voices) interrupted by bursts of bell-ringing or a chorus of percussion – huge drums made of wood suspended from the ceiling and brightly painted with a lovely design of red, gold, blue, purple and green dragons and flowers round the rims, cymbals with orange tassels, conch shells (these make a hooting sort of noise and only a few monks used these) with the most beautiful wrought silver work on them, and leather and wood rattles. There were some old men and women who were still devout and were telling their beads and joining in the chants. There were also a lot of little children their grandparents had brought along, as well as just people on a Sunday outing come to see the sights. One young woman was going round the temple shrines and at every place where she touched her head against the holy writings she touched her tiny baby's head against it too.

The Mongols, I think, are very light-hearted. Tonight is dance night in the hotel restaurant. There the band will 'play'. The band here is prehistoric and makes me roar with laughter every time I hear it. A Hungarian musician here to help a state orchestra was asked to pass judgement on it. He said, 'I will give it –50'. When asked –50 out of what, he replied '–50 out of 200'. It consists of a bass saxophone who is always one beat behind everybody else, a tenor sax who is good (comparatively), a trumpeter who is always flat and out of tune and completely misses out some notes and never tries, a piano-accordionist who tries hard but can't make himself heard, and a drummer who is the leader but does nothing, but *nothing*. I hope you are both well and having good spring weather. Here it is cold, sunny and exhilarating.

西藏西藏

Jane's account of the temple ceremonies can be supplemented by excerpts from a dispatch I wrote to the Foreign Office in October 1965 (PRO/FO371/181 166).

西藏西藏

The lama church is normally treated here as a sight for tourists. There are today only some 100 monks in the whole of the Mongolian People's Republic. They are congregated at the Gandantegchinlen monastery where three small temples, a library and a few stupas and images survive at the side of the dilapidated shell of the great Ariavalo temple in what was once the seat of higher Buddhist theology and learning in Mongolia and the second largest monastery in the country with 7000 monks. Two monks are detached from Gandang to look after the temple museum of Erdeni Dzu at Kharkhorin, the oldest monastery in Mongolia, founded in 1586. As far as I know, there are no monks elsewhere. Services are conducted at Gandang every day and there is always a little crowd of spectators, including a few old people who prostrate themselves on the prayer boards, spin the prayer wheels, touch their foreheads to the pillars and furniture of the temples and give presents of matches to the monks. The performance (it cannot be described as anything else) never fails to fascinate visitors. The monks, seated cross-legged on cushioned benches in attitudes of long-suffering indifference, intone their prayers and readings from the scriptures in a hoarse muttering, broken every few minutes by the banging of drums and gongs, ringing of hand bells, blowing of conches, twisting of *ochir*s (something like a small mace, the symbol of power or of the elemental force), and on great occasions by the blowing of the great temple horns three or four yards long. There are frequent tea breaks when the monks pull their old wooden *ayag*s or bowls from the folds of their dingy yellow and red robes and noisily enjoy their *suutei tsai*, or milky tea, carefully wiping their bowls with dirty old cloths before putting them away again in their bosoms, running their hands over their shaven heads and resuming their mutterings at a word of command from the master of ceremonies.

The High Lama Gombojav appears to be a genuinely devout man, learned in the Buddhist scripture, who has devoted his life to his religion and no doubt lived through many horrors in the 1930s when leading lamas were tried and shot in substantial numbers and monasteries were laid waste and destroyed. He would probably make a favourable impression on any visiting Buddhist leaders whom he received in his large ceremonial *ger* at Gandang, perhaps the finest *ger* to be found in Mongolia today. Distinguished lay visitors usually meet Gombojav only as guests in his tent, where he expresses to them his dismay over American policy in Vietnam, enquires (if they are English) after the Lama Hewlett Johnson,[5] and asks if there are many monks, especially Buddhist

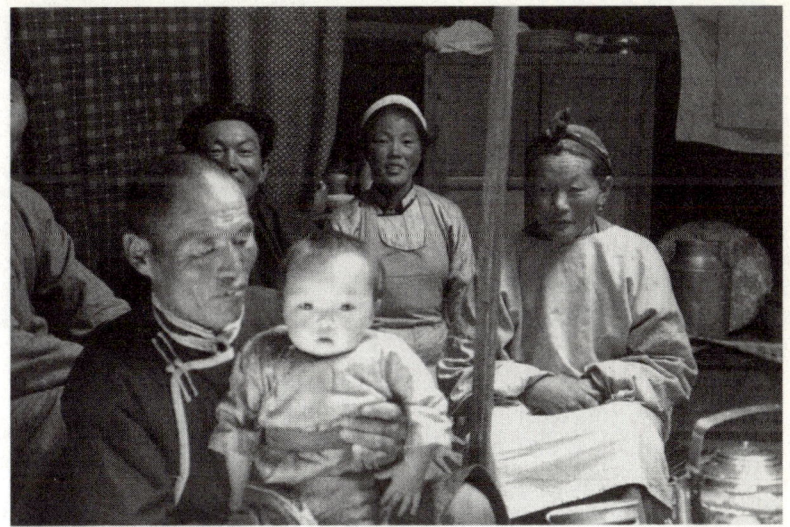

9. A Mongolian family in their *ger*.

ones, in their own countries. For all other purposes a younger monk, who looks as though he were formerly a wrestling Titan, looks after visitors.

西藏西藏

Ann to Reginald's parents

12 April 1965

So far the children have had a really quite interesting time and have quickly adapted themselves to the limitations of this place. It is a good thing they all like reading and doing jigsaws because otherwise they would certainly find themselves at a loose end from time to time.

The weather has become very changeable now with many cloudy days. Today, for example, started off with a beautiful blue sky but it has now clouded right over. Sometimes when the wind blows we get terrific storms of dust so that you can't see a hundred yards. It is most unpleasant to be out in it: you get grit in your eyes, mouth, hair and.everywhere else.

This is a really poverty-stricken place. George has come out with only two shirts. I thought we would buy him a cheap cotton one here but there just was not one in his size of any sort. So I am reduced to washing and ironing a shirt every day, which is a bit of a bore.

I am afraid we have caused a lot of bother with the children's journeys. It is a pity that my mother should have been taken so ill when we are so far away and have to rely on our families for so much help. I shall be glad to get home in September and stay for a little while to have an eye on things.

Reginald to his parents

26 April 1965

The children leave here on Thursday and will already be back at school when you receive this. No doubt the staff at Cliveden will have been able to cope with them.

We took them on a long journey last week to Kharkhorin (Karakorum), the principal site of the Great Khan's court under the successors of Chingis Khan in the thirteenth century, and the site also of the oldest Lamaist monastery in Mongolia, established in 1585. Kharkhorin is over 250 miles from Ulan Bator and it took us more than 13 hours to cover the distance. The tracks are in poor condition as the spring approaches. The ice and snow begin to melt and the surface crumbles and grows spongy at the bottom of the valleys. Sometimes there are wooden bridges over watercourses and often not, and sometimes a river runs round its bridge instead of under it. However, 13 hours of bumping in the Land Rover got us there. It was cold and snowing in the empty steppe, but the weather improved as soon as we were there.

We stayed at a trade union 'sanatorium' at a place called Khujirt. It is really a rest place for deserving workers built on the site of some mineral and mud springs. We had hot sulphur baths, which were relaxing, but the children felt boiled and objected to the smell. We spent Easter Sunday fishing in the river Orkhon, which is one of the historic cradles of the Mongol people. Like the Tuul River at Ulan Bator its waters flow northwards to reach Lake Baikal and thence join the Yenisei to reach the Arctic Ocean.

We visited a state farm and toured the ancient monastery of Erdeni Dzu, where two shabby old monks are still allowed to officiate to show foreigners like us that the practice of religion is still tolerated in Mongolia. Through our own initiative we managed to find the site of Khubilai Khan's palace round which the

10. Jane, William and George beside a stone tortoise or turtle that survives with two or three other such remnants on the otherwise desolate site of Kharkhorin, once the principal seat and encampment of the great khans. In the background is the wall of stupas enclosing what remains of the old monastery of Erdeni Dzu.

tents of the Great Khan's court used to be gathered. Nothing remains of it but a few foundations, some odd undulations in the ground and some small, scattered fragments of green, glazed roof tiles. Nevertheless, it is moving to stand there and think that this place, in the middle of the huge and splendid stillness of the Orkhon valley, was once the centre of an empire stretching all over Asia and eastern Europe. The valley cannot look much different today from its thirteenth-century appearance, except that the centre of the valley is now ploughed under the virgin lands scheme and 24,000 hectares of it are sown to wheat. That figure will show you how vast the valley is – like a great wide plain bordered by mountains.

The monastery within its heavy white walls with stupas set in it like towers is an evocative place, but I would find it more acceptable if it were a straightforward museum, without the pretence of being a temple actively served by lamas.

We returned by a more southerly route, skirting the northern edge of the Gobi country. It was supposed to be shorter but it took us longer. The length of the journey was relieved for all of us by the sightings one has every now and then in Mongolia of wild animals and birds – foxes, marmots, innumerable hamsters, a bear-like creature, geese, ducks, eagles, hawks of all sorts. And of course we passed herds of horses and camels and sheep and goats and cows. It must have left some strong impressions on the children.

We have done plenty of other things while the children have been here. They have been inside *gers* and temples and out in the wide open, empty spaces. At any rate all three want to come back at the end of July.

Our present plan is that Ann should travel back with them in September (8, 9 or 10). We have given our tenants at Hampton notice. Ann would move straight into our house. It is not long ahead – only four months away! I shall probably be home by the end of November for some leave.

The children much enjoyed celebrating Easter on the Tuesday evening when we returned from Kharkhorin. I am not sure whether I shall be asked to return to Ulan Bator in 1966. It is not yet decided. I think the FO may have difficulty in filling the post during a leave period. It may be easier to replace me with a new man when I go on leave.

Reginald to Ann's father

28 April 1965

You may like to have some preliminary information about our plans for the summer. We are asking the FO to arrange for the children to fly to Moscow on 26 July and to Ulan Bator on 27 July. They would have to be collected from their schools by car on Sunday 25 July. At the end of the holiday Ann will travel back with the children and move into our house at Hampton. She will get Jane back to Roedean, William to St Wilfrid's and George, we hope, to Charterhouse. I shall come on leave in November or December.

The children seem to have enjoyed their stay here, including, perhaps especially, our trips in the countryside. But a month is about as much as our administrative arrangements will stand. It is not easy running a family in a hotel, especially in the only inhabitable hotel in UB. Ann has been very busy keeping them organized. From tomorrow onwards we shall be able to pull out of the line for a few days to refit.

We were glad to learn from your letters received at the weekend that Mo has been continuing her improvement; but your news about Bill's health was disappointing, and we are very sorry that Bronwen has this anxiety.

Jane, George and William to Reginald and Ann
29 April 1965 (a postcard from Omsk)

Superman has entertained us all very well. This is sent from Omsk: Mongol time 3.30 p.m. Russian time 10.30 a.m. (!). We are all drinking mineral water – Borjomi!

西藏西藏

As well as being signed by all three children, the card was signed by Hela Kolman, the wife of the Yugoslav ambassador, who was also on the flight and was evidently doing what she could to help the children enjoy it.

西藏西藏

Ann to her parents
British Embassy, Ulan Bator, 4 May 1965

Thank you for sending the telegram about the children's arrival. It seems that they got there roughly at the time we expected. We had heard that they had reached Moscow according to plan as the wife of the Yugoslav ambassador who was travelling on the same flight from Ulan Bator telephoned her husband from Moscow that evening. It is interesting to reflect that, now that there is a growing amount of coming and going here, the Mongolian People's Republic may one day become a regular tourist resort.

It has begun to rain here – the first rain Reg has seen since the beginning of last October. The clouds came lower and the rain turned to snow, and when the clouds lifted again the hills round the town were as white as they had ever been during the winter. However, the snow soon melted and presumably this little bit of moisture will help to hurry on the greenness, which we are promised in the summer.

So far the grass remains almost entirely brown, but there are one or two flowers growing, the most common of which is a really lovely crocus-mauve pulsatilla, growing in clumps of up to five or six together, dotted about the hillsides. I have dug a few up for

Kew, which was quite an effort as their roots go down an immense length and usually between rocks. I am not very impressed by my efforts at pressing, as they look rather miserable and withered up. Perhaps Kew can make something of them. The things that grow here at the moment are plants that one usually sees in rockeries. We have made a little collection of some of the smaller plants and are forcing them on the windowsill where they get heat from the sunshine and the central heating. I have a round, fleshy, spiky thing, a sort of rock rose perhaps, which I am particularly pleased with, which I picked up when it was a tight little button and which has now opened right out and come up in a tall point in the middle and looks as though it will open out into a flower at any moment. It is an amusing hobby and gives some of the interest of gardening without the hard work!

I hope you found the children looking well. They had plenty of fresh air here. We get out as much as we can and climb the hills round about. Reg is very fit at the moment and climbs uphill at a terrific pace, which I find impossible to keep up with, my main trouble being shortness of breath. While the children were here I did not have time to do my exercises and I have probably slipped back a bit in general fitness. But I am now back on my old regime and hope to lose a bit of weight again. The food here is not calculated to make one slim – far too much bread, rice and potatoes. This does not seem to affect Reg who is remarkably slim. He puts this down to his having taken regular exercise in the winter and he may be right, but I think it is also a question of metabolism. On our trip to Karakorum we got so shaken about in the Land Rover that we both had a bit of old disc trouble, Reg in the back and I in the neck. However, with exercise we put this right in about ten days.

I am nearly half-way through to coming home and shall look forward so much to doing what I can to help you – even if it is only entertaining you with a few traveller's tales.

8 May 1965

No sooner had the children left than we were pretty well drowned in a sea of communism. On May Day there was a 'demonstration' in which the populace as a whole takes part 'voluntarily'. Unfortunately the excitement is not confined to 1 May alone. For two days beforehand and two days after we had to endure continuous and very loud music and lecturing over the radio, which is relayed over the whole town. Two loudspeakers point directly at our windows from across the road. The programme starts at 6.30 a.m. and finishes at 11.00 p.m. You can imagine it is pretty exhausting. Fortunately for me I cannot understand anything that is said, but Reg has the added irritation of hearing repeated invectives against the capitalist world and abuse over Vietnam, the Dominican Republic and the like.

On 1 May we were called to turn up with all the other diplomats and stand in tiers on either side of the mausoleum of Sükhbaatar (their red hero) in front of the building that houses the government and Great Khural.[6] All the bosses of party and state stood in a row on top of the tomb (as in Moscow). The parade went on from 10.00 to 11.30 with people streaming past carrying banners and the various insignia of organizations and factories. It became a little tedious at times, but Reg has given me a Japanese ciné camera and I used up my first film on this parade (the first part of the film having been used to record the children). All the town was decorated, that is to say that all the main buildings had red flags and strings of electric lights all over them and elephant sized pictures of the leading Mongolian and Soviet bosses and Marx and Lenin. In the background were regiments of women with red and blue flags, who waved them in unison according to the directions given by a man on the roof of the government building who signalled with his red and blue flags.

The town looked very gay – as gay perhaps as Piccadilly Circus 100 years ago. Reg and I went out for a walk in the evening and found that they had installed simple time switches here and there so that some strings of light could be made to wink.

They took everything down on Monday and on Friday put a lot of it back up again. And today we found ourselves watching an almost identical parade, except that this time it was entirely children. This was the fortieth anniversary of the foundation of the Mongolian Pioneer Corps, which is a sort of communist Boy Scout/Girl Guide organization. This celebration was also hailed by an outburst of noise from the loudspeakers, but it was also distinguished by a rehearsal, which started at 3.00 a.m. on Thursday morning and took place to a large extent right outside our hotel, going on until about 5.30. Thousands of children were being drilled in the dark, laughing and shouting and running about underneath our windows. You can imagine how much communism endears itself to us. I haven't seen anything like this semi-military organization of children since the Hitler Youth. This afternoon we went officially to an exhibition put on by the Pioneers. It consisted almost entirely of photographs as exhibitions mostly do.

We now start celebrating the Soviet defeat of Germany, which was apparently carried out single-handed by the glorious Red Army. No mention is ever made of any allies. It is rather nauseating. Reg has to go to something at the theatre this evening called a 'solemn meeting', at which I suppose he will have to listen to endless speeches about the marvellous achievements of Soviet Russia. Then tomorrow morning we diplomats are summoned to lay a wreath at the Soviet war memorial, which commemorates the Soviet victories over the Japanese, at Khalkhin-Gol[7] before the war and in 1945 at the end of the war. And in the evening we go to the Soviet Embassy for a reception to congratulate the Red Army on its defeat of the Germans. The ambassador who seems most upset by this one-sidedness is Stane Kolman, the Yugoslav, who rages about it. Reg is fed up with it but takes it calmly. In Soviet eyes the Yugoslav is almost a capitalist, so what he says doesn't count.

In the midst of all this we have six Americans here. They belong to the Wildlife Preservation Trust, the organization headed by Prince Philip. I think the Mongolians find it difficult to understand that they want to wander in the wilds to search for the original horse that is supposed to roam somewhere in the far southwest, and not to visit factories and state farms. And the Americans find it hard to understand that they can't just charter a plane and fly wherever they like. Their visit was a little complicated by the fact that their leader, an ex-ambassador by name of Crowe, something over 60 years old, arrived here after travelling about the world for four months and decided he didn't feel well. He has had two heart attacks and as he had a cold feared he was going to have another. Being the only Westerners here and having, as it turned out, mutual acquaintances, Reg and I were naturally roped in on this problem – our advice asked and supplies of fruit juice and so forth provided from our stores. Fortunately, after two days in bed, he decided he was well enough to continue with their programme and the whole lot took off today to go to some site in the Gobi approved for foreigners by the Mongolian government.

They will be back at the end of the week to tell us their adventures. Ambassador Crowe is going to London and may give you a call.

Our new Ambassador arrives in Peking on the 12th and soon after comes up here to present his credentials. There is always something on in Ulan Bator!

Ann to Reginald's parents

10 May 1965

They have changed the schedule for the QMs. The bag will leave London as usual on Mondays, but the second QM will not leave London until the following Sunday, carrying a second bag, to join the first QM in Hong Kong. The two will then travel together to Peking and Ulan Bator, arriving here as usual on the following Saturday. So on 22 May we shall receive a bag that left London today, 10 May, and a bag that will leave London on 14 May. This means that some letters can arrive in just over a week, and a similar speeding-up occurs in the opposite direction. This is a great improvement.

Here the weather has suddenly turned very warm and today is like a lovely English summer's day, except that the hillsides are still brown. Some flowers are beginning to appear and along the sides of streams it is quite green, but there is still ice in some valleys that get little sun.

I wonder if you could visit George and William later in the term and take them out. The school could tell you which weekends would be suitable.

Reginald to Jane

19 May 1965

Spring, or perhaps summer, is here. They have turned off the town heating system for a 'remont' and there is not a drop of hot water to be had in the hotel or in any other modern building in Ulan Bator. Only our electric kettle keeps us, and those who come to beg from us, in touch with the soapy civilization of the West. There will be no hot water for at least a fortnight. Zogsood said it would be a month, but we let her use the eyebath in our first-aid kit and she brought it down to a fortnight. The manager said we could have arrangements made to bathe occasionally in the town's public baths. I did not know it had any. We may take him up on it just to see what they are like. For the moment we jump in and more quickly out of very cold baths. We fill the bath the previous evening so that it is chambré by the morning.

Mongolia is turning green at last. In the past week Bogdo Uul has changed colour, and the trees have begun to come into leaf around Lenin, and the grass is growing in the verges by the pavements. The wild flowers are coming out so fast that Mother is being beaten by Nature and there are going to have to be some things that will never be reported to Kew. The blue variety of pulsatilla has been succeeded by yellow and white, and we have found wild pansies and violets and hundreds of miniature iris and all sorts of other flowers. George's iris flowered yellow – Mother is pressing the flower and sending it to him.

A group of Americans was here last week hoping to look for the wild horse (*Equus caballus przhevalsky*). They were frustrated but, I think, enjoyed themselves in a sort of way – the Mongol way. They were treated as ordinary tourists, and of course the centrepiece of their tour was our dear old 'Sanitary' at Khujirt. They did a day's fishing and went to Erdeni Dzu and picnicked by the waterfall, which we failed to see. They were taken south into the Gobi for a night and slept in Zhuulchin's special *ger* encampment for tourists, not far from the places where the Chapman Andrews expeditions found dinosaur skeletons. They thought that was marvellous. In fact by the time the Mongols had finished with them they had quite forgotten about *Equus caballus przhevalsky*, which no one had any intention of letting them see even if anyone had known where to find it. They had an interpreter whose favourite answers were 'yes' and 'tomorrow'. 'Is it black or white?' 'Yes'. 'Can we go to the state store?' 'Tomorrow'. They thought he was unable to speak English and completely stupid; but I think they were beautifully chosen answers. Our friend Yondon [who escorted us to Kharkhorin] showed much less finesse.

One of the Americans was a Mrs Oswald Lord. She was here on the day of the Pioneers' fortieth anniversary. She joined in the monster procession of children past the leaders of party and state on Sükhbaatar's tomb and past us standing next to it. She was allowed in because she looked like a Russian schoolteacher. She marched past the presidium taking close-ups with her ciné camera. If we had known, we might have photographed her waving, with an anti-American slogan behind her! Apparently she was in Irkutsk on 1 May and took part in the May Day procession there.

When she talked to me she always spoke in a whisper to show respect for POLITICS and SECURITY. She was a lively old thing and very resourceful. When the party flew to Övörkhangai in one of those little biplanes of Mongolian Airlines all the Mongol passengers were sick; and this is dealt with in Mongolia by passing round a bucket. The bucket finally finished up next to Mrs Lord, who promptly whipped out a polythene cover to fit over it and followed that with a lavender aerosol spray to sweeten the atmosphere. No wonder Old Glory leads the free world!

I expect Mother told you about our celebrations of the Soviet Union's lone victory over Nazi Germany 20 years ago? At the Soviet Embassy reception I stood, by a freak of wrong placement, within two yards of the Soviet Ambassador and Tsedenbal while they contrived to say nothing at all about the Western allies in two long speeches. My failures to applaud when everyone else in the room (except Mother) was showing wild enthusiasm must have been very obvious. Perhaps I ought to adopt the Chinese Ambassador's habit of lifting his hands ostentatiously and fluttering his fingertips together when he disapproves of what is being said. It is the most insultingly indifferent form of applause I have seen, and he does this right under Tsedenbal's nose. When he agrees with the speaker he applauds with his whole hands. I can read the state of Sino-Soviet relations on any given subject by watching the modulations of the Chinese ambassador's handclap.

西藏西藏

The east German ambassador was Herr Willerding. He was much the most able and well informed of the eastern European ambassadors. I often rubbed shoulders with him at the Mongolian government's official occasions, and in this way I had one or two interesting conversations with him. But I had no official or personal relationship with him. The British government did not recognize the German Democratic Republic (GDR). He extended invitations to me on one or two occasions but I refused. Finally, he asked if Ann and I would lunch privately with him and his wife one day. I agreed. He was well informed about us as well as about Mongolia and he knew that Ann had served in the Auxiliary Territorial Service (ATS) in the war and that I had been in the army in

Albania and Italy. He surprised us during lunch by rising to his feet and saying that he knew that both Ann and I had been in the British army in the war against fascism and that we had therefore both made our contributions to the victory of socialism in Europe. He toasted us for those contributions. Ann had not previously realized how far-reaching the consequences could be of being an ATS driver and then a subaltern on the staff of the ATS OCTU at Windsor.

I continued to have useful and informative private exchanges on Mongolian affairs with Herr Willerding. Many years later in the late 1970s when, as political director at the FO, I was visiting east Berlin for talks with the deputy foreign minister of the GDR, I asked if I could call on Herr Willerding, who I knew was then a senior official in the Foreign Ministry. It was evidently found difficult to accede to this request, but after some delay Herr Willerding was produced and came to see me briefly. He was no longer informative or interesting. He was busy subverting the third world in Africa.

西藏西藏

Reginald to his parents

19 May 1965

We are now busy preparing for a Foreign Service inspector, who visits us next week, and a main board director of ICI. Early in June we are holding a Queen's Birthday Party, and shortly after that our new ambassador comes to present his credentials. Then in early July it will be the Mongolian National Day, and at the end of July the children will be here again. Our summer is already full for weeks ahead.

For the first time after six months we are beginning to see the green Mongolia that travellers have usually described. There have been two or three showers of rain and the grass, plants, flowers and trees have started to burst out in all directions. The wild flowers on the hills are already blooming in thousands and Ann is finding it difficult to keep up with them in her collection of specimens. Very few people climb the hills, and none of the country's bosses or any of our diplomatic colleagues; but it is only by climbing to the top that one finds the finest carpets of flowers. They all grow like rock plants, close to the soil and stones, and they all have huge roots to tap the scanty moisture deep down.

They must be incredibly hardy to survive the Mongolian winter so well. But obviously plants can survive where animals can.

We are doing much better for food these days. We at last have a satisfactory supply line running from Hong Kong. We can obtain stores from there in six weeks or so and the range of supplies available is enormous. We still eat lunch in the hotel restaurant because the problem of cooking in our rooms is insuperable, but we always have breakfast in our rooms and we nearly always have supper there too. Provided one can afford it, it is possible to buy almost everything in a canned or bottled form. We now have smoked salmon and Parma ham and shrimps and eels and Matjes herrings and olives and salami and sardines and chicken and tongue and ham and foie gras and celery and beans and asparagus and beetroot and peas and all sorts of dried and tinned fruits and spaghetti and baked beans and various precooked meals from America and of course an infinite variety of soups. The inspector's job, as I see it, is to make it possible for us to afford all this. You can imagine that the costs are high out here. Freight charges from Europe are about 100 per cent of the value of a consignment and from Hong Kong at least 50 per cent. Unfortunately, we cannot store much at a time, so that we are not being such gluttons as we perhaps sound. But it makes a great difference to have the variety.

I expect you have heard something from the children either directly or indirectly. We have not yet been able to receive news of their arrival in England, other than a telegram from Sir Alun Pugh.

西藏西藏

On 22 May Ann received a letter from her father announcing that, because of her mother's incapacity following her stroke, it had been decided that they could no longer maintain their home in Hampstead, and they were going to move to a large old rectory at Dunsfold, near Godalming, and Gwyneth and her partner, Ron Barry, who had settled in that area, would live in half of the house and keep house for them. This was upsetting news for Ann who felt that, if we had been nearer home, an easier solution might have been found for her parents' problems. Ann's letters in late May and June were largely focused on this upheaval, which was going to be completed before she could arrive in London in September. I was very busy with visitors and official matters at the time and hardly wrote any letters at all. One of the complications was that arrangements needed to be made for the children's departure from London at the end of July. Various items of their and our property were stored at the Hampstead house and needed to be extracted before the move took place.

One curious aspect of the affair was that the old rectory into which Ann's parents were to move had been the home of one of Ann's friends at Oxford and Ann knew the house. This gave her more a feeling of being involved, while in fact being unable to do anything to help or advise in any way in this important family event.

To make matters worse, Ann herself fell ill with hepatitis at the beginning of July. The standard of hygiene in the hotel, its kitchens and dining room had undoubtedly deteriorated during the weeks of no hot water. Our rooms were kept clean, but it was difficult to be confident about the handling of food elsewhere. Even the milk, which Ann bought at the diplomatic shop, tended to have a sediment of fine dust and sand, picked up presumably on its journey through clouds of dust from some state farm or other in a battered tanker truck. The milk often curdled as we tried to boil it. Adequate cleanliness was difficult to achieve with very cold water. We would probably have been better off at this period if we had been able to live in simple Mongol style in a *ger* outside the city – the sort of *ger* that Zhuulchin had set up for tourists in the Gobi. But this was inconceivable.

西藏西藏

Ann to her parents

23 May 1965

Thank you, 'Nhad, for your letter of 8 May. You can imagine how pleased we were to get this first news about the children since they left. It sounds as though Bron managed to look after everyone very well for the weekend at Cliveden. It was certainly very thoughtful of her to invite Mr and Mrs Hibbert. What a pity you fell down the stairs! I am glad you didn't break anything.

I am, of course, very anxious to hear what has been decided about where you are going to live. Must you really give up Pilgrims Lane? ... There seem to be so many pros and cons, but perhaps if I were to put my oar in I should only complicate matters.

To add to the joys of Outer Mongolia they have now cut off

the town's supply of hot water – for a month! I may take advantage of our Yugoslav colleagues' offer to have a bath in their embassy, as they have an independent boiler.

We have had a telegram from London saying that I cannot be allowed to travel to Moscow on the Trans-Siberian Railway with the children in September, unless accompanied by another adult. So we shall have to fly, probably on 2 September.

We have had some amusing letters from the children. Jane complains that no one at school wants to hear her stories about Mongolia. She is learning that people on the whole are not keen to learn anything much that doesn't concern them – one of the hard lessons of life!

Ann to her mother

31 May 1965

Thank you so much for writing to tell me of your plans. ... As you can imagine, I am very sad to hear that Pilgrims Lane must go, but I can quite understand that some sort of decision had to be taken.

Ann to her parents

6 June 1965

We would be very grateful if you could soon give us some idea of the time element in your plans to move. It seems possible that you will already have moved by the time I come home. ...

Now, about the children's journey out here. Where will they be able to stay for the night of 25/26 July? The easiest thing might be if they could go to Cliveden, which is so convenient for London airport, in which case there are various things of theirs at Pilgrims Lane, which will need to be taken over. ... I will write to both G and Bron and see if they can help. It is ghastly being so cut off, not being able to telephone and so on. I am afraid we are compelled to ask for help, though we don't want to be a nuisance. It is a question of fetching them from their schools by car, driving them to wherever they are going to spend the night, seeing that all their belongings have already been assembled there, and then next morning getting them onto the aircraft. I hope this will be the last time this will have to be done.

We have had a pretty hectic week, which reached its peak, or perhaps its nadir, on Tuesday. Last Saturday the inspector arrived by train from Peking (at 7.30 a.m.) and Mr and Mrs Harold Smith of ICI arrived in the afternoon by plane, also from Peking but via Irkutsk. He is the director of ICI in charge of business with communist countries, and he came here partly to top up his collection of out of the way places but also to see if any business could be done with the Mongols. He and his wife are the sort of people who are used to living very comfortably, so the shock of finding themselves on hard beds in rooms without proper curtains, with no hot water and condemned to eat greasy stewed mutton on cold plates for five days was a little hard to bear. However, they took it surprisingly well, and we helped them out with breakfast and the occasional kettle of boiling water, and we had them in for supper one evening, opening two precious jars of Shippam's chicken breasts in jelly.

Sunday was spent dealing with the inspector, who seemed a bit dreary and with the wrong attitude to life. We offered him breakfast when he reached the hotel (9.00 a.m.), but he said thank you very much but he had had a ham sandwich on the train – a sandwich that had of course been made in Peking two days earlier. Inspectors are supposed not to be seduced by hospitality from those they are inspecting, but by Monday he was glad to eat breakfast with us. His cheeseparing ideas were definitely at variance with those of the Smiths. When he attempted to make a comment such as, 'Well, this mutton really isn't at all bad', or 'After all, hot water is really rather a luxury' or 'At least you are not shot at by bandits whenever you go out, as we were in La Paz', there would be a few astringent comments from Smith, which got things back into proportion again.

Anyway, things jogged along until Tuesday morning, when the inspector left by the early train to Peking and the Smiths and we set off for a state farm not far from Ulan Bator (about 60 or 70 kilometres). It was a lovely day. We had had two days of rain, so the air was fresh and the sunshine clear, and everything was turning green and flowery. We met a herd of yaks, and the Mongolians who were accompanying us set off in pursuit in their *gazik*, making the poor things stampede towards Mr Smith, who was able to film them comfortably from his car (provided by the Mongols). Later we came across a couple of camels and Mrs Smith (60 next February) climbed on, much to the animal's disgust, and was photographed by her husband. I was allowed to do the same. And so the journey went merrily on and at about midday we rolled up at the state farm. Here we were introduced to the headman and the chief Party man, as one always is, led into a room and sat round a table, as one always is, and given the usual lecture about the farm's statistics – so many horses, cows, men, women, children and so forth. Meanwhile, a girl in a white cap and overalls was doling out huge bowls of *airag*, fermented mare's milk (*koumiss*). I find it unpleasant and in any case have been warned that it can upset the stomach, so I left the bowl in front of me and said nothing. Mrs S who doesn't like milk of any sort made a bit of a fuss insisting loudly that she couldn't drink it. Reg had forgotten to brief Mr S that in Mongolia if you do not want any more of something, you leave your bowl full and not empty. Mr S, at the other end of the table, was quietly trying to empty his bowl and had already drunk two bowlfuls. Reg, seeing this valiant effort and wanting to distract attention from Mrs S's anti-*airag* demonstration thought he should keep Mr S company. The Mongols were delighted and told them that the custom in Mongolia was to drink three. They finished up by drinking four. I can't think how they did it. It smells more of ammonia than of milk.

We were then taken round the farm, and a demonstration of horse racing and a sort of rodeo, to show how horses were plucked from the herd and broken in, was put on for our benefit. Mrs S had brought some sugar for the horses and was disappointed when, being quite unused to such delicacies, they spat it out. By this time it was about 3.15 and we were led in to lunch. On this sort of occasion the meal is frequently punctuated by toasts to peace and friendship and the men are expected to empty their glasses each time. Mrs S again started protesting and kept emptying half her glass into her husband's or Reg's. The result was that we were all definitely under the weather by the time we left. We had a couple of hours of fearfully rough and zigzag driving, in the middle of which the drivers halted, pulled out some bottles and announced that they wanted to give us a party too. Soon after that, as we careered on, Reg passed out with a terrible groan and cannot remember much about the sequence of events. At this point we drew up unexpectedly at a chicken farm and factory. Amazingly, Mr S was still on his feet, but having staggered round the place lurching from door post to door post, he was again made to drink a glass of vodka and he was invited to join a singsong (his contribution – Drink to me only with thine eyes)! This was the last straw. Reg had woken up by the time we started off again, but Mr S was taken very ill before we got back to Ulan Bator and then had to spend two days recovering. I can't imagine what his memories of this country will be – not pleasant, I should think. What a life! Our prestige with the hotel staff went up when they heard about our exploits. The women *dezhurnaya*s told Eric Cheyne that men always behaved like that when they get together.

Reginald to his parents

7 June 1965

I have been too busy with visitors to have time to write, and we are now preparing for a reception next Friday for the Queen's Birthday. It takes a long time to arrange such things here.

We are going to be without hot water until about 20 June. To aggravate matters we have burned out our electric kettle and are having to wait for a new one from Hong Kong.

The Soviet spaceman Nikolaev and his wife Tereshkova, the space woman, were here last week and we met them on several occasions. They are charming people. Their programme was exhausting. A great deal of political capital is being made out of them.

Ann to Jane

13 June 1965

I am writing to wish you the very best of luck in your exams [O level]. We shall send you a telegram in time for the start.

The British Embassy, Ulan Bator, is quite large at the moment. Alex Thompson has arrived with his wife Grace to replace Eric Cheyne, who will leave in a few days. The Thompsons are Scottish. They are taking the difficulties of living here with admirable calm.

We had a terrific storm yesterday evening with lightning flashing down onto Bogdo Uul, a pitch-black sky and torrents of rain. But of course the more it rains the greener everything becomes. All my flower presses are now full and I have a blister on my hand from digging, so I am concentrating on photography instead for the moment. Yesterday I was able to take some pictures of them milking the mares. It is a very attractive sight, as all the mares have their little foals beside them and some of them have beautiful colours.

We had a very successful Queen's Birthday Party on the 11th. Father made a speech in Mongolian and Russian! I drank plenty of champagne and a good time was had by all.

西藏西藏

As our Queen's Birthday reception on 11 June was the first ever to be held in Mongolia, I sent a brief report to the Foreign Office to record the event (PRO/FO 371/181168). The following para-graphs are taken from it.

西藏西藏

Our small British cell of three was warmly supported in drinking Her Majesty's health by some fifty or sixty dignitaries and officials of communist countries with some twenty or thirty of their wives.

The principal Mongolian guest was the newest deputy chair-man of the Council of Ministers, Mr Damdini Gombojav. The chairman of the Great People's Khural (and Secretary of the Ulan Bator town committee of the Mongolian People's Revolutionary Party), the Ministers of Foreign Trade and Culture and the Chair-man of the Executive Committee of Organizations for Peace and Friendship were also present. The Foreign Minister was unable to be present because he was preoccupied with preparations for the Afro–Asian summit meeting at Algiers, but a newly appointed Deputy Foreign Minister who will in future supervise relations with non-communist countries represented him. There was a good attendance of Mongolian officials from the Ministries that are allowed to have dealings with foreigners; but the Protocol Depart-ment seemed to have invented a rule that Mongols from outside these Ministries who had accepted two previous invitations from me should absent themselves on this occasion.

I decided to adopt the local practice of making a short speech at the beginning of the party. It seemed a valuable opportunity to say a few simple things about the establishment of diplomatic relations between Britain and Mongolia and to secure a sort of public endorsement of the normality of our being here. I warned the Protocol Department in advance and let them copy my manu-script. The first part of the speech was in Mongolian and the second part in Russian. As souvenirs for the record of a somewhat unusual occasion, copies of the two texts are attached as annexes (needless to say I was greatly helped by my Mongolian teacher in establishing a correct Mongolian text). The theme was our pleasure at celebrating the Queen's birthday for the first time in Mongolia, our gratitude to our guests for doing honour to our country, our satisfaction at the hospitable and helpful way in which we have been received here, the British desire to build normal, mutually advantageous relations with Mongolia on a foundation of good understanding and on the pattern of the mutually profitable relations that have long existed between Britain and the other communist countries, and the importance that the British attach to traditional diplomacy at a time of sharpened international tension. Here and there it seemed expedient to adopt local terminology, for example in the use of the adjective 'socialist', in order to indicate our realistic acceptance of the situation that exists in this part of central Asia.

I am glad to say that the speech was quite well received by the Mongols, who were gratified to hear themselves addressed by a foreign diplomatic representative in their own language for the first time in their experience. I fear that some of the heads of missions will regard me in future as a blackleg, but I must confess that it was enjoyable to see the Soviet and eastern European Ambassadors, who had not brought their Mongolian interpreters, unable to tell whether or not they were listening to heresy. The Chinese ambassador was unusually affable afterwards: he seemed to be short-sightedly gratified by proceedings conducted in a language other than Russian.

The deputy chairman of the Council of Ministers replied with an amiable speech in Mongolian, which one of the Mongolian students who was recently at Leeds University and who is now working in the MFA translated ably into English. No translation into Russian was offered and once again most of the diplomatic corps had to guess what was being said. Mr Gombojav's theme was that the MPR had established diplomatic relations with Great Britain within the framework of the policy of coexistence, that the Mongolian people were peace-loving, and that he hoped and indeed was sure that the presence of a permanent British diplomatic mission in Ulan Bator would facilitate the development of good Anglo–Mongolian relations in many fields. He ended with a toast to peace, Anglo–Mongolian friendship and the British people.

Unen, whose editor had been present, carried a short para-
graph reporting the reception and Gombojav's presence at it on
the back of the foreign affairs page on Sunday. All in all, I think
we can be satisfied that the Mongolian authorities treated us with
the exact degree of courtesy the occasion demanded.

西藏西藏

Ann to her parents

22 June 1965

I am very glad that Bron has offered to organize the children's
departure. She will be getting together with you, 'Nhad, about
passports, visas, tickets and so on, as you have been dealing with
Travel Section at the FO. Jean Brimelow in Moscow is expecting
them on Monday 26th. Thank goodness we shan't have to do this
again – at least I sincerely hope not.

G tells me that she expects to have you safely installed at
Dunsfold before I get back. It has been a momentous year, but like
most of the big things that happen in the family, I just don't
happen to be there for them. I certainly feel remarkably rootless at
the moment.

We have had the new Ambassador here since last Saturday –
Mr Donald Hopson.[8] He has been presenting his credentials. The
trouble for Reg and me is that in the hotel visitors are on top of
you the whole time and seem to forget that our rooms are the only
home we've got. Anyhow, the presentation ceremony was very
amusing. It took place on the broad terrace in front of the
parliament building. The Ambassador and the Chief of Protocol
stood side by side and Reg and Alex Thompson behind him –
wives lurked in the background. The military band then played the
British and Mongolian national anthems – very well actually – and
then the officer commanding the guard of honour stepped up to
the Ambassador and reported that the guard of honour was very
pleased to welcome the British Ambassador, and then the Ambassador inspected the guard. He had then to stand in front of it and
shout in Mongolian something like, 'Soldiers! How do you do?'
and they all shouted back, 'Very well, thank you', just like the
soldiers in Turkey. Then the Ambassador went into the building
followed by Reg, bearing the letters of credence, and Alex
Thompson. I took a film of this on my new movie camera, espe-

cially of the Union Jack flying in front of the palace of the Great Khural.

In the afternoon we had to lay a wreath on the tomb of Sükhbaatar, hero of the revolution and father of the Mongolian People's Republic. Wives were allowed in. This meant walking behind a couple of soldiers carrying an enormous wreath of paper flowers on a wooden framework into the mausoleum where the tombs of Sükhbaatar and Choibalsan are. Once inside, the ambassador and Reg took the wreath and stood it between the two tombs. The Ambassador somehow managed to get himself shut in between the wreath and the wall and took a second or two to extricate himself from the bits of greenery that had got entwined around his face and neck. Of course, we kept our heads bowed in solemn silence.

We are now trying to organize a dinner party for the Ambassador, which is proving more difficult than usual (which is saying something!). They are having the hotel completely redecorated, so apparently there will be nowhere where 20 people can sit down to eat. It is all very trying, especially as we are now five weeks without hot water!

The Ambassador flies to Moscow on Thursday and then on to London and will bring this letter with him.

Ann to Jane

28 June 1965

Last week we had the Ambassador and his daughter here. You know what it's like here when we have visitors – we don't have a moment to ourselves.

The Ambassador hosted a dinner party on Wednesday evening. There were 21 of us and we had to have it in the bar at the end of the restaurant, so everyone having supper in the main hall (which is being redecorated) could see us enjoying ourselves through the glass screen. The soup and main course were from the hotel, but I managed to make an hors d'oeuvre with ham, smoked salmon (tinned), prawns, crab, caviar, pâté de foie, asparagus and salami, and it really looked quite nice. We had some of our tinned fruit at the end. The Ambassador was lucky. The Swedish Ambassador who came from Moscow to present his credentials had nowhere to give a dinner. We have been eating on the landing of the floor below ours. The girls have had to carry everything upstairs.

Anyway, the Ambassador entertained us and the Thompsons on the landing on one evening and left us the bottles of wine that he had brought from Peking and were left over from his 'official' dinner. On the next day his aircraft was delayed and he left at 6.30 p.m. instead of in the morning.

I hope my writing isn't too awful. I am in bed with a mysterious 'fever' that came upon me a couple of days ago and won't go away. As you know, Father is wary of drugs and doctors, particularly here, so I just lie and wait. I had a sore throat before the ambassador arrived, so I have been a bit under the weather lately. I shall no doubt be hale and hearty by the time you arrive – not long now!

We have got lots of rather gushy American tourists here – also a young French woman who has come from Peking to interpret for a Frenchman who comes from Moscow on Wednesday to see if it is possible to set up a French embassy here. She is very bored as she thought she was going to spend her time galloping romantically over the steppe. Father of course has befriended her. We have also had these two funny Dutch businessmen here. They speak like a comedy turn, saying 'dis', 'dat' and 'dem'. One of them lives near Barcelona, and I have an open invitation to go and stay with him!

I am sorry if my letters seem few and far between – I am thinking of you.

Reginald to Ann's father

3 July 1965

The news of the week from here is that Ann has gone down with jaundice (infective hepatitis) and is now sampling Mongolian hospital life. She first felt ill last weekend and we thought it was a sort of flu, but it got worse instead of better, and when we called on the Bureau for Servicing the Diplomatic Corps to produce a doctor on Wednesday, a Russian woman appeared who said it was jaundice. She said that Ann must go into hospital, which we resisted, and she added engagingly that the hospital for infectious diseases was much too dirty to be suitable. She said she would speak to her head doctor at the 2nd Hospital (which is the top people's hospital) and see what could be done.

Next morning she came again, examined Ann again, said it was definitely jaundice – do you see that green tint? – and then announced that this was her last visit and that the Ministry of

Foreign Affairs was putting the case in the hands of another doctor. You know what they are like, she said, they will forget and you will have to keep phoning them.

This proved an accurate forecast. I telephoned several times in the afternoon, but the only informative answer I received was when an inexperienced junior told me unguardedly that she thought they were discussing the problem with Badarch in the Central Committee (that is the secretariat of the Party).

In the evening a committee of doctors arrived – first a Russian (from Kharkov) in red, open-necked shirt and sandals, second a Mongol in a blue silk shirt and a white straw hat (which continued to be worn right into the presence of the patient), and third another Mongol with a much scarred face whose job was to carry the bag, wipe the thermometer and produce the stethoscope. It soon became clear that the Russian knew his job. He gave Ann a thorough examination (her third by now) and he carefully drew the attention of the Mongols to the main symptoms and the main points of the case history. I took the two Mongols to be senior medical students. Once again the conclusion was that Ann must go to hospital, and once again we asked for her to be treated in the hotel. So far we have had only one prescription, which was written out by the first woman doctor. Perhaps they will not have it in the Apteke, she said. She was right. They sold us something with a quite different name, to which the committee of three said there was no objection (a Russian phrase expressing approval).

The committee urged me to think over the question of hospitalization and said that the senior medical student (as I took him to be) would return or telephone at 8.30 a.m. the following morning for a further consultation. Of course, nothing happened. As the morning wore on I managed to get through to the 2nd Hospital on the telephone, finally spoke to the first woman doctor and was assured that the committee of three was grappling with our case and seeing if they could clear a section of the hospital for Ann (I had asked some questions about the accommodation that could be offered).

Finally, after lunch, the senior medical student arrived, introduced himself as the Deputy Director of the hospital (150 beds) and invited me to come and inspect the special room that was waiting to receive Ann. I was to arrive in half an hour. The half hour had been put to good effect because when I arrived every part of the hospital was standing to attention as for a divisional commander's visit. I was shown a private corridor cut off from the main hospital corridors and provided with a side entrance of its own – obviously designed for the accommodation of very important people. A host of white-coated peasants was lounging around, but leaped into action with mops, dusters and pails of disinfectant as soon as we appeared.

We were being faced with the choice between treatment in hospital and no treatment, so Ann had to go in. I went back and fetched her in the Land Rover, and she was now thoroughly examined for the fourth time by what I suppose was the duty doctor. He carefully recorded her life history on a form of many pages, cheerfully offering us, by way of relaxation from this long and arduous task, occasional excerpts from medical lectures on some of the principal scourges of mankind, including jaundice. Did we use this procedure of recording a case history in England? Of course, yes, we replied. What were the social and economic circumstances of Ann's childhood and upbringing? Were they comfortable? No, said Ann, ungratefully. 'Comfortable', he recorded. Like most things in Mongolia, it was a joke for both sides. Finally, when we had allayed his anxiety that we might have forgotten to tell him something important he adopted a solemn tone and pronounced, 'You are suffering from infective hepatitis and your treatment will be initiated as follows. ... If there is anything you want please ask for it. These women are here to serve you.' The women giggled and disappeared.

By this time it was becoming clear what lay behind all the rigmarole. Political and diplomatic considerations demand that Mongol doctors should treat Ann. They also demand that no mistakes should be made and that she should have first-class attention, that is attention from the leading Russian consultant physician in Ulan Bator (the doctor from Kharkov). These two requirements could be met simultaneously only in hospital where the consultant could be present unobtrusively. Today her treatment has gone into top gear, even if the nursing remains haphazard.

Last night, after Ann had gone into hospital, I was visited at 11.30 p.m. by a team of white-capped and white-coated Mongols who had come to disinfect Ann's bedroom. They had a sort of stirrup pump and they sprayed some sort of chemical solution, leaving the bathroom floor under water and the bedding thoroughly damp. I had to sleep on the sofa in the sitting room.

This morning the Ulan Bator public health director visited me. Where did Ann contact jaundice? I accounted for our movements and meals over the past few weeks. Then he asked, 'Do you get letters and parcels and telegrams from England?' Yes, but I think the telegrams are written out in the Mongolian post office. There was rapid conversation in Mongolian on this point with a hotel official. Return to the charge – 'Do you get letters and parcels from England and do any of your correspondents have jaundice?' 'No, jaundice is not a problem in England.' I then divert his attention to the staff at the diplomatic shop, not because there is anything wrong with them but simply because there is clearly going to be some more stirrup-pumping and it might as well be in their *gers*. Finally, he comes back to wondering where jaundice comes from. I lower my voice and say that I think it is the Soviet Union. This thought leaves him speechless and he quickly leaves.

The heroine of this comedy seems much better today and remarkably good-humoured for a jaundice patient. She is quieter and better cared for medically than she would be in this hotel. She is supposed to stay where she is for up to two weeks and she is to keep still and not undertake any activity. She will be bored long before then. But a lot of boredom is probably good for jaundice.

The Russian consultant says that there is no need to alter the plans for having the children here – thank goodness. And the family's return home can take place on 3 September as planned. Ann may not be fit enough to handle the move into 79 Broad Lane single-handed, but I will see if my brother can take a day off to help at that stage.

It is a great pity that we are so far away at just this critical time: you must be frantically busy at the moment with preparations for your move. I hope Mo is continuing to make gradual progress.

Reginald to his parents

4 July 1965

In hospital Ann has virtually a private staff. Of course they are simple peasant women who have no idea of time or routine. They washed the floor four times yesterday but could not remember to fill the bottle of drinking water. They are relaxed and good-natured like most Mongols and Ann gets on well with them. It is pathetic to see how thin the hospital's material resources are, touching to see how they put themselves out for us and hilariously funny to experience some of the resulting situations. The comedy is good for Ann's morale and she seems very cheerful.

Thank you for taking Jane out. We heard from her that she enjoyed her outing.

Reginald to Jane

5 July 1965

This is the last letter I can write to you by bag before you leave for Ulan Bator. Aunt Bronwen will send a car to collect you and George and William on Sunday 25 July. You spend the Monday night with the Brimelows in Moscow and arrive here on the Wednesday morning 28 July. Tadcu [grandfather] has your passports and tickets and will see that you get these and some pocket money at Cliveden. You know the Aeroflot routine. Happy journey!

Mother will only just have recovered by the time you get here. She will have to take things quietly. We have not managed to go out of town much recently, mostly because of demanding visitors. I shall try to arrange at least one expedition in August.

Mrs Fort wrote to me about your sixth form course. She seemed a bit woolly. I hope your O-level results are reasonably satisfactory; not that O levels matter much – except as a stage to A levels.

Ann to Jane

Undated

This is just one more short note before you leave to come here. I am likely to be in hospital for another week or so, but I don't mind at all as in the circs it is much more comfortable than the hotel. Pity I am missing all the fun of the National Day, but I feel that is mainly a tourist attraction. This is the real Mongolia!

Reginald to Ann's father

5 July 1965

[This letter merely contained numerous details about final arrangements made for the children's journey, and for Ann's return to London in September with the children, and for having our stored possessions delivered by Cox & Kings to our house at Hampton

on 6 September so that Ann and the children would be able to
take up residence there from that date.]

西藏西藏

The Mongolian National Day was celebrated on 11 July with the
usual mass parade and government reception. Between the morning and evening events the *Naadam* or national games provided
some colourful spectacle in the shape of the three manly sports of
the Mongols, horseracing, archery and wrestling. The horse races
are horse marathons and the jockeys are children (girls as well as
boys). The archers were mostly middle-aged or old. The wrestlers
are the only competitors who look like athletes – big, beefy men in
skimpy wrestling costume, doing their eagle dances before their
fights and after victories.

Several non-resident ambassadors came from Moscow or
Peking for the occasion. The routine of the recently redecorated
hotel was rearranged to impress them. The usual clientele of the
bar and restaurant were banished to a basement room and the
quality of the food served to them became very poor. The visiting
ambassadors and other delegates from abroad were offered an
improved menu in the restaurant. Alex and Grace Thompson and I
were classed as regulars and relegated to the basement room,
which we quickly labelled the drivers' pull-in. In a way this was
flattering as it meant that we were fully accepted as part of the
Mongol scene. But it was irritating to celebrate the National Day
with poor food and to be segregated from the *chers collègues* from
the rich outside world. Fortunately, one or two of the ambassadors, those from Scandinavia, invited me to join them once or
twice upstairs, so that I was able to sample the high as well as the
low of Mongolian efforts to please. After the visitors had left we
all returned to the restaurant and normal service resumed its
erratic but monotonous course. Ann, of course, missed this
experience.

西藏西藏

Ann to her parents

18 July 1965

Here I am back in the hotel again after two weeks in hospital. And what an interesting experience that was. There's nothing like getting to know the country well and trying everything!

I have now been in bed three weeks and must have one more week actually in bed – in fact the Russian doctor says I should stay in bed for another week and a half, which would take me up to the day after the children are due to arrive. I shall then have their five weeks of holiday in which to get my strength up for the journey home and the move into our house at Hampton.

They certainly did their best for me in hospital according to their lights and gave me VIP treatment. I had a little bare room to myself with a curtain on the window that only went half way across because three rings were missing. There was a modern washbasin, though for the first ten days there was no hot water. There was no bell, but this was of no importance as of course nobody would have come if I had rung it. I had a sister and a maid permanently on duty entirely for myself, for there were no other patients anywhere near (it was a secure suite of rooms and had been cleared for me). The maid did the cleaning and brought my food (a very severe diet) and changed the sheets every three days (roughly). The nurse handed out pills at irregular intervals and took my temperature and came to ask me if I had a temperature. She also gave me glucose and vitamin B12 injections, glucose transfusions, and one plasma transfusion, took blood samples and as a last refinement carried out a ghastly test in which a tube was given to me to swallow so that acetone could be extracted from my stomach for analysis. I am told that the nurses here have no real nursing training. I can quite believe it. They tackle these jobs like confident children who are happy to undertake anything without knowing the basic principles and therefore unaware of any risks. Half the time I was terrified, not of the treatment but at the thought that they had not properly sterilized something or might just temporarily forget what they were doing. However, I seem to be none the worse, in fact a great deal better.

This has meant more work and worry for Reg. We are very fed up as the wife of the man who has taken Eric Cheyne's place has done nothing to help. She came to visit me only when specifically invited and has not offered to cook anything for Reg or to relieve him of any other chores while he has been on his own. The other morning when the QMs arrived, Reg asked her if she would give them breakfast, as we normally do on their first morning, and she burst into tears and there was quite a scene. Our strange way of life seems to be becoming a bit much for her. We are waiting until the weekend is over and the QMs have gone to have it out with her and her husband. We live at such close quarters here that that sort of emotion must be overcome, and we are so isolated that there cannot be any question of not helping one another when difficulties arise.

Thank you for your birthday card. I spent my birthday in bed. I had a telegram signed Jane, George and William, but I can't make out how it came to be sent as I don't suppose that Jane had enough money to send it off her own bat.

We are of course delighted with George's success in Common Entrance. He is to go into Saunderites at Charterhouse, and his marks were good enough for him to go straight into the Remove, which means that he should be taking O-levels in two years' time. I think his life will broaden out very much now.

By the way, if you happen still to have any interesting and amusing letters from here, would you please hang on to them? They may come in useful for reference later on.

Ann to Reginald's parents

18 July 1965

The weather here is terrible, very changeable and stormy with hardly two nice days together. Yesterday we had a great dust storm followed by a tremendous downpour. It has now been raining in torrents for over 24 hours without a stop. These poor people living in their tents must be in an indescribable state. The whole place is awash. No wonder rheumatism is such a prevalent disease here. There have been some very long delays on the flight from Moscow recently. I very much hope the children do not have the additional anxiety of being held up.

Many thanks for the magazines you send. They do the rounds here and are very much enjoyed.

西藏西藏

Ann's hepatitis had a sequel some thirty years later when she was due to undergo an operation at the Acland Hospital at Oxford. It was announced at the last moment that blood tests showed that she had had hepatitis B, and the operation was held up while precautions against infection were taken. The Ulan Bator public health director would have had something to think about if hepatitis B had been known in Mongolia in 1965.

西藏西藏

Reginald to his parents

19 July 1965

Life is a bit of a grind at present. Looking after a sick person here is hard work, as nothing goes according to plan. Assembling three meals of suitable food and washing up three times a day in an ordinary hand basin is not my idea of fun, particularly when I have all my official work to do as well. I wondered if I ought to cancel the children's visit, but there is nowhere they could go in England. We shall be able to manage no doubt. I must confess that I am looking forward to having some time on my own here as the winter begins in September. It becomes a bit tiring after a few months when one has had to be the factotum of every English speaking person who happens to turn up simply because none of them speaks any language that is useful in Mongolia. The Mongolian winter keeps people away, which makes the winter much nicer than the summer.

Ann to her parents

2 August 1965

I hope our telegram reached you saying that the children had arrived safely. They seemed in good spirits and said that they had enjoyed the trip more than the first time. I think they knew what to expect and were more confident. All the same, George was sick on coming down at Irkutsk and again on landing here. Apparently he had refused to eat on the journey for fear of being sick. I am afraid he is and always will be the most sensitive and suffers for it. It took them a full two days to recover from their tiredness.

I am not allowed to go bumping around in the Land Rover, and Reg is very busy at the moment. So this morning they have been driven by Batsukh to somewhere out in the nearer hills and are amusing themselves wandering about there. They should certainly enjoy a sense of freedom in these wide spaces, which they cannot get at home.

I am really very much better at last. But I don't get up until about 11.00 and then go back to bed again after lunch until about 5.30. It is very boring for everyone, but I must be completely fit again by September.

18 September 1965

This letter will not have been brought to London by the Queen's Messengers but by a woman member of the United Nations Secretariat who is returning to London after a UN seminar on the status of women in public life that has been held here and in which I have been participating as an assistant observer for the UK.

It has been an amusing interlude in our lives and we have thoroughly enjoyed meeting the ladies from all the south, east and southeast Asian countries – India, Pakistan, Nepal, Ceylon, Afghanistan, Iran, Thailand, Cambodia, Japan, Western Samoa and New Zealand. Reg and I have had one or two little parties for them, one of them a Commonwealth party, and I felt like the queen entertaining the Commonwealth prime ministers, especially as the chief UN official present is a Canadian and there are several British people on his staff. It was very nice to hear English spoken so much, for of course it was the lingua franca of the seminar. All spoke English except the Cambodian and the Afghan who spoke French and, of course, the Mongolians who spoke Russian. I think it was a good thing for the people here to see on what frank and friendly terms the people of all these nations are compared with the relationship between the peoples of the communist countries, who obviously never trust one another further then they can see them. The star of the meeting was Mrs Menon, Minister of State for Foreign Affairs from India – a most impressive personality. She was outspoken against the communist system, which must have shaken the Mongols a bit, though they probably don't think her attitude is typical of her country (the non-resident Indian ambassador affects a more ingratiating style towards them).

It has been a pretty strenuous fortnight for me as I have been going to either a morning or an afternoon session of the seminar each day. Fortunately, as I was only assistant observer, I was not expected to play a very active part. However, I did at one point make a speech – or statement as it was called – on the position of women in the UK. It was very well received: in fact the delegate from Japan has taken a copy with her back to her own country to read it to some of her Japanese ladies. We had two Japanese who were the smallest ladies I have ever seen. When they came to cocktails they were able to sit side by side on one armchair, something I would have thought impossible except for children of two and a half. I think they came up to William's shoulder.

Reg and the children went off yesterday for a week's trip to the north of the country, their objective being a big lake on the Soviet border in an area reputed to be the Switzerland of Mongolia. That will give me a restful week, but I am sorry to miss the trip.

4

Trip to the North

The following pages contain the text of the report on our trip to the north, which I sent to the Foreign Office under cover of my dispatch no. 16 of 4 October 1965 (now available at the Public Record Office, PRO/FO/377/181154). It gives a typical impression of the way in which our journeys away from Ulan Bator were organized and conducted.

西藏西藏

**Notes on a journey to Lake Khövsgöl in Khövsgöl *aimag*,
17–23 August 1965**
Lake Khövsgöl is 819 kilometres or 512 miles to the northwest of Ulan Bator, about as far as from London to Inverness. It was obvious before we started that it would need four or more days of hard motoring simply to complete the round trip. This made it necessary to set off as soon as the Queen's Messengers had left on a Tuesday morning, in order to be back by the next week to prepare for the next Queen's Messengers. In order to allow for the usual Mongolian delays, I asked that we should start at the weekend. The Protocol Department of the Foreign Ministry, which is responsible for arranging all excursions requested by foreign missions at Ulan Bator, moved more quickly than usual and arranged for us to start on the Monday. It was a bit troublesome having to ask for Monday to be changed to Tuesday, but in this way we managed to leave on the day we wished instead of two or three days later, as is more usual.

Mr Dologrin Purev, at that time the desk officer for Great Britain in the second department of the Ministry of Foreign Affairs, was appointed to be my escort. This was a pity. Although personally amiable, he is a not a very active or capable man and seems destined to be a thoroughly dull communist official for the rest of his life. I took my three children with me, as they had come out for the holidays, but my wife was recovering from jaundice and had to stay behind. Purev knows a little English but he managed throughout the journey never to take a conversational initiative with any of the children (I knew before he came that he would be careful not to initiate conversations with me – Mongolian officials expose no front). At the same time he understood enough English to inhibit our conversations among ourselves. With our driver, we were six in the Land Rover. In addition to normal baggage we took fishing rods, gun, tent, sleeping bags, picnic materials, drinks and various Land Rover spares. It is wise to provide against many eventualities when travelling in Mongolia.

The first day took us to Bulgan, the centre of Bulgan *aimag*, 211 miles northwest of Ulan Bator. Some 15 kilometres out of Ulan Bator we left the tarmac road that runs northwards to the Soviet Union. We saw no more made roads until we returned a week later. During the morning we ran through the territory of a collective farm, touched the edge of a state farm and by the early afternoon were near the centre of another collective farm. The pasturelands were in fine condition, with grass and wild flowers stretching to every horizon.

August is a wet month, so the herds could be well scattered without finding themselves too far from water. We passed several large areas of wheat and there were signs of machinery being concentrated and slogans hung up in preparation for the harvest; but much of the wheat was still green, although it was already the second half of August. I heard in Bulgan and Khövsgöl that there had been too much rain this summer and not enough sun. Everyone assured us that the harvest would begin at the end of the month. The growing season is very short. It does not start until about mid-May, and I was told that some of the sowing had not been completed until late in June. By the end of August everything begins to turn brown rapidly, as September is dry and the night temperatures start dropping to around zero. The green wheat we saw has presumably turned brown with the grass and is now (late September) being harvested.

In the afternoon we crossed the Tuul River 140 miles from Ulan Bator, the river having made a great loop west and north since leaving the capital. About 40 miles further on we crossed the

Orkhon River, the longest river in the Mongolian People's Republic, into which the Tuul runs. The bridge over the Tuul, standing
in the middle of a vast and empty landscape as a solitary reminder
of human activity, is a timber construction, mended last spring (in
February we could not cross it but drove across the river on the
ice). The bridge over the Orkon is a simple concrete bridge of
fairly recent construction (the old wooden bridge still stands
nearby) and it has a few buildings (the centre of a wheat-growing
brigade) at one end. During the afternoon we ran through some
completely empty areas, reserved perhaps as winter pastures. At
any rate they seemed to have plenty of grass, which by now will
have become standing hay.

The 'natural' road from Ulan Bator to Bulgan is a good one,
running mostly over firm, rolling hills where it is easy to start a
new track if the old ones seem badly worn. We were able to keep
up a good speed and completed our 211 miles by about 7.30 p.m.
The Secretary of the Bulgan *aimag* Executive Committee of the
Khural of Workers' Deputies met us at the ornamental wooden
arch or gateway to Bulgan (all towns, *somon*s and farm centres in
Mongolia have ornamental arches standing some distance away
from the town in the middle of the steppe, with tracks running all
round them). I knew him already from my visit last February. He
escorted us to the town hotel or guesthouse and installed us in the
VIP suite, which is incongruously furnished with modern Czech
furniture and Chinese carpets. Bulgan is a relatively advanced
town. The hotel had pulsating electricity from a diesel generator
and indoor plumbing, which worked after a fashion when the
water supply was turned on. We were asked to say what we would
like for supper, as though there were a choice, and we finished up
as was to be expected with meat and milk products and the
inevitable *arkhi* or local vodka.

Bulgan *aimag* covers an area of 50,000 square kilometres and
has a population of a little over 30,000, of whom 42 per cent are
children. The population of Bulgan town is 10,000. The *aimag*
contains 16 collective farms and one state farm, each of which is
also a *somon* (administrative district) making 17 *somon*s in all. It
also contains three Animal Husbandry Machinery Stations (which
in practice are equipped almost entirely with machinery for grain
farming) and three animal breeding stations for cows and sheep.

Twenty per cent of Bulgan's surface is covered by woodland,

mostly in the northern, more mountainous part of the *aimag*. The north is rich in horned cattle, while the centre and south are rich in sheep and goats. The total head of cattle of all sorts in the *aimag* is about one million, of which 80 per cent are collectively owned. The rest are privately owned, but private animals are herded with the collective animals. The *somon*s have collecting centres for butter and milk in the summer. It is claimed that the *aimag* produces 400 tons of butter per season. 40,000 hectares or virgin land have been ploughed in Bulgan, and the *aimag* delivered 10,000 tons of grain to the state in 1964. The map that I was shown of the *aimag*'s virgin lands indicated that the bottoms of most of the broader valleys had been turned over to wheat growing. These must in earlier years have been the best pastures.

Bulgan town has a small brick factory, a motor transport base, a construction department, a sewing cooperative (organized in three divisions) and a mill. The latter has a capacity of 24 tons a day and receives grain from parts of the Central, Selenge and Arkhangai *aimag*s as well as from the whole of Bulgan *aimag*. Although it has been running for a few years, it still has two or three Soviet technicians controlling operations. The majority of its employees are women. It seems to work for much of the time well below its capacity. The *aimag* is soon going to have a small coalmine built in Saikhan *somon*.

Bulgan town has a ten-year school with a separate boarding house. There are four seven-year schools with boarding houses in the *somon*s and 16 four-year schools. All schools start at the age of eight. There are two evening schools and one general cultural school for adults in the *aimag* centre, which also has a local museum, a cinema (rather like an old-fashioned village hall in England), a library, a dispensary, a hospital with 75 beds and allegedly 15 doctors (no information available about their qualifications), children's kindergartens, crèches, and a maternity centre with 25 beds. The most eloquent comment on housing is that even the secretary of the *aimag* executive committee lives in a *ger* (Mongolian tent).

The *aimag* centre is connected to Ulan Bator by telephone and radio. Aircraft call three times a week on the Ulan Bator–Bulgan–Mörön run. The post lorry arrives from Ulan Bator four times a week, and post trucks visit all the *somon*s three times a week. Each *somon* is said to have a club, a reading room and a medical

centre (mostly with doctors but some with orderlies only). The
facilities claimed to be available are very modest.

In the old days there was a very big monastery two or three
miles from the site of present-day Bulgan. There are allusions to it
in the museum, but it is claimed that no trace of it survives. We
passed a group of two or three old buildings with Chinese-style
gables not far from Bulgan town, but any connection between
these and a former monastery was firmly denied.

I was told that an old 1921 partisan whom I visited in February was looking forward to seeing me again, but there was no
time for calls, only for a stroll down the dusty main street, which
is very wide and laid out rather like a little park with propaganda
boards every few yards and piped music coming through badly
tuned loudspeakers. Strolls of this sort are not encouraged and one
is of course very conspicuous. The general aspect of these little
townships from street level reminds me very much of the scenarios
of westerns on the films.

We drove off next morning at 8.15 a.m. and found ourselves
struggling with a very bad road. As we moved north into the
hillier and more wooded area the ground became softer and we
were frequently hemmed into defiles where we could no longer
pick our own way but had to bump slowly over the single, pot-
holed track. By 2.00 p.m. we had covered only 86 miles to the
banks of the Selenge River (into which the Orkhon flows and
which itself flows into Lake Baikal). The scenery was very fine,
with some deciduous forest in the valleys descending to the Selenge
and wild flowers growing in profusion everywhere. We passed
only a few herds and only one brigade centre. The Selenge is a
broad and swift river and for some reason Purev expected to find a
bridge over it. We were astonished as we approached it to see a
notice saying 'TO THE HOTEL'. This led us to a tumbledown one-
room cottage with a couple of *ger*s outside, which was evidently a
sort of drivers' pull-up. There was a wire across the river with a
skiff attached to it but no indication of a crossing for vehicles.
There was no one there and no one in sight in any direction, and
no one answered our shouts. A few yards along the bank was an
old wooden Chinese-style pavilion, which must have been there
since pre-revolutionary days, but there was no means of discover-
ing its history. It was very hot by the river and there were swarms
of flies and gnats. We decided to follow a track upstream as the

river seemed to be more closely confined between hills and cliffs in that direction. Very soon we arrived at a ferry, where a herdsman was sitting patiently beside his horse under some trees. The ferry (two large wooden boats with a wooden platform built across them) was on the other side of the river and no ferryman was in sight, although we could see some sheep and cows and a group of *yurts* not far away. We made a noise and settled down to a picnic, and while we ate a herdsman galloped up to the far bank and brought the ferryboat over. The ferry ran on a well-anchored hawser that bore against a spindle made of a tree trunk, the ferryman doing no work except to set the rudder against the fast current. But he must have had to change the tree trunk very frequently because the hawser bit deeply into it. On the other side we met a *gazik* carrying a Russian and a well dressed Mongol official from the Ministry of Agriculture. We exchanged greetings but fraternization was clearly discouraged and we pressed on into Khövsgöl *aimag*. As we rose from the Selenge valley the road slowly improved. We passed through the centre of a collective farm in a broad valley where dozens of herds were grazing and immediately afterwards were stopped by two men standing by a *gazik* just off the track. One of them was the Deputy Secretary of the Executive Committee of the Khural of Workers' Deputies of Khövsgöl *aimag*, who had come well over 100 miles from Mörön to meet and escort us.

By now we were running well on the slopes of broad, firm hills from which we occasionally had distant views of the Selenge River winding towards and below us in the distance on our left-hand side. By 6.00 p.m. we reached Ikh Uul *somon*, an unusually large collective farm and *somon* centre in a fertile plain by the river, 163 miles from Bulgan. We were shown into two rooms, each of which contained three or four iron beds, in the headquarters of an animal husbandry machine station. Purev confessed that he did not know what was happening but half an hour later it was announced that we were going to stay the night. We were told to rest and drink the *airag* (*koumiss*) provided for us while a meal was prepared. All sorts of officials stood around outside; obviously it was impossible to go for a walk, so we did as we had been told. An hour or so later we were called to supper in the *somon* dining room, a battered wooden structure uncomfortably full of flies. Eight or nine local dignitaries were present. They spoke only when spoken to, as is often the case when rural Mongols face foreigners. In those situations one relies on the Ministry of Foreign Affairs man to help create some semblance of conversation, but this was beyond Purev's capacity and I had to do all the work, racking my brains to think of questions that could not be answered by 'yes' or 'no'. The children and I drank and ate far more than was good for us in order to show our appreciation of their hospitality, but I discovered afterwards that all the alcohol, at £4 a bottle, was put on my bill. There were innumerable toasts and speeches by the *aimag* representative, the chairman of the collective farm and me.

After supper it was announced that we were going fishing. We careered across some meadows to the river and everyone started fishing noisily with the oddest assortment of equipment. Of course no one caught anything and the mosquitoes were unbearable, but it was a beautiful spot and a fine sunset. Back in the animal husbandry machine station the diesel generator failed and we went to bed in the dark, but two jolly country girls under the tuition of our driver struggled to the last to behave like maids and brought us hot milk and tea.

Next morning we set off at 9.00 a.m. for Mörön, the centre of Khövsgöl *aimag*; the going was good and we covered the 73 miles in three hours. The road soon turned away from the Selenge River and the landscape became more mountainous, with coniferous forests and occasional lakes and pools, many of which were covered with duck. Grain growing areas petered out as we moved northwards. All the way to Mörön we passed scattered herds. Yaks and *hainag*s (a cross between a yak and a cow) began to appear in some numbers. Sheep predominated, but there were also plenty of horses.

At Mörön we were taken to a small hotel/guesthouse, built in 1959, consisting of one corridor with rooms opening off it, each room containing several beds, and everyone sharing a sort of washstand in the corridor with water fed by gravity from an old oil drum. *Airag* and several other milk products were served to refresh us while Purev disappeared to talk about our programme. He returned to fetch me to the offices of the *aimag* executive committee where a number of officials were waiting to receive me. With much drinking of *airag* they gave me a short exposé about the *aimag*. A man who had been introduced to me simply as a member of the Khural of Workers' Deputies soon began to take control. When I heard his name I knew that this was the First Secretary of the *aimag* committee of the Mongolian People's Revolutionary Party. He chipped in with correct and intelligent answers when the others stumbled, and by the end he was prompting the others – 'Tell him about medical care', 'Tell him about education' and so forth. After the exposé we went off to lunch in a private room behind the town's principal public dining room. There were speeches and toasts as usual. Thanks to the party secretary, but not at all to Purev, conversation was much easier than at Ikh Uul the previous evening.

After lunch we visited the local mill, which was similar to the one at Bulgan. It too had its little cell of Soviet specialists. We also visited the local museum, which contained several interesting diagrams illustrating the movement of Red Army troops into Khövsgöl in 1921 and the locations of the former monasteries. There was a good display of local flora and fauna. In the evening we were allowed an hour or two of free time in which we were able to wander on foot round the town, a process that took about 15 minutes if one kept moving. Two local officials, one a young woman doctor and the other a young official of the executive committee had by this time become part of our suite. They had obviously been selected because of their ability to speak adequate Russian and their knowledge of city ways. They were good company and much more help than Purev. The day finished with a concert by local performers in the town's club or cultural centre (a small theatre is being built but will not be ready until next year). Every *aimak* has a group of amateur musicians, singers and dancers who travel around the farm and brigade centres giving concerts rather like wartime ENSA concerts for the troops. The core of these groups seems to consist of performers who are amateur only in name and have become full-time entertainers; but they gather round them wherever they go a number of genuine amateur performers. The performances are uneven but pleasing and consist mostly of traditional Mongolian material; but every programme will contain at least one Soviet song. The audience at these concerts is in a way more interesting than the performers. All one's senses become aware of what the words 'toiling masses' mean.

Khövsgöl is one of the older *aimag*s. It was formed in 1931. It is the largest of the northern *aimag*s and has a population of nearly 70,000 in an area of just over 100,000 square kilometres. The population of Mörön town is approximately 10,000, like that of Bulgan, but Mörön has a less developed appearance. The *aimag* contains some two million livestock, over half of which are sheep. Mörön itself is not very high and stands at 1200 metres above sea level, but the highest mountain in the *aimag* reaches 3700 metres. The *aimag*'s sown area is 30,000 hectares, mostly in the southern area along the Selenge River. The grain yield on this land in 1964 averaged one and a half metric tons per hectare and is expected to be a little lower in 1965. The *aimag* is divided into 24 *somon*s, of which 23 are coterminous with collective farms and one with a state farm. There is one other state farm that is not a *somon*. One of the state farms specializes in grain production, the other in breeding cows.

Mörön's industry consists of its mill (capacity said to be 15 tons per shift with three shifts a day, which is larger than the capacity claimed for Bulgan mill), a construction department, and a food combine. I was not shown the latter, but it presumably makes various milk products and bakes some bread. The mill has a small wood-fired electricity plant, which provides some current for the town. There is also a diesel generator. I found a copy of the Mörön telephone directory in a drawer. It gave an interesting picture of the number of branches and offices of central ministries and organizations that fill the permanent buildings in the town centre. Virtually the entire population of Mörön seemed to be housed in *ger*s.

The *aimag* has three ten-year schools, of which one is in Mörön and one in Ikh Uul. There are more than ten seven- or eight-year schools of all types. This means that there must be at least 15 four-year schools; in other words, the majority of the *somon*s have four-year schools only. The 30 or more schools cater for over 10,000 children. They seem to work in two shifts a day, as in Ulan Bator and indeed everywhere else. Each *somon* is said to have a doctor, and it was claimed that every *somon* had a share in a small hospital, which means that there are small hospitals in not more than half the *somon*s. There is a general hospital in Mörön but there was no inclination to let me see it. Each *somon*, that is each farm, is said to have a fully qualified veterinary surgeon, and most brigades have a veterinary 'feldsher', namely an orderly with middle school education.

On the next day we set out for Khatgal, a little town at the southern point of Lake Khövsgöl, 65 miles from Mörön. The track ran through some fine mountain scenery with substantial forests running well down into the valleys and bare, rocky crests rising above them. There were many large herds and after a while we became aware that nearly all of them were moving slowly north-wards. About half way to our destination a track ran in from the west, which my driver told me was the main road from Javkhlant (the old Uliastai), the centre of his home *aimag* Zavkhan, and beyond that from Khovd, the far southwestern *aimag* of the Torgut Mongols. From this point onwards we passed many very large herds of sheep, cows and yaks and a few herds of horses moving steadily northwards with camels, horses and sometimes yak carts carrying the drovers' tents and stores. We had come upon one of the old-established trade routes of the Mongols, and the thousands of animals we saw were being exported on the hoof to the Soviet Union. This was the main artery of west-central Mongolia.

It emerged when I questioned my driver and others that anyone driving to or from Zavkhan and the far west would normally take the route we had been following. This was astonishing because we had come a long way northwards and had met or passed very few vehicles all the way from Ulan Bator. I had imagined that all the traffic for the far west was driving through the Khangai Moun-tains via Tsetserleg in Arkhangai *aimag* or round the southern edge of the Khangai Mountains via Arvaikheer in Övörkhangai *aimag* to Bayankhongor and Gobi Altai. It seems that this is not the case. The roads through and round the Khangai Mountains are very difficult. This explains why everyone who is supposed to know about such things has told me that it takes ten days to drive to Bayan Ölgiy, the westernmost province where the Kazakh and Tuvin minorities live, and that no one in his senses thinks of trying to drive there from Ulan Bator. The fact is, as I was to realize at Khatgal, that the west-centre and far west of the Mongolian People's Republic depend more on their own overland routes to the Soviet Union than on their overland routes to Ulan Bator.

Purev showed a curious unwillingness to admit that the herds were on their way to the Soviet Union. They are just changing pasture, he said. But he could not explain why they all changed pasture in the same direction at once. Other Mongols in Khatgal, when Purev was out of earshot, were much franker.

Khatgal is a rare phenomenon in Mongolia – a town that is not an *aimag* centre. In Mongolian terminology it is a *khoroo* and not a *somon*. It looks more Russian than Mongol, consisting of a single main street lined with log cabins and wooden houses, but there are two or three rows of *gers* enclosed in high stockades behind the log cabins. The population totals between 3000 and 4000. It is simply a trading post. It receives produce from west central Mongolia, ships it on barges up the lake to Turta (called Khankh on the official Mongolian map: Turta is probably a Russian name – it is the one commonly used). Turta is said to be roughly similar to Khatgal and stands at the northern point of the lake about 20 kilometres from the Soviet frontier. From there a road about 200 kilometres long carries goods to Irkutsk; in winter sledge trains run over the frozen lake between Khatgal and Turta. Cattle follow a track round the lake on its eastern bank, but the cattle track is said to be impassable to vehicles.

We were lodged in a timber house surrounded by a high stockade with a militia man to keep the gates to the enclosure shut and a silent old woman to fetch water and wood. The various milk products provided in our rooms were made mostly of yak's milk. We started with the usual *airag*/exposé session with the local dignitaries, and this was followed by a lunch in the local dining room, which was closed to the general public for the occasion. There were toasts and speeches and much vodka drinking. Purev distinguished himself by declaring that the people of Khatgal lived by animal husbandry and that trade with the Soviet Union was not particularly significant to them.

In the afternoon we were taken up to the top of a local mountain and shown the view up the lake; and after that we visited Khatgal's industry – a wool-washing factory. This was built with Soviet help in 1932, namely before the first workshops of the industrial combine at Ulan Bator, which is usually claimed to be the first industrial installation in the Mongolian People's Republic. The machinery at the factory is still the 1932 machinery. It produces 5000 to 6000 tons of washed wool annually and has its own plant to generate electricity (wood-fired). The wool washed at Khatgal is drawn from Khövsgöl, Zavkhan and the western *aimag*s (this was obvious when one saw the wool, as much of it was of the coarse brown colour that is peculiar to the regions beyond the Khangai Mountains). There is as yet no wool-washing plant further westwards. Most of the washed wool is exported to the Soviet Union across the lake, but a little (Purev tried to say 'most', but there was ample evidence to the contrary) is sent to the industrial combine at Ulan Bator for processing into tent felt and for spinning. The wool-washing plant employs 300 workers, of whom more than 60 per cent are women.

Our next appointment was on board the Mongolian People's Republic's merchant navy – a 400 horsepower tug (wood-fired) called the *Sukhbaatar*. It was received from the Soviet Union in 1956 and tows three barges, each of 400 tons capacity to and from Turta, the ship's main base being at Turta. The trip takes ten hours with barges or six without. The navigation season opens in mid-June and closes at the end of November, but from the end of October the main wharves at Khatgal are iced up and loading and unloading are carried out in November at a spit of land two or three kilometres north of Khatgal where the deep part of the lake begins. The *Sukhbaatar* made a special trip out into the lake for our benefit and the captain, who was a fluent Russian speaker, obligingly explained many things to me. He pointed out for example a petrol depot about five kilometres north of Khatgal on the western shore of the lake, containing about 18 cylindrical tanks lying horizontally, which he said was the petrol depot for the western *aimag*s of Mongolia. One of his three barges is a petrol tanker. He also talked freely about the export of cattle to the Soviet Union while we inspected through glasses the huge concentration of herds resting in the meadows between the forests and the lake on the eastern bank.

There appeared to be two main wharves at Khatgal, presumably an import and an export wharf. A barge was being loaded at the wharf where the *Sukhbaatar* lay. It contained bales of washed wool, barrels of butter, bales of hides and skins and some boxes whose contents I could not imagine. It seemed to take a lot of people to do a little loading. There were several Russians about. In the town there were various motor transport parks and yards where goods were piled and covered with tarpaulins (most bulk storage in Mongolia is in the open air, even in Ulan Bator). There were armed civilian guards at every depot, and fences were mostly too high and too solid for people to see in.

Lake Khövsgöl is over 100 kilometres long and very deep. It is said to be associated geologically with Lake Baikal, into which its

waters flow by a long detour through northern Mongolia via the
Eg River, which flows into the Selenge. Through Lake Baikal its
waters eventually reach the Angara, the Yenisei and the Arctic
Ocean. Only a few miles from where we stood on the bridge of the
Sukhbaatar, on the other side of the mountains that form the
western rim of the lake, a small stream rises, which, when it
crosses the Soviet frontier, is already called the Little Yenisei. This
is the remote corner of Mongolia where the Tsaatan live, very
primitive people who sustain themselves by breeding white reindeer. It would have taken us two days to visit the Tsaatan and
Purev made it clear that they were not one of the exhibits of the
building of socialism. Three final points about Lake Khövsgöl are
that its colour is a translucent, pale, greenish blue of great beauty,
that its temperature never rises higher than seven degrees centi-
grade, and that it forms a wind tunnel down which a very cold
Siberian wind blows into the Mongolian People's Republic.

After our trip on the lake we were invited to a formal dinner
given by the municipality. They presented me with a whole boiled
sheep in a dish, the various parts disposed as prescribed by ancient
ritual and the head (cooked whole) pointing towards me as guest
of honour. I was handed a Mongolian dagger and it was my duty
to carve the sheep and distribute the meat to all the company, the
fattest meat being the most highly prized. There is a complicated
set of rules about the carving, but Purev was not disposed to help
me with them. He said that he was surprised to find that such old
practices still survived. However, everyone else enjoyed the occasion and some of the older men took the meat from me with a
reverence that in England would be reserved for Holy Communion.
Again there were toasts and speeches and much heavy drinking.
Afterwards we retired to the local club where we saw a dimly lit
film about the 1921 revolution, with the toiling masses sighing
and yawning and muttering hoarsely to one another in the darkness.

We began our return journey next morning; but we had no
sooner started than we stopped by the river Eg where it runs
southwards out of Lake Khövsgöl and were commanded to fish.
There was a strong, cold wind and brilliant sunlight and the fish
could not be expected to cooperate. After a while Purev could
stand the cold no longer and we pushed on; but for once we were
left to our own devices, Purev being in the other vehicle with the
woman doctor and young *aimag* official. We dawdled here and

there and at midday caught up with the others. They appeared to
have met an old friend in the middle of nowhere. This turned out
to be the chairman of a nearby collective farm who, said Purev,
had heard we were in the neighbourhood and wanted to entertain
us. We drove off in the general direction indicated, this time out-
stripping the others. After an hour or so we came to a group of
three *yurt*s where everyone seemed to be standing around in their
best clothes. We decided this must be in our honour and introduced ourselves. By the time Purev caught up we were comfortably
installed drinking bowls of *suutei tsai*, the universal beverage of
the Mongols, which is made by stewing a handful of tea in a
mixture of milk and water with some fat added. For the next two
hours we drank *airag* (*koumiss*) and *arkhi* (a sort of vodka
distilled from *airag*) and ate *urum* (dried cream), *aaruul* (dried,
caked milk) and *byaslag* (a sort of cheese), all made of sheep's
milk, as our hosts were shepherds. We ate *buudz* (a sort of meat-
filled dumpling) only to find that I was being presented with
another whole sheep in a dish and was once more required to
carve and distribute it. This time, among country folk, it was
much more important to do it according to the rules, but Purev
was again unhelpful. We moved from *ger* to *ger* and finally
everyone was so well feasted that it was decided that we must have
a break for a ride. The horses were untied from the *uyan* and we
ambled and cantered up the valley and back. We had to have one
final drink for the road and I was presented with an old blue silk
khadag (ceremonial scarf) while the children were given lamb-
skins. We produced presents in return (we distribute presents
wherever we go in Mongolia, chiefly silk or chiffon scarves for the
women and picture books about Great Britain for the men) and
we finally set off, as we thought, for Mörön.

The chairman of the collective farm was leading in a *gazik* into
which I had seen him stowing a large churn of *airag*. After a while
we descended to a river and were told that we were going to fish.
It was a well-chosen spot and in an hour we had taken three large
taimen, each weighing between 15 and 25 pounds, and several
lenok, which are like large trout. A tremendous storm overtook us,
with hailstones like mothballs, and the chairman of the farm
decided that this was the time for more *airag*. We sat in the cars
drinking *airag* until the storm cleared and then at last we made for
Mörön where we arrived as night fell.

Next day we were due to leave very early for Bulgan. We said we would have breakfast at seven o'clock. When we reached the municipal dining room Purev told us that the *aimag* authorities had intended to give us a farewell dinner on the previous evening (Saturday) but we had arrived back too late. They were going to entertain us to breakfast instead. At 7.15 a.m. on Sunday morning we sat down to the previous evening's dinner, with a full set of courses, vodka and wine, the only concession to breakfast being that huge *taiman* steaks were substituted for the main meat course. There were speeches and toasts and finally I was presented with a silver *ayag* full of *airag* on a blue silk *khadag* (the *ayag* is the traditional Mongol drinking bowl), and the children were given little models of animals. I in turn presented our gifts and we were at last free to start the hardest and longest day's journey of our tour, 250 miles from Mörön to Bulgan over the bad tracks of the Selenge River and its associated valleys. We reached Bulgan exhausted after dark, but a member of the executive committee of the *aimag* nevertheless visited us at the guesthouse and came to see us off to Ulan Bator next morning.

We had traversed in the week the whole of the river system of northern Mongolia, which is in fact a catchment area for Lake Baikal and the Yenisei. Back in Ulan Bator I sit about a mile to the north of the river Tuul, which drains into the same system. Beyond the river Tuul and the Bogdo Uul massif, which rises behind it on its southern bank, there are no rivers draining into any ocean until one reaches the Yellow River in China.

The broad intervening space consists of steppe and Gobi. This is usually thought of as the homeland of the Mongols; but in fact the area through which we had travelled and its extension to the east in the Onon and Kerulen River system (draining into the Amur) are the true homelands of the Mongols. Travelling through it one senses that the Russian colonization of Siberia was bound in time to bring the Mongols under Russian influence. The development of Siberia under the Soviet regime is exerting a powerful force on all the old trade routes between Mongolia and Siberia. These trade routes penetrate directly into the west, centre and east of Mongolia and do not run through Ulan Bator. The advantage this gives the Soviet Union seems to be of considerable importance in the Sino–Soviet struggle. There is virtually only one route into China on the general line of the railway and the old caravan route

11. Mid-morning break by the Kerulen River.

to Kalgan. It runs through the parts of Mongolia that are least suited for modern development. It seems to me that the forces of geography are nowadays working strongly in the Soviet Union's favour, even if many other forces work in the contrary direction and make Mongolia a costly dependency.

Shortly before starting our journey I fitted new rubber bushes to the front shock absorbers of the Land Rover. When we returned, after a total of 1125 miles, they needed to be renewed again. Such is the state of Mongolia's 'roads'.

5

Family Separation

Ann and the three children left Ulan Bator by the weekly Aeroflot flight to Moscow on 2 September. They spent a night in Moscow, arrived in London, much delayed, in the early hours of 5 September instead of on the evening of 4 September, and stayed briefly at the St Ermin's Hotel at Westminster before moving into and taking over our house at Hampton.

Many of the letters exchanged between Ann and me in the next three months dealt with jobs that needed doing at the house, arrangements with and for the children at their schools, and Ann's involvements with her own and my families.

西藏西藏

Ann to Reginald

79 Broad Lane, Hampton, 8 September 1965

I hope you got my cable saying that we had arrived safely. We were fearfully late in arriving. We got to Moscow only 15 minutes late, having been delayed about half an hour in Omak. The flight was uneventful and quite pleasant.

Jane and I stayed with Miss Wood, the consul, and the boys stayed with the Brimelows. Everyone was very nice to us. We heard from Miss Wood about the Brooke case and how she dealt with Britons in distress. I was invited to lunch at the embassy, where Sir Geoffrey Harrison[1] and his wife had been installed for just over a week. They naturally had other things than Mongolia on their minds. It is not true that he doesn't smile or laugh; he does both, but with a sort of grimace as though he shouldn't be giving in to such weakness. I admired a lovely Ivon Hitchens in the drawing room, but they both said they thought it was hideous, couldn't make out what it was and had no idea who had painted it. Fitzroy Maclean and his wife were there, on their way to Central Asia (Samarkand and so forth) but in fact were doubtful about getting there because of an outbreak of cholera. Fitzroy didn't seem interested in talking about anything except Bron and Bill. She seemed more ready for ordinary conversation.

I hurried back to the Brimclows expecting to leave at 3.30 p.m. only to hear that the BEA plane had not yet left London because of the bad weather at the Moscow end. Takeoff would be some time after 9.00 p.m., so we found ourselves involved in a cocktail party for English teachers of Russian, and we finally left for the airport at 8.15 p.m. We took off a little after 10.30 p.m. feeling pretty weary, as you can imagine. The air was turbulent and we bumped and swayed across Europe for three and a half hours, but the children managed to get some sleep. Who do you think we met in Moscow? It was our little American teacher friend who had disembarked at Irkutsk on the previous day hoping to fly to Khabarovsk. The connection had not turned up and the teachers in her group, needing to get back to the USA for the beginning of term, had decided to come to Moscow and join the flight to London and to catch a flight from there to Chicago. By the time we parted from them they were absolutely exhausted but had another 11 hours flying to do.

We had just finished with the customs at London airport at about 2.00 a.m. when we heard someone calling to us and there were my parents. They had come to meet us at 8.00 p.m. and had stayed on! They had a hired car and we drove with a good deal of hilarity to the St Ermin's. We got to bed at 3.30 a.m.

On Saturday we bought George a bicycle at a shop at the Elephant & Castle recommended by a taxi driver. The shop undertook to put it on the train, and there it was at Hampton station on Monday morning. On Saturday afternoon we went to see the Beatles film *Help* and laughed our heads off. On Sunday morning Godfrey Davis brought us a car – a Corsair – and we went to Westminster Abbey for Morning Prayer (though a bit late). And then we went to see the parents at Hampstead. Monday morning we got to the house at 9.30. Cox & Kings didn't arrive with all our stored possessions until 10.30 (a burnt-out starter motor). Your nephew Christopher arrived to help. The men were in a hurry to get away, so we were left with everything unpacked from the cases by lunch time, surrounded by rivers of sawdust and hundreds of glasses. We aired some blankets and had a good night's sleep.

[The letter continues with details about garden help, heating engineers, builder and decorator, and Jane's O-level results.]

Reginald to his parents

Ulan Bator, 12 September 1965

We have had a 'cultural delegation' here for the past fortnight, that is someone from the FO and someone from the British Council to negotiate an agreement for future cultural exchanges. Perhaps we shall succeed in getting in a few English books and films and people. We signed and exchanged notes on the subject, which in its way was an historic event as it was the first agreement ever signed between Britain and Mongolia. I found the fortnight quite exhausting, for the delegation needed a good deal of attention. Now there are two Queen's Messengers here. Perhaps tomorrow we shall have a quiet day. If so, it will be the first for two or three months.

The autumn is advancing very rapidly. Frosts have started at night and we are told that the hotel's heating will be turned on on Wednesday. The larches are dropping their needles fast. There is almost no green grass left. The landscape is reverting to brown, grey and yellow, which were its only colours when I arrived at the end of last October. Father Masters[2] (now chaplain at Helsinki and Moscow) wrote a little while ago to say he is going to try to come here, but he has not arrived. I think he would be wise to abandon the idea. The journey via Irkutsk is very tiring and unsuitable for a man of his age and physical condition. I am not sure that I would have time to look after him properly.

Reginald to Ann

12 September 1965

I have been told that I can leave here on 2 December and travel home via Stockholm, where I want to see the collection of Mongoliana assembled by the Scandinavian expeditions that visited both Inner and Outer Mongolia in the 1920s. I shall hope to reach you on 7 December. We do not have to be back in UB until 29 January, so that you will be able to travel back with me via Hong Kong and Peking. We are expected to stay for only a few months in 1966.

The visit of the cultural mission was strenuous. Old man West of the British Council went out of his way to be considerate and helpful in practical ways. Richard Speaight of the FO expected to be looked after in detail. We concluded the first ever agreement between Britain and Mongolia and we had a little ceremony at which Chimiddorj and I signed and exchanged notes – quite fun. I had to do a bit of speechmaking in Russian and we had the usual amount of drinking. The Khujirt trip was cancelled, to my secret relief, and they went to Terelj instead. Incidentally, the colours on the way to Terelj were very beautiful – light green and yellow and brown. There was a long delay over their departure yesterday.

We have two of the better QMs here at present, so I have had them to dine in our suite on duck à l'orange and pheasant, giving thanks for our tins.

Grace Thompson has now become an employee (locally engaged) and works as my personal assistant. This has made her more cooperative but she and Alex still find it hard to fit in with Mongolian rhythms and the Mongolian environment. Their own order from Hong Kong has arrived, so they can begin to eat well in their own way.

I had a cold after you left, but it has cleared up. I do my exercises strenuously and I feel very fit. Perhaps it is just as well that the Mongols don't allow telephone calls to London. I would be spending a fortune if they did.

PS. The bag for UB closes on Thursdays at 2.00 p.m. on 16 and 30 September, 14 and 28 October and 11 November.

13 September 1965

[Letter mostly about getting Christmas and New Year cards printed with the royal arms, repairs to items of cold weather kit, clothes and books.] Some Czech musicians gave a very good concert of national music on Saturday, very folksy, of course, but well done. It was good to hear a thoroughly European style again, although of course they had to fit in a Mongol song and two Russian ones. The concert was very badly attended. I was sorry for Gaidosh, the Chargé d'Affaires.

I am looking forward very much to tomorrow, which will be my first day not under pressure for ages. Unfortunately, a long cipher telegram has just come in, which looks ominous.

西藏西藏

By this time our operation had become more sophisticated. I had received some ciphers, but it was very time consuming to use them. Their use had to be kept to a minimum. When we were in the hotel I kept them in my security cupboard, but when I was going out of town I either left them with the Thompsons or carried them with me in a little bag strapped to me. I kept a minimum of paper in my cupboard, shredding nearly everything I received once I had read it and, if necessary, answered it. I kept copies of most of my own reports in order to be able to maintain a consistent reporting thread. I was not worried that the Mongolian or Russian authorities might find some way of getting access to them. I assumed that we were watched and listened to. They were welcome to know what I thought. There was nothing they could do about it. And some of it might jolt them into unaccustomed reflections.

西藏西藏

Reginald to Ann

13 September 1965

Just a stop press to tell you that Father Masters turned up this evening, having set out from Moscow yesterday with only a single ticket to Irkutsk in his pocket. They grumbled in Irkutsk that he was not entitled to travel cheaply, but they sold him a return ticket by Mongolian Airlines to Ulan Bator and a single ticket back to Moscow. His whole travel bill is about £50. We would pay some £200 on the same route.

Sodnomdorji was phoned from the airport and told that there was an Englishman there who must be a tourist. Sodnomdorji came to me and asked if I knew who it might be as no tourists were due. I said I thought I knew, so we fetched the Land Rover from the garage and drove to the airport, and there was the padre complete with clerical collar and broad black hat. The hotel has fixed him up with a 35-tugrik room, which I expect I shall have to pay for, he being unable to afford such luxury. It has to be recognized as an extraordinary performance, although I could do without an extra presence at the moment. He was the only passenger on the plane from Irkutsk – they must have put him on a service flight! It is wonderful what obstinate innocence can do. I will let you know what it feels like to have a private chaplain.

Ann to Reginald

79 Broad Lane, Hampton, 14 September 1965

We have at last got all our bits and pieces under one roof. But we seem to have collected an enormous number of things over the last few years and we shall have to acquire more cupboards and book-cases if we are to clear our glass and bed linen and books out of the way.

The Treasury Medical Adviser, Dr Medvei, arranged for me to see Professor Sheila Sherlock at the Royal Free Hospital last Friday; she said she thought I had made a remarkable recovery in such a short time and that my liver seemed pretty well as good as new. I should try not to get overtired, but I needn't bother about my diet, except no alcohol for six months. When all the children have gone back to school, there should be nothing to stop me having a good long rest.

Reginald to Ann

Ulan Bator, 18 September 1965

Being at last free from looking after other people, I write to you. At least, I hope I am free. Padre Masters flew off this morning two days earlier than he had expected, but I have just had a phone call from him in Irkutsk saying that he is in difficulties because his Soviet visa is not valid. Goodness knows what happens now. He has no visa to come back here. It is only 7.15 a.m. in Moscow, so I shall be unable to rouse anyone to do anything there for an hour or two. I did not examine his passport other than to check his Mongolian visa. It seems a bit feckless to travel in these parts without making sure that all documents are in order. The whole visit has been a bit trying.

This seems a fine time of year to have some leisure in Mongolia. The days are brilliantly sunny as in winter, and the nights are crisp and fresh. The night sky is marvellous – more stars than blackness, an amazing brilliance. The yellow colours everywhere have turned to copper and brown and many of the trees are already quite bare. I am surrounded by things to read, accumu– lated over many weeks. I have plenty to keep me busy.

PS. Stop-press from Irkutsk by phone. The Padre is having to wait in the airport hotel until a visa appears from somewhere, which won't be from here.

Reginald to Ann's father

24 September 1965

I have been writing all week and have emptied my cupboard. I can now start writing a few private letters. I seem to owe a great many.

I send you and Mo my most affectionate congratulations on your golden wedding, but I am very sorry to say that I have no note of exactly which day it is. Ann will have to represent me on the day itself. I hope you have many more.

One of the curious features of this post is that our pattern of living is always changing. I am now living a sort of undergraduate life – something quite different from anything I have experienced here so far. It is now I who am the single member of our little team. My assistant and his wife live their rather static life by themselves, and I go my own way alone. I am managing to do a welcomely large amount of reading and writing, which makes it possible to consolidate much of my experience here; but it is an austere and not very stimulating way of living, not really suitable for someone over forty.

Ann to Reginald

79 Broad Lane, Hampton, 25 September 1965

It was a joy to get your letters on Tuesday morning and feel that at last we were once more in a form of contact, though terribly tenuous. The children have gone and here I am all alone in our house.

I drove George to Charterhouse on Friday, calling in at Dunsfold on the way to see how the parents were settling in. It was utter chaos there. G has been having so much done to the house that there has not been enough time to get it finished. ... I found it all rather depressing.

George and I made our way to the school and asked the school sergeant where Saunderites' temporary quarters were. He said, 'You can't miss it – it looks like an 'oliday ome'. It does rather – a one-storey building, mostly windows, with a very temporary look. There was no way of telling the front from the back, and we found ourselves going in through the kitchen quarters, which was a bit disconcerting. However, it didn't seem to matter, and I took to the housemaster, Mr Harrison, immediately, and also to his somewhat shy wife. Matron, a plump woman, seemed sensible and practical, quite severe but not unreasonable. George seemed to get on well with the house tutor, a nice, skinny young man who introduced himself as the housemaster's dogsbody, and the house monitor who was a northcountry boy. After the housemaster's tea party I called on Van Oss, who was very friendly, told me to call again and to bring George next time. George is already in the choir.

William was not at all keen to go back to school, saying that the masters were horrid and the other boys too rowdy. He cheered up when he found that he was to be a 'substance', looking after a new little boy whose parents are in Ghana. Also he has been invited out to Watson's birthday party. I had a good talk with Darwall-Smith.[3]

On Sunday we spent quite a lot of time at the airport waiting for Jane's friend Patricia who had missed her connection at Amsterdam from the Philippines. She and Jane kept each other in fits of giggles and violent indignation about the school. They did some shopping in London and finally on Wednesday afternoon caught the train to Brighton and Roedean, leaving me all sorts of jobs to do, parcels to post and general mess to clear up.

I have ordered Christmas and New Year cards with the photograph we wanted, royal arms, ribbon and so forth – ready in three weeks. I have arranged for your anoraks to be cleaned, and I am looking for the books you want. It is not easy to find the right sort of picture books for giving away. They are all full of olde England and don't show much of the modern country. I am sending you three booklets from the Young Farmers' Club, which might go down well with the herdsmen.

Reginald to Ann
Ulan Bator, 26 September 1965

It was a great relief to come out of the tunnel and have two letters from you yesterday.

My hand and arm are worn out by writing. At last I am up to date. I have even had time for Mongol lessons and to read a novel or two, a great relief after months of reading products of Leninism.

I climbed Bogdo Uul twice this week, once from the front and once from Nukht. A QM came with me the second time. All the larch needles are dropping, turning from saffron to brown. Everything underfoot has withered. I saw a fox or two and some little groups of deer. The air is marvellous – crisp and hard, but not yet really cold.

It looks as though we are soon going to have the offer of some accommodation. I think the end flats, one on top of the other for four floors, in one of the blocks the Russians have built behind your hospital. It might be a solution. We must wait and see what it looks like.

Ambassador and Mrs Hopson will bring the next bag from Peking and Sarah and Tony Blishen[4] too. I shall be grateful for the Blishens. They will help time to pass. I find I am getting a bit bored with auto-entertainment.

The end of the Padre Masters' story was that he was detained at Irkutsk visa-less from Saturday to Monday and then flown to Moscow where a visa was to be issued to him. I have written to Moscow to make it clear that it was his adventure and not mine. I think Bill Masters is too old for this part of the world: he is losing his sense of proportion and becoming expensive to keep.

I was glad to hear that George helped you so much. He wrote and told me that he and William provided you with breakfast in bed. As Mrs Chabbaria[5] used to say, 'He is a good boy, really.'

Last night I had to go to one of Bora's[6] boring parties. Many people were asking after you. In the coming week we have China's National Day and a state visit by Mr Kadar from Hungary.

Reginald to his parents
27 September 1965

Did you hear that Mr Masters did in fact turn up? He is 67 and a bit unsteady on his feet. We should have had real trouble on our hands if he had fallen over, as he constantly seemed on the edge of doing. He celebrated Holy Communion in his hotel room, which must have been the first time for many years that the Christian liturgy had been heard here: I suppose Russian priests used sometimes to officiate in Mongolia before 1917, and two or three Protestant missionaries from the West tried to proselytize in Mongolia in the nineteenth century.

I feel ready for some leave. Mongolia is a rare experience, but like all rare experiences it is very strenuous. I imagine that many people outside think that we sit here peacefully with nothing to do. If Ann is meeting them she is, I am sure, disabusing them.

Ann to Reginald
79 Broad Lane, Hampton, 27 September 1965

[A long letter with comments on various proposals for work to improve the house.] I am sending through the next bag the various give-away things – scarves, dress jewellery, picture books and so forth.

Reginald to Jane

Ulan Bator, 26 September 1965

Thank you for your letter with your O-level results. Your good subjects are very good and your bad subjects are very bad. I think Aunt M[7] and I would probably agree that a little more effort to do things you do not much like would be desirable. However, from now on you can concentrate on the things you like. You should do well.

Yes, Mr Landreth shot four *ovis ammon*, but I did not see them. Since then the Swiss ambassador from Peking has been here to shoot deer. He told me it was like trench warfare. He was put in a hide, and the Mongols on horseback drove the deer towards him. There were no good heads among them. He refused to shoot and said it was murder not sport. They suggested that they should shoot for him and he would pay for the head they shot! At one little wood the Mongols said there were certainly deer inside. They rode round to flush them out; the Swiss Ambassador cocked his gun and out came a herd of horses.

He told me that he had seen people being deported. I was able to tell him that they were just students going off to help with the harvest on a state farm.

When the cultural delegation was here Mr Sodnomdorji put a little Union Jack on our table and now it seems to be there to stay. It ensures that we always have a table, but it seems a bit unnecessary to have the flag up to eat our mutton soup.

Zogsood came in the other day looking miserable and with a bandage on her hand. She cheered up when I pointed to the medicine chest. I insisted on looking under the bandage. There was nothing there. She tried to pretend she had banged it. She would have stood more chance if she had said she wanted it for a friend. I told her you had passed your exam. She was very pleased, she said.

Best wishes for a good career in the sixth form!

Reginald to Ann

27 September 1965

I have written all my official letters and all my duty letters and letters to the children, and I have been to the airport to welcome Mr Janos Kadar, the Hungarian boss, and I am soon going to the Chinese Embassy to see one of their bad films. For a few minutes I can write to you. ...

It is going to be a full week. All the better. It will go more quickly. A Polish song and dance company, over 80 strong, moves in here on Wednesday. I imagine we may be banished from the restaurant to the drivers' pull-up.

6

Yak Hair for the Cavalry

At about this time I was asked by the Foreign Office if I could investigate the possibility of obtaining some yak hair for the Household Cavalry. I was told that the plumes on the helmets of the Blues and Royals were, or should be, made of yak hair. But yak hair was in short supply, partly because powdered yak hair was in demand in the film and television industries as an ingredient of cosmetics to simulate five o'clock shadow. I received a specimen plume through the bag and approached the Mongolian Ministry of Foreign Affairs. There the local connoisseurs of yaks judged that only belly or tail hair could produce hair of the length required, and said that they would see what could be done. How much was required? A ton? Having been told that not more than ten plumes would be required per year, I indicated that much less than that would do.

The matter languished for a while, as tended to be the case with many matters in Mongolia, until in the spring of 1966 I was told that there was a technical difficulty. The yaks in Mongolia were shorn annually and a yak could not grow hair long enough on its belly in a single year. Two years of growth would be needed. The officials in the MFA could not see any way round this difficulty except by having a dedicated herd, a Mongolian–British Friendship herd, which would be shorn only in every second year. This gave the question a political tinge and would need careful consideration. There the matter rested for the rest of my stay in Mongolia and remained unresolved when I left. A better result might have been obtained by asking one of the British firms buying cashmere and furs from Mongolia to add a bale or two of two-year yak belly hair to their order. Trade channels would perhaps have been less obstructed by considerations of 'Friendship'. I am reminded of Mongolia every time I see sentries from the Blues and Royals on duty at Horse Guards. The correspondence on this subject is at the Public Record Office (FO377/187205).

西藏西藏

Reginald to Ann

7 October 1965

I have been working on the Land Rover this afternoon, changing the ball joints of the steering drag link. I managed to do it without Alex coming to watch me. He passed his driving test this morning but did not deserve to. I ought to charge for my interpreting in such cases. After a great struggle we completed the third quarter's account this week. He managed to slip in new mistakes at every stage. Admittedly the biggest difficulty was that the State Bank had given us a wrong exchange rate in August and corrected themselves at our expense in September.

We had a surge of diplomatic activity last week – Kadar's visit from Hungary, the Chinese National Day and visits by Bulgarian and Polish ensembles of singers and dancers. The best thing about China's National Day was that our Yugoslav colleague, Stane Kolman, was put down on the seating plan as *Gospodin* Kolman and not *Tovarich*. I was the only other *gospodin* present. This joke was much enjoyed by all. Kolman managed to smile but was discomforted. Of course the Chinese are always rude to the Titoists. We had a chopsticks competition at my end of the table – a Chinese speaking Russian won – and all the Russian and satellite people were on the lookout for chances to be sarcastic about the Chinese, laughing at the things one normally sees them doing themselves. The Chinese ambassador ended up with a toast that was translated as 'Goodnight'! All the Russians and Mongols found this a collector's piece of stupidity. At any rate it got us home early: no, not home, just to my rooms.

It became a bit exhausting turning out for Kadar once or twice a day for several days running. The Hungarians threw a terrible party in the hotel. They had not done their staff work properly and the hotel staff cheerfully messed up the few dispositions they had made. For half an hour the diplomatic corps was without a drink. In the end I got two or three of the waitresses whom we know well to go with me to the distant bar and bring back a supply of bottles. The Soviet chargé hailed me as an 'activist'. Unfortunately my Russian was not good enough to say, 'No, only an old lag'. Mrs Andrasfi finished up working in the kitchen. She was admittedly more at home there than at the top table, but as all the food she cooked was eaten straight away by Hungarians, it seemed a bit pointless.

The Polish troupe was too Russian to be true. I have now had enough evenings of mindless folk music to last the rest of my life. The Bulgarians were all opera singers and classical ballet dancers. Their programme was thoroughly corny – *Madame Butterfly*, *Tosca*, *Rigoletto*, the *Barber of Seville* – but it seemed miraculous in Ulan Bator to hear a programme of Western music reasonably well sung, and to see an excerpt from *L'après-midi d'un faune*. The Mongols in the audience were out of their depth and received it coldly.

Ronny Schouten, the crazy Dutchman who buys third-grade sausage casings and has them transformed to first-grade in Spain, has been here for a week. He was good company up to a point, but he sometimes went beyond it. He said we must have a barbecue on Sunday. I had misgivings, but it was a great success. I now know how to do it. The steaks (meat bought from the diplomatic shop and then shaped and processed by Ronny) were delicious. We went out to the north, beyond the hospital and the shelters of the cattle brigade. When we climbed to the crest of a hill in the middle of nowhere we suddenly came upon a Mongol in his best Sunday suit making love to a girl in her best Sunday *del*. They must have walked for miles to get there, and goodness knows how many *subbotnik*s and political meetings they were missing. But I thought it showed that the spark of humanity still lives here. I think Alex and Grace enjoyed our great outdoors for once.

The Hopsons and Blishens arrive the day after tomorrow. Grace and Alex go off on leave to Hong Kong on Tuesday. I am busy negotiating with the Foreign Ministry for a trip to the Gobi with my visitors.

10 October 1965

It was marvellous to get three letters from you yesterday. I had to read them in odd moments, like riding in the Land Rover, until I could read them properly after I had got to bed.

The three specimen picture books you sent were not at all bad. Perhaps you could send me several copies of the general book on Britain and the book on London. I have written to Information Executive Department at the FO asking if they can help.

The Hopsons are here. They are not as exacting as the Garveys used to be, because Mrs H more or less opts out of most things. She expects inconvenient services at times, but she does not interfere. Indeed she is happy to leave it to Sarah Blishen and me to cater for her husband. He seems to assume that this is the natural order of things. However, he did volunteer to wash up this evening, which shows that he is getting to know Mongolia.

With people who clearly have no intention of putting themselves out for anyone, I find it possible, when alone, to retaliate with the same attitude. I felt unwell last night (the result, I think, of a very uneven day with much rushing about and irregular food and drink). I was still a bit queasy this morning, so I announced that I was not going down to lunch and left them to fend for themselves while I had some soup and toast upstairs. I think this was the first lunch I have missed in a year, except when I was confined to bed soon after you arrived. This evening I offered everyone supper in my rooms at 7.00 and made it clear that I had writing to do afterwards – hence this letter to you and letters to the children. Incidentally, Hopson ignores the Thompsons completely, just as they ignore everyone else. So we have had a sort of tit for tat period.

Reginald to Jane

10 October 1965

I enjoyed your account of the Hibbert family party at Alan's rooms in Lincoln's Inn Fields. I had another lively description of it from Mother.

We have had same chaotic parties here too recently. I mean official receptions of course. The Hungarians gave one where the food was on one side of the hall and the drink on the other and everyone collided in the middle carrying plates or glasses or both. And you know how people rush for the buffet here. The Chinese gave a party that ended abruptly with a dismissal just as most of the guests thought it was starting to warm up. And the Mongolian government gave a party in a room whose window would not open. The heating was on and we all roasted or boiled. Tsedenbal spent most of the evening wiping his face and the back of his neck with his handkerchief. A Polish folk song-and-dance ensemble has been here, 86 strong. We regulars were exiled to the lower restaurant where the food was very poor (namely poorer than ordinary poor).

I hope you are not really finding everything as ghastly as you say. Have a good term!

Reginald to Ann

11 October 1965

The day after tomorrow we fly to the South Gobi *aimag*. Batsukh has to set out with the Land Rover tomorrow. I am busy making sure that he takes with him everything we can possibly need. We come back on Saturday, and then I have to arrange a cocktail party for Monday. I am glad for your sake you are not here, as you would be much put upon if you were. For my part, I can plod through the routine fairly steadily. It all amounts to diplomatic activity. The Blishens are helpful and likeable.

17 October 1965

The great news of the week is that I have seen *Ovis Ammon* with my own eyes and through binoculars. He looked splendid. We saw two rams and seven ewes at one place and a single ram at another. The single ram ran up to the skyline and posed as a silhouette with his great scroll of horns lifted up in full view against the blue sky. It was an exciting sight, and I could catch the thrill that Carruthers[1] and the other old hunters must have had. The horns are up to a yard or so across and weigh about ten kilos. The animals have powerful necks and shoulders to carry them, and they run like trained athletes, agilely and gracefully, carrying their great weight before them. The full grown rams appear to be charcoal grey grizzled to white on the face, back, rump and legs, and the ewes are a finely shaded dark brown. We also saw two big herds of the wild goat, which has fine, large, knobbly horns sweeping backwards. They are only about half the weight of the horns of the argali (*ovis ammon*).

We saw all of this at about 7000 feet in the mountains south of Dalandzadgad in the South Gobi *aimag* (the Gurvan Saikhan Uul or three beautiful mountains). These are the last eastern extremity of the Altai range.

We had a very good tour in the Gobi and were very well treated. Mrs Hopson is a Frenchwoman, capable of occasional moments of charm, but quite unfit for Mongolian conditions and therefore a bit of a nuisance to all around her. And he, as you know, tends not to notice one's existence except as a superior sort of servant. You can guess that, in spite of having Namsraidorj as our escort, the trip lacked the good-humoured, easy-going atmosphere of our earlier trips here. However, I was fascinated to see the Gobi and its people (there are not many of them), and I was able to get most things done in the way Mongolian conditions and habits require. While I hate interpreting, especially for ungracious people, it has the advantage of conferring a certain power to influence the course of events.

We flew down in a little AN-2 and back on an IL-14. The air journey was very easy and afforded wonderful views of southern Mongolia. The whole landscape was camel-coloured, with all the shades of which a camel is capable from pinky beige to burnt amber. It was extraordinary to see animals dotted about on it here and there apparently finding things to eat.

We stopped at Mandalgov, the centre of the Middle Gobi *aimag*, which was small even by Mongolian standards and piercingly cold with a powerful wind. Dalandzadgad was bigger than Mandalgov but only about the size of Bulgan. The Hopsons and I had to share a two-room suite with a Bulgan-style bathroom. I was in the corridor room and managed to preserve a certain freedom by going to bed last and getting up first. There was a bit of a fuss about getting hot water in a suitable receptacle for Mrs H, but nothing serious. I quite enjoyed getting up early and wandering about the town.

We did the usual *ger* crawls. Mrs H behaved a bit like Mrs Smith. Mr H told everyone how taken Danièle was with Mongolia when she came with him in the summer (you remember what a rotten time she had hanging about). We saw camels and sheep and horses and goats and even a few yaks in the mountains. We were shown a little stretch of Gobi sand but mostly it was dark brown, flinty gravel with a sparse growth of all sorts of interesting desert plants. You could see for miles and miles, and there were mirages in every direction. Movement and direction were largely determined by the incidence of wells, and there seemed to be camels (Bactrian, of course) in little scattered groups everywhere.

I was glad to get back to UB. I hate being expected to act as a servant, with only a little condescension being offered as a substitute for thanks. When I visit the FO in December I shall have something to say about the situation in which the man in UB finds himself when visited by non-resident superiors who insist on seeing Mongolia but are not prepared to rough it.

Sarah and Tony have been doing well here and keep the place human. They are very nice people. Sarah is having another baby. How young they are!

We are already in the second half of October, past the halfway mark of separation. I think so much of coming home on leave.

18 October 1965

I have been busy with arrangements for a cocktail party tonight. You know what it is like. Everything is uncertain but, as always, our visitors from outside demand certainty. I have the comfortable feeling that this will be our last social burden until well into next year. Viewed from this point of view it is an easy run.

We had a cold spell a week ago, but now it is warm and very sunny. I expect we shall soon have a downward turn. All the local experts are now giving their prognostications for the winter, but they differ widely. Those who judge by the behaviour of the hamsters say it will be a bad winter, but those who judge by the birds say it will be good. You take your choice. I say it will be good because I shall be at home with you.

22 October 1965

Yesterday was the anniversary of the day on which I left you in London last year and flew to Moscow. Since then I have been away from you for five months, soon six. It is a lot of time to lose in our life.

The hotel is being redecorated and only our floor and the one below are now working. This means that there is no room for the Blishens tomorrow. So they will move into our bedroom and I shall sleep in the 'office'. Mongolia always has a fresh surprise. Zogsood and the nice *dezhurnaya* on our floor are horrified that I should have to sleep anywhere so uncomfortable. They do not realize that I do not really care where I sleep when I am alone.

The Blishens have been good company and Sarah has been

cooking very good breakfasts and suppers. The only trouble is that
we sit and talk too long. But it is a relief to talk intelligent gossip
about normal (and abnormal) human beings again.

The Hopsons went off on Tuesday last on a cold and snowy
morning, unbending and cold to the last. She could not even put
herself out to the extent of appearing in the corridor to wave
goodbye. It puts a strain on loyalty. I have arranged that we shall
stay with them for one night on 26 January. You will find one
night acceptable, even interesting.

I have heard from London *by telegram* that I need not expect
to stay here beyond next June. It shows that it sometimes pays to
make a bit of a fuss. They must have thought that I was feeling a
bit neglected.

Lord Furness is going to visit Ulan Bator in November. Ugh! So
is Mr Green of Anning, Chadwick & Kiver, the fur people. A
Time correspondent is here at present and a Canadian press
correspondent arrives on Sunday. I think the Thompsons and I
will be required to move upstairs temporarily while our corridor
and rooms are redecorated. I am putting in a new order for supplies from Hong Kong so that whomever replaces me when I am
on leave can eat satisfactorily in December and January. There is
always work to do in Shangri-la.

The Finnish ambassador and his wife have been here from
Moscow. Hopson seemed to want to monopolize them as ambassador to ambassador, but I had met them in Moscow on the way
through and they insisted on seeking me out. I took them to
Sangino to fish on Wednesday and we each caught a large *lenok*,
which tasted delicious. Sarah and Tony were delighted to have a
trip in our fabulous countryside. It was cold but sunny.

Reginald to Jane

23 October 1965

I have enjoyed all your letters, but if you have a lot of work, don't
bother to write to me. Mother will send me your letters to her.

At the end of our visit to the Gobi the *aimag* authorities gave
the ambassador a pair of *ovis ammon* horns and me a pair of wild
goat's horns. The ambassador's was not a very large pair but
nevertheless weighed eight and a half kilos. Mine weighed four
and a half kilos. My horns have grown maggots and I have had to
hang them out of the window to dry. Some flesh tissues must have

12. Raising water from a well in the Gobi.

been left in the crevices of the skull bone. Paradoxically it shows how fresh they were. We have been laughing at the thought of the ambassador and Mrs H finding maggots in his *ovis ammon* horns on the way back to Peking. He would not be able to hang the horns out of the train window.

I was fascinated by the mirages all round us in the Gobi. You think you see buildings and hills and lakes, and when you draw near they become a group of camels. Although the vegetation is very scarce, there are very few areas with no vegetation at all. Mostly, the surface is of a black, brown or dark red gravelly mixture. Some of the plants are very pretty in a spiky, thorny sort of way. We saw hundreds of camels but virtually no cows. There were the usual sheep, goats and horses. Do you remember how the Turkish sheep used to eat dust, or so we thought? The Mongolian sheep must do the same.

We rode camels and horses. There were the usual toasts and speeches. I think the ambassador found it difficult to enter into the spirit of these Mongolian drinking sessions. I had to interpret solemnly into Russian, and in order to keep the exchanges alive I sometimes put in things he did not say and left out things he did say that would grate on the Mongols. It worked out all right in the end.

We flew to the Gobi in one of those tiny green biplanes. It was like a London taxi with wings. It was great fun. We had to come down for fuel at Mandalgov, halfway. It was the most miserable little town I have seen in Mongolia.

Reginald to Ann
25 October 1965

The 'office' has been my bedroom for the weekend, due to the 'remont' that is going on. The Blishens had to turn out of their room and were offered no substitute. So I have put them in our bedroom and am spending time in my little cell. This evening I had to go to a Romanian reception and when I returned at 8.00 p.m. the Blishens were giving themselves baths and going to bed, so I was unable to get any of my things from our room or the bathroom. It is nice to have occasional visitors and we try to make them as comfortable as Mongolia allows. They ought to try harder to avoid giving us a bonus of extra discomfort. Perhaps I should devise a special training programme for visitors to UB. But I am afraid the only effective training is to spend weeks or months and not just a few days here.

The Thompsons have returned from Hong Kong laden with treasures. They have evidently relaxed a bit, but they remain somewhat out of reach. I shall have to work hard in the next month to get them to believe that, while I am away, whoever takes my place temporarily will take care of their interests, and that anyway they now know Mongolia well enough to look after themselves.

PS. The Young Farmers' booklets are very good. I shall write to the FO for more.

Ann to Reginald
79 Broad Lane, Hampton, 27 October 1965

Sitting in Mongolia you will be surprised to learn that I, sitting in London, am a bit disappointed at the difficulty of getting anything done efficiently and on time here. When one is abroad one (or I do) tends to think that everything is much easier in England. It is disillusioning to come back and find oneself constantly battling to get anyone to do anything when and how they say they will.

[A long letter follows with news about the children and their schools, our two families, the house and Ann's efforts to get things done.]

Reginald to Ann

Ulan Bator, 31 October 1965

This morning I have been here for just one year and the weather is almost exactly as it was when I arrived with Eric Cheyne 12 months ago, −12°F last night and brilliant sunshine in a clear blue sky this morning. It was my intention to go for a walk and climb on Bogdo Uul today, but I have a heavy cold and sore throat (left behind by Sarah Blishen) and I think it wiser to stay indoors and read.

A week that would otherwise have been a peaceful one has been spoiled by the redecoration going on in the hotel. I have had to move out of our room and am now installed with all our possessions in total disorder in 430 upstairs. A team of some 40 or so Chinese is now in possession of our corridor and the dust and disorder are at their height. Alex and Grace are still there, and I have insisted that they should stay until I can get back into 331 and so become the pivot of the embassy again. It is ironical, and I fear typical, that the anniversary of my arrival should find me virtually as unsettled and rootless as I was then.

Next weekend we shall have the QMs again for the first time for a month. We shall also have the anniversary celebrations of the Great October Revolution. I hope I shall be back in my own room by then. A week later, on the 17th, Lord Furness will be here to keep me busy, and sometime after the 20th, Mr Green, the fur man.

I took Alex and Grace to see the *Three Hills of Sorrow* at the opera on Friday. I think they enjoyed it. At any rate I did. It was pleasant to be able to do something unofficially again. The tempo of life here has begun to slow down again as winter approaches. There is much less activity outside in the early morning and the streets are fairly empty after nightfall. The hotel population changes less rapidly, and the hotel food grows rapidly less varied.

5 November 1965

I hope William enjoys his fireworks at St Wilfrid's tonight, and George too, but I doubt if the fireworks at Charterhouse are official or organized.

We have heard that the QMs are not coming tomorrow. They

have been delayed somewhere south of China. So there will be no letters from you or anybody else tomorrow. I am sending Alex and Grace to Peking with our bag, so that you ought to hear from me without delay. They will be back on 13 November with our inward bag seven days late. I hope you do not need any answers to questions, because I am afraid you can't have them.

There now seems to be a chance that I can move back into 331 on Sunday – the anniversary of the Great October Revolution, when I shall be busy attending parades. As soon as I move in, Alex and Grace move out so that their room can be done. It will be convenient for them to be away for a week.

There are various January dates you should know. We shall have to leave London on 21 January for Hong Kong ... and take the train in Peking for Ulan Bator on 27 January.

It looks as though Alex and Grace may find themselves alone here for Christmas (ten days). No one from Peking seems to be prepared to volunteer to come out at that time (which is understandable) and Hopson and Wilford seem disinclined to 'volunteer' anyone (which is disappointing for us here). They tried to revive Garvey's idea of packing up here and going to Peking. I have resisted that hard. It is up to the Foreign Office to post someone temporarily. If I were Alex and Grace I would willingly accept being the service's orphans and having a quiet Christmas. But of course I would object officially and make sure my objections were registered.

Can you arrange to advertise the house for short-term tenants to take it over when we leave in January? Perhaps you could ask the Foreign Service Wives' secretary if she knows of any possible candidates in the service. They could have it at a reduced rent. I am afraid I am out of touch with such matters. And at the moment all my regular contacts and routines have been removed simultaneously. It is difficult to know where and how to attach oneself to some sort of material regularity again. Fortunately I have feelings of security built in from my earliest days.

7 November 1965

I am now back in our own rooms and have managed to restore nearly everything to its right place. I am glad to have our own things round me again and to re-establish a relationship between my inward and outward lives. It has been a most disorderly 24 hours, with October Revolution ceremonies requiring me to appear every so often correctly dressed, while it was shirtsleeve order to carry out my move. The Thompsons have now moved out from next door and I have their office equipment in with me.

It has turned sharply cold. The parade took place in a temperature of 12°F. We all put our woollies and furs on. The poor populace did its trudge past, but rather quicker this time to keep warm. A little snow fell, but later the sun came out again. I have to dress now for a reception at the Soviet embassy.

Everyone asks me if I am counting the days until I leave. In fact I try to avoid doing so because the answer still sounds so big.

Ann to Reginald

79 Broad Lane, Hampton, 16 November 1965

I write this airletter to tell you how terribly distressed I have been to receive back the letters I wrote for the bag on 11 November, marked 'LEAVE'. The bag room obviously had the date wrong, so I am afraid you must have been disappointed not to receive anything. However, Lord Furness should have brought you a little note with a Beatles record. I rang up and complained, as you can imagine, but there's nothing to be done.

I had an amusing though strenuous weekend taking Jane and William out. George spent an earlier weekend with me. I have visited our families, cultivated our neighbours, bought Christmas presents for everyone, so that we shan't have to bother with these things when you arrive. There are already various fixtures for you and me in December.

Reginald to Ann

Ulan Bator, 19 November 1965

I should reach London airport from Stockholm at 10.55 a.m. on 6 December.

I had a mysterious cable from you today – at least I assume it was from you as it comes from Hampton and calls me 'darling'. There is no name on it. It says 'expect airmail only'. I am not sure what it means. Perhaps it means that you have not written by the bag? I shall know tomorrow when the bag arrives.

I enjoyed your letters by the delayed bag last week. I am sorry to hear that Mo is in such poor shape. I wish I were there to help you with these things.

It is amusing that you are going to see Margaret King and that Hilary[2] is at St Antony's. Strictly between you and me, the FO has been thinking of sending Hilary and Margaret to replace you and me next summer. Well, not strictly to replace: he would be the first resident ambassador. I would probably replace him at St Antony's. Of course, none of this may mature. For one thing, the Mongols are being hopelessly slow over making an offer of permanent housing. It is not at all sure that the situation will be ripe for an ambassador next June or July. And the post may always disappear in the economy drive. But be careful what you say about Ulan Bator. For goodness sake, don't run it down. As far as I know, the Kings know nothing about this. I am not supposed to know. Hopson kindly told me. So don't tell anyone. Just enjoy the situation.

I went to dinner at the Czech residence last night, with the Soviet Ambassador, the Kolmans and the Cubans. We had to drink ourselves into a stupor and the food was excessive and muddled. I have been feeling off-colour all day today. I even went to bed for two hours after lunch.

Lord Furness is here and we all have to call him Tony. He brought armfuls of good things from Fortnum & Mason. Best of all he brought a letter from you.

I find myself bothering less and less to make all the efforts required to keep on top of Mongolia.

20 November 1965

Now I see what your telegram meant. Not a single letter in the bag from you or the children or anyone at all. Apart from the letters you wrote on 27 and 28 October and the note you sent with Lord Furness I have had nothing from you for a month. You must not depend on airletters. It is even more puzzling because Grace had a letter from you. She showed it to me. I see that you say that you contemplate coming back here with misgivings. You ought to write such things to me rather than to her.

西藏西藏

Coming so soon after interruptions in our bag service, the inexplicable sudden stoppage in the flow of private letters from London was a disagreeable happening. In addition, Ann's enigmatic cable appeared to suggest that she had decided to stop writing letters other than empty airletters. All of this was well within the norms of unwelcome events in Mongolia, and of course it was my thirteenth month. It was not until I received Ann's airletter of 16 November a few days before my departure from UB that I was able to understand what had happened. The outward bag room's blunder made the end of my spell in UB somewhat uneasy.

西藏西藏

Reginald to Jane

22 November 1965

This letter is really a birthday card for 3 December. It is also plastered with a collection of new Mongolian stamps.

A few days ago I went up Bogdo Uul and came across many deer looking very fat and healthy. They need to be fit and strong with the winter beginning. The lowest we have had so far is –8°F. I have to turn out tomorrow for the QM at 6.30 a.m., but this will be the last time until next February. I am getting a bit end-of-termish and cannot be bothered to work very hard. Alex Thompson says that sailors call this 'the channels'. Apparently sailors grow restless and find it difficult to bother about their work at the end of long voyages because they are thinking of home. 'The channels' seems to me a good name for it.

22 November 1965

I can confirm that I shall arrive at London airport from Stockholm by flight SK 505 at 10.55 hours on Monday 6 December.

3 December 1965 (a cablegram)

Still stuck Ulan Bator bad weather will telegraph eventual ETA.

西藏西藏

Although my departure from UB was delayed, I still managed to visit the Mongolian collections in Stockholm of the Scandinavian expeditions (Sven Hedin, Haslund and others) of the 1920s and early 1930s. I arrived in London only a day or two late – nothing unusual in Mongolian terms.

Ann's and my places in Ulan Bator were filled in our absence by John and Fionn Morgan from Moscow. He had served in Peking in the mid-1950s and was now a first secretary in Moscow. Speaking both Russian and Chinese, he was admirably qualified for Mongolia. In January John Boyd,[3] a second secretary from Peking, relieved John Morgan.

Before departing on leave I sent a dispatch to the Foreign Office summarizing my general impressions of Mongolia at the end of a year's experience. Most of it is reproduced in the following paragraphs; but the second, third and fourth paragraphs are taken from another dispatch I had written in May 1965 on the more limited subject of diplomatic relations with the MPR (dispatches no. 5 of 4 May and no. 22 of 17 November 1965, PRO/FO371/181 156 and 181 153):

西藏西藏

Having now resided at the Mongol capital for more than a year, longer I think than any previous diplomatic representative from a western European country, not excepting even Friar Giovanni Del Piano Di Carpine, disciple of St Francis of Assisi and legate of Pope Innocent IV, and Friar William of Rubruck, Ambassador of St Louis of France, each of whom spent several weeks or months at the capital of the Great Khan at or near Kharkhorin, some 250 miles west of Ulan Bator, in the years 1246 and 1254, I have the honour to celebrate the occasion by summarizing in this dispatch, before I return on leave to London, some of my general impressions of Ulan Bator and the Mongolian People's Republic. In doing so, I begin with some reflections on Mongolia's foreign relations in general.

The Mongolian People's Republic began to have relations with countries other than the Soviet Union in 1948 and 1949 when diplomatic relations were established, perhaps through a poor sort of Stalinist joke, with North Korea and Albania. But the real beginning of Mongolia's foreign relations came shortly after the proclamation in Peking of the Chinese People's Republic and immediately after Stalin had agreed with Mao Tse-tung in February 1950 that the Chinese People's Republic, recognizing the independence of the Mongolian People's Republic, should establish diplomatic relations with it. In the past few weeks in Ulan

Bator there have been celebrations of the fifteenth anniversaries of the establishment of diplomatic relations with Poland, Czechoslovakia, Hungary, Bulgaria, Romania and the German Democratic Republic. Stalin evidently lost no time in seeing that Chinese diplomatic relations with Mongolia were diluted by a copious if weak admixture from eastern Europe.

The eastern European countries did not at first send permanent diplomatic representatives to Mongolia. Perhaps the point Stalin wished to make was simply that the independence of the Mongolian People's Republic was a fact accepted by other states and not the result of a Chinese concession. His successors soon found that the rapid growth of Sino–Soviet rivalry, especially after 1957 made it desirable to have the physical presence of eastern European embassies in Ulan Bator in order to show beyond doubt that the Mongolian People's Republic was on the one hand sovereign and independent and on the other a member of the Soviet Bloc.

The first eastern European ambassadors in Ulan Bator must have endured much for the Soviet communist cause. Since living here I have learned to appreciate how cleverly Molotov's place of exile was chosen by Khrushchev. The Polish ambassador, who is now the Dean of the Diplomatic Corps, has been here since 1960 and he tells me that when he first arrived there were virtually no paved roads in Ulan Bator; he had to live in the old Hotel Altai without any running water; the camel caravans used still to unload from time to time on Sükhbaatar Square. It is only in the past three or four years that the Mongolian People's Republic has acquired the physical facilities for receiving a few foreign diplomatic missions and providing them with simple but adequate accommodation.

In these somewhat rudimentary circumstances I have had and still have the feeling of leading an expedition rather than conducting a diplomatic mission. However, I now have the advantage of knowing the Mongols who look after foreigners and being known by them. If something breaks in my room, someone else's room is cannibalized to replace it. If I demand service from the restaurant, someone else waits while my wants are met. If I want to book tickets, see the management, put the Land Rover over an inspection pit, send telegrams and so forth, I am invited to jump the queues or scrums of other aspirants. If any sort of Mongolian functionary is not at his post to deal with the public, (this is depressingly common here – there is no concept of serving the public) he will be sought and fetched if I want him. This is not entirely due to the fact that I am a British chargé d'affaires. It is also in part a case of being a personal acquaintance. The Mongols have few of the graces of civilization, but they retain many of the virtues of a simple people, especially loyalty and mutual help among family and friends. They will work extraordinarily hard on the impulse of helping a friend or acquaintance but seem to be completely without conscience when it is a question of working for a living or for the general good. To put it at its lowest, if you want to eat at all adequately in Mongolia you have to flirt with the waitresses.

The lack of order and routine and the importance of the personal connection in Mongolia often give the feeling that the Mongols are playing like children rather than working like grown-ups. They play at running a hotel, at shops, at post offices, at exporting, at every activity one can think of, even at being a state. There is a baffling lack of seriousness and purpose in the way they do their work. It would take a Gogol to describe the overwhelming incompetence, slovenliness, deceit and apathy with which public business is conducted here. Communism has subjected the Mongols to a system of bureaucratic control that can function only after oracles have been consulted in the Central Committee of the Mongolian People's Revolutionary Party and, beyond that, in Moscow. This system is not altogether strange to the Mongols because it has affinities with the old Shamanism that is deeply rooted in this part of Asia. But the oracles are guided by rules of historical divination that have virtually no relevance to conditions in Mongolia, and when they pronounce their rulings in the circumlocutions of Leninism there are very few people in the MPR who can understand what is required and fewer still who feel personally involved. The MPR still does not have that thick layer of well-schooled career seekers on which all modern bureaucracies, and communist bureaucracies most of all, depend. This is the fundamental weakness of the attempt to move straight from 'feudalism' to 'socialism' avoiding 'capitalism', which is supposed to be Mongolia's contribution to the science of government. The social structure of princely families and lama church, which used to provide a focus of personal service, often unfortunately an unworthy one, for the lives of the Mongol people was swept away more than 25 years ago; but a new and intelligible focus capable of engaging the personal loyalties of the Mongols has not yet been put in its place. Experience and concepts that cannot be encompassed within the circle of a *ger* have small meaning for most Mongols. And a *ger* encompasses very little.

The Mongols have often been described as lazy and incapable of working. This does not seem to me to be true. Men and women who look after large herds of animals in the wastes of Mongolia through the six formidably frozen months of winter cannot be described as lazy. They are a tough, frugal people with immense powers of endurance and a hard-bitten sense of humour to help them survive their heroic relationship to the forces of nature. But they are accustomed to rhythms of life and work that have nothing in common with those of urban communities, and their way of life is primitive. The industrialization and urbanization being thrust on them by communism cannot be quickly assimilated. The attempt to force them rapidly into a new way of life seems to be resulting in a comedy of universal inefficiency.

It is more or less the result of an accident that a Mongolian state exists at all. Had the overthrow of the Manchus in China not occurred just at the time when the Russian government was systematically strengthening its hold on Transbaikalia following its defeat in the Russo–Japanese war, the Mongolian state would probably never have come into being. For many years it had almost none of the attributes of an independent state. It had a few leaders, mostly members of the old ruling families and the higher ranks of the lama church, but these were 'liquidated' in the 1920s and 1930s. The MPR's population is very small, comparable to that of Glasgow in an area as big as the whole of western Europe. To make matters worse, it is the population of Glasgow with virtually everyone who was ever a civic dignitary, leading public official, priest, magistrate, or leading citizen removed and usually 'liquidated'. The Mongolian communists now pretend that it was the 'capitalist' states that refused to recognize Mongolia until the early 1960s, but it is clear that the country was not in a fit state to have diplomatic relations with any country other than the Soviet Union until the late 1950s. It is hardly in a fit state to have useful diplomatic relations even now; but the rise of communist China has caused the Soviet Union to give such priority to the task of establishing Mongolia's independence on surer international foundations that very considerable resources, cadres and cash and precious accommodation in Ulan Bator have been devoted to foreign policy. This has produced superficially successful results in giving the Mongolian People's Republic the appearance of having the attributes of a fully independent state. But underneath, the emptiness and lack of resources remain. The population of the Mongolian People's Republic is simply not big enough to exploit its huge territory by any standards that could be regarded as adequate in the modern international community.

I think it is likely that the leaders of the Mongolian People's Republic appreciate how lucky the Khalkha Mongols are to have a separate state at all. They know that they are the only people of central Asia to have a state of their own (unless the Afghans are counted as central Asia too). The present regime in Mongolia is doing all it can with its limited resources and within the confines of Soviet-directed 'proletarian internationalism' to exercise this independent statehood. It is surprising how much diplomatic activity is generated in Ulan Bator. Delegations come and go ceaselessly; there seems to be a new official cultural or sporting exchange taking place every week or so; official statements are issued and press conferences held on all sorts of subjects remote from Mongolia's interests; the diplomatic corps is summoned to turn out for innumerable little ceremonies and celebrations. All of this activity is squeezed out of the MPR's relations with a dozen other communist countries that are hardly free to withhold their cooperation. The government of the MPR would like to develop, discreetly and steadily, greater diplomatic activity with non-communist countries. The problem is how to induce the non-communist countries to take the initiative and to undertake the expenditure required to maintain active relations with Mongolia. The MPR is going to find that it cannot have these relations entirely on its own terms. It is going to have to make a much bigger effort to provide suitable accommodation, services of all kinds, speakers of Western languages and above all a greater degree of freedom.

There is one frustration in life at this post that is particularly unfortunate. Mongolia is a spacious and empty country of great natural beauty, with abundant fish, animals, birds and flowers to be looked at, caught, collected or shot as the case may be, and with no installations that need to be kept secret. It will, however, be some time before anyone can enjoy the Mongolian countryside without great expense and difficulty. Although the country is so empty no one is free to please himself in it. So far, the Mongolian authorities have been able to claim that they must keep tight control of foreigners' movements because no suitable facilities exist outside Ulan Bator, and foreigners could easily come to harm in the empty distances and savage climate. This excuse is beginning to wear thin. Once this mission is established in quarters of its own with one or two more UK based staff, so that it can become normal to take turns at having free weekends, it may prove possible to wear it even thinner. I have had the advantage of being a pioneer and have been afforded attentions by the Mongolian Foreign Ministry that could not be afforded to several non-communist missions simultaneously. Some way will have to be found of making the lives of foreigners less restricted if the MPR is to develop the wider diplomatic activity for which it seems to be hoping.

The history of the Mongols consists of one century of triumphant infamy followed by several centuries of ignominy deepening almost to extinction. They have not, so far as I know, made any contribution to the general store of human knowledge and human civilization. If some of their current research is successful, their first contribution may be instant *koumiss*. They have now made a new start in the world with the help of the Soviet Union. They have two invaluable qualities, courage and fortitude. It is difficult to predict their future, but at least it now seems certain that they will have a future and that their position as the only disposable independent country in central Asia will be one of growing importance. In the thirteenth century envoys from the west came here because it was feared that the Mongols were about to make a bid to take over the whole of the known world. In the twentieth century the position is exactly opposite: envoys from the west can come here to watch bids being made to take over Mongolia. The interest of watching the rivalry between the Soviet Union and the Chinese People's Republic is probably the factor that will determine whether other Western countries will open missions in Ulan Bator. But I venture to suggest in conclusion that it is beginning to be worthwhile to cultivate diplomatic relations with the Mongols for their own sake. They are determined to play a part in the world, especially the Afro–Asian world, and it would be a pity if they were not helped to learn to play it on the broadest possible basis. Of course, my advocacy of more Western missions in Ulan Bator is not disinterested. It would be a great relief to have some free colleagues.

7

A Spell in England and
Back to Ulan Bator

Ann and I had a busy Christmas holiday with the children in our house at Hampton. We had a burglary two days after I arrived – a reverse cultural shock for someone coming from Mongolia. We enjoyed as much as we could of all the things that London has to offer. We visited our ageing and ailing parents and tried to think of ways in which they could keep in touch with the children in our absence without being burdened by them. We commissioned various works on our house.

I had meetings at the FO, British Council, Board of Trade and so on between 10 and 17 December. A principal subject was of course the future of our mission in Mongolia. Murray MacLehose,[1] who had been the head of Far Eastern department when I first went to Ulan Bator and was now principal private secretary to the Secretary of State, told me that my bid to report directly to the Foreign Office, challenging Terence Garvey's ruling in my early days, had caused some senior eyebrows to be raised in the FO. I told him that anyone who thought I was wrong should be invited to do two months solitary in UB. Everyone in the FO seemed to accept that the next incumbent of my post should be accredited as Ambassador. The viability of a mission at Ulan Bator appeared to have been demonstrated adequately. I had to make a few official visits outside London, for example to firms interested in cashmere and camel hair and other trade possibilities.

We decided that Ann should return home for the Easter holidays and then rejoin me for my final weeks in UB. We saw the children back into their schools and set off back to UB via Hong Kong and Peking in late January. A colleague in the diplomatic service took a short lease on our house for the period of his and his family's home leave.

西藏西藏

Reginald to his parents
Hong Kong, 24 January 1966 (a postcard)

We had a good journey – New Delhi at dawn, Everest in the distance in mid-morning, over Rangoon to Bangkok at lunchtime. We are doing a lot of shopping. We set out for Canton tomorrow morning.

Ann to her parents
British Embassy, Ulan Bator, 31 January 1966

We were very well looked after in Hong Kong by an old friend of Reg's in the diplomatic service, Anthony Elliot.[2] His job in UB seems an enviable one to me – Political Adviser. Our service is of course now amalgamated with the Commonwealth service.

The journey in a Boeing 707, first class, was very comfortable. Landing in Hong Kong is a bit like landing on an aircraft carrier as the runway sticks out into the bay. You come down low over the roofs of the town and even between some tall buildings. You feel you could recognize friends in the streets.

We stayed at the Peninsula Hotel in Kowloon and crossed to Hong Kong Island by ferry. Our friends live in the peak district, where it is cooler than in the town and has wonderful views when it is not blanketed in cloud. We had a shopping spree on the 24th – cameras, silk shirts, a suit for Reg and some cultured pearls.

We went by train from HK to the border. There we walked across the bridge over the little river that divides Hong Kong New Territories from Red China. There were masses of Chinese who were visiting relations for the Chinese New Year, carrying heavily stuffed string bags on the ends of bamboo poles on their shoulders. They seemed to be taking everything you could imagine with them, but those coming back again had scarcely any luggage at all. In China everything was orderly and regimented in contrast to the happy-go-lucky untidiness, dirt and informality on the HK side. We were all shepherded into various waiting rooms and made to wait an hour or so while they copied out our passports in longhand, or whatever they do. There were bananas and bougainvillea growing everywhere, though it was cool enough to wear a jacket. We were given lunch (Reg and I are getting quite good with chopsticks) and then we got into a train for the four-hour journey to Canton. We found ourselves staying in a new hotel away from the Pearl River, which was a pity. However, we were driven along by the river, which was certainly a busy scene, though now that the government has built workers' flats for the port workers, there are not so many people living on the water, so it is probably not as picturesque as it used to be. In the evening we were taken to a performance of *The East is Red*, China's *West Side Story*, a musical version of the revolution – it was quite impressive.

At lunchtime on Tuesday we took off by air for Peking and flew for four hours above clouds. Peking was cold and grey. It was comfortable at the embassy, and we did some shopping and bought some flower paintings. From Peking we took the train on Thursday night and arrived like QMs before breakfast on Saturday morning. Nothing seems to have changed here. Everyone appears pleased to see us back. It has been a much colder winter this year than last. Many deer have come down from the woods, and we are told that bears' footprints have been seen in the woods where we go for our afternoon walks.

This evening there is a Russian film show, so we shall be starting again with all our diplomatic colleagues.

Reginald to Jane

14 February 1966

I have not yet written anything to you about our journey out. We had a first feeling of early spring at Rome, after which we flew all through the night to New Delhi, where the dawn was rose and lavender. Delhi airport was seedy and depressing, being in a style that can best be described as run-down British. There were soldiers about in faded khaki and notices saying that we were in a military area and must not take photographs.

After Delhi we saw the Himalayas to the north in sunlight and a worn and faded countryside below us, until we came to the tropical sea between Calcutta and the Arakan coast of Burma. The mountains behind the coast were covered with jungle for hundreds of miles. Over Rangoon we looked down on the boats clustered in the Irrawaddy and soon afterwards landed in Bangkok in the middle of a great stretch of tidy paddy fields and canals. The airport was full of US Air Force planes, and the airport shop tempted us with precious stones and alligator skins and silk.

In Hong Kong the shops all seemed to sell jewellery and cameras and clothes. You begin to wonder if anyone ever buys anything else. It is an altogether Chinese city. Everyone wished us a happy new (Chinese) year. The servants were always on the lookout for a tip, and the whole place seemed to be air-conditioned at too low a temperature. It was a wonderful place for tourists like us recovering from a burglary.

China was its inimitable, blue-ant self, girding against US monopoly capitalism and crammed full of toiling masses on bicycles. Canton is a vast city with no obvious centre except perhaps the Pearl River waterfront. We were taken to a performance of *The East is Red* – 4000 strong and loud and brutal and marvellously organized in brilliant colours. Our guide was no taller than William and spoke poor English – she turned out to be 26 and a teacher of English.

After that it was Peking and Mongolia again.

Reginald to his parents

31 January 1966

I have been too busy all the weekend to attend to letter writing. We arrived back exactly according to plan after a most enjoyable journey.

It has been very cold here. It was −18°F (−28°C) on the morning we arrived, but today it has snowed and is only 0°F (−17°C).

My missing suitcase turned up the day after we returned. It was apparently untouched, but the contents were very cold.

We do not feel so far away now that we have been home to England, but the journey was impressively long.

西藏西藏

During our absence on leave, in January, Tsedenbal had had his finest hour in a visit to Ulan Bator by L. I. Brezhnev, accompanied, among others, by Y. V. Andropov, A. A. Gromyko and Marshal Malinovsky, the Soviet Minister of Defence. A new Soviet–Mongolian treaty of friendship, cooperation and mutual help had been signed, tying the Mongolian People's Republic to the Soviet Union for the next 20 years. A year previously, Tsedenbal had been under challenge in his own Central Committee Plenum. Since then his standing had been steadily buttressed by the Soviet leadership. He himself had been to Moscow; A. N. Shelepin had visited UB in January 1965. Marshal Sudets had come in July; G. Voronov, another member of the Presidium of the Central Committee of the Soviet Communist Party, had come with several high-ranking Soviet officers in September. All of this was a steady year-long build-up to the supreme event of the visit by Brezhnev. Brezhnev received, so to speak, the keys of Mongolia, and Tsedenbal received promises of massive aid. China was, of course, the ghost at the feast – a sufficiently real ghost to cause the Soviet Union to parade its military commitment so ostentatiously in the shape of the marshals and generals who accompanied the leaders from Moscow.

西藏西藏

Ann to Jane

10 February 1966

We have had a few warm days, which melted the snow in the streets. For a couple of days it was just as though it had been raining and cars going by made a swishing noise. But as soon as the sun went down it all froze again and the swishing turned to crackling. Father managed to have one day's skiing. He had to walk a long way uphill in order to have a decent run down. The hotel has been unbearably hot and the water is quite dangerous as it comes out of the tap boiling.

We had some colleagues in to supper the other evening and gave them a meal entirely out of tins – asparagus soup, roast pork with peas, carrots and onions, roast potatoes and, finally, pear condé. How's the food at school this term? Come to the British embassy in Mongolia for a really delicious diet!

Reginald to his parents

14 February 1966

We were sorry to hear that Mother has not been well again.

I have had a busy fortnight getting settled back into the routine. There is plenty to read and write, and I have numerous questions to answer.

Our chauffeur is ill at present, which means that we have to put the Land Rover away in the garage ourselves. The garage is about a kilometre from the hotel. The other night I had to take the Land Rover there and walk back to the hotel against a wind in a temperature of –25°C. It was paralysingly cold, although I was well wrapped up in my sheepskin coat and furs. It is difficult to conceive how animals stay alive in it, and yet they do. On these colder nights the streets of Ulan Bator are almost totally deserted. The whole town seems to hibernate for the night.

Ann to her parents

14 February 1966

I must give our plastic flowers a wash in time for Dewi Sant,[3] though unfortunately there are no daffodils among them.

Reg and I are both keeping well, but I sleep badly here. The beds are abominably uncomfortable, hard and uneven and a bit sloping, so that I slide slowly down. We have been spared diplomatic functions for a few days, except for a Russian film show, which fortunately didn't go on too long. Apart from the facts that I couldn't understand the dialogue and my chair was unbearably hard and there were no ashtrays so one couldn't smoke, it was quite enjoyable.

The food in the hotel is as awful as ever, but we have now got a fairly decent reserve of tinned stores, so we eat upstairs in our room every evening. Some of our menus are delicious, and we have some reasonable wine as well.

On Saturday night we had the extraordinary experience at the theatre of seeing *Lear Khan* by William Shakespeare. The interesting thing was that the audience must have been very like the audience that Shakespeare was writing for. There was no question of appreciating the poetry or sophisticated acting. The straight drama of the play came out, expressed of course in contemporary Mongolian, and the audience threw themselves into it like true Elizabethan groundlings. There were sharp intakes of breath at the disgraceful way the daughters behaved to their aged father. There were angry mutterings over Edmund's villainy and cheers when the traitors met their deserts. It was really highly entertaining. The Mongol actors had made themselves look characteristically European by sticking false Roman noses on and wearing fuzzy wigs of grey cotton. They threw themselves into their parts with great gusto rolling their eyes and waving their arms about and making

13. An excursion for the heads of diplomatic missions and their families organized by the Foreign Ministry at Terelj, a holiday camp for senior cadres and meritorious workers in the foothills of the Khentey mountains. The scene is of a shooting competition, which, to the general astonishment, was won by Ann.

great play with swords and cloaks. One disadvantage was that it was very cold in the theatre (in spite of a full house), and in the storm scene they had such a powerful wind-machine in the wings that it became really uncomfortable in the auditorium. I was glad I had my long woolly pants on! The princesses looked as if they had come straight out of a harem, and for once the rather stuffy jokes of Fool were received with gales of laughter, which I am sure cannot have happened for about 400 years.

Yesterday an outing was organized for the diplomatic corps to Terelj, a government rest house about an hour's drive from UB. We all set out in a convoy at about 8.30. Reg took his skis, but there was not much snow. He found a slope he could slide down, but he could not really ski. The Mongols who came with us (mostly from the Foreign Ministry) were delighted with the simple fun of tumbling in the snow. The sunshine was glorious. In the afternoon they organized a shooting competition, and much to my and Reg's amazement I won! I beat by two points an old Mongol who claimed to have shot in his lifetime more than 300 wolves.

The prize was a bottle of cognac, which of course I couldn't touch. However, everyone else was glad to have the opportunity of drinking a toast to something or other.

At 7.30 we set off home again in such a thick cloud of dust that it was like driving over the Sahara in a London fog. At one point we got completely lost and ended up in a deep gully in a snowdrift. However, we got safely back. The fishermen in the party had very little success, as there was scarcely any water. They had to make a hole through nearly two metres of ice. I imagine that the fish were having to crawl along the bottom, poor things.

Ann to Reginald's parents

14 February 1966

We had a day in the country yesterday. I drove the Land Rover up and down a hill so that Reg and a couple of Mongols could do a bit of skiing. It gave us an appetite for lunch, which even the sight of Reg gnawing a huge hunk of sheep's spine with the Deputy Minister for Foreign Affairs demonstrating how to eat in the true Mongol style did not altogether take away, though you can imagine it was a pretty messy sight.

Reginald to Jane

28 February 1966

It sounds as though the *Macbeth* you saw was not as good as the *King Lear* we saw recently here. It was like the players in *Hamlet* putting on *King Lear* – wonderfully emphatic and rhetorical acting. The emotional response of the audience was most exciting. Thrills of shock and horror ran through the house when the Goneril and Regan were rude to Lear or when other bad things happened. There were spontaneous cheers when the baddies were dealt with, one by one. I saw this production last year. The audience reacted equally enthusiastically then.

We have been celebrating Mongolia's new treaty with the mighty Soviet Union, guardian of peace and protector of the peoples. It has not been very interesting. Most people watch the Chinese to see if they show any signs of displeasure, but they (the Chinese) do not flinch and smile vacantly and enigmatically.

Poor William feels a bit out of touch with the world. He writes that he did not know that something had landed on the moon until he heard the priest mention it in his Sunday sermon. It is rare for sermons to be so usefully informative. I much enjoyed Sir Bernard Lovell doing a crib of the Russians' signals and the Russians pompously saying that his answer was not quite right. Curiously, we have not had a meeting of the Mongolian working masses to celebrate the occasion.

On 3 March the Bulgarian Ambassador is giving a party to celebrate the anniversary of Bulgaria's liberation from the Turks. Perhaps I ought to give a party to celebrate Britain's victories in the Boer War, or perhaps in the Afghan wars. I suppose anything can be made to supply an excuse for drinking vodka.

Batsukh has been away sick for a couple of weeks or so, allegedly in hospital; but I think he is probably on a spy course. I have obtained a temporary replacement, called Dambaravchaa, from the MFA. He is a much better driver than Batsukh, but does not seem to be so well connected with generals and colonels. Zogsood is also away, after walking around holding her ear and drawing her breath sharply through her teeth for two days. Perhaps we did not give her enough aspirins.

I have asked for your visa for Prague.

Ann to her father

27 February 1966

Both Reg and I were relieved to hear that you are going to retire in June. We have been anxious all this winter about your commuting from Dunsfold. It has been a strenuous routine after your short Hampstead journey.

Reg was very pleased to get your joint telegram for his birthday. He will write as soon as he has time.

I have only another month to go before I come back for the Easter holidays. We have had a good deal of wind and dust, which is the precursor of spring here. Reg went out yesterday for the first time this year in his heavy London overcoat with an extra padded lining.

We must go down to the restaurant for lunch. Another meal of tough, greasy mutton and pickled cabbage!

Reginald to his parents

28 February 1966

During the last fortnight we have had the coldest weather I have known here, with sharp north winds to make the very low temperatures unbearable. The winds have also brought dust storms. However, there has been a notable improvement in the last day or two and we begin to think of spring.

The work pressure shows no sign of abating. Too many people are getting round to the idea that we are here and write asking what to us are silly questions about Mongolia.

We have at last received a payout from our insurance company for our losses in our Hampton burglary.

It looks as though Mr Wilson will win the election, which will be going on by the time this reaches you. It won't affect us.

8

Upgrading the Mission

There began to be some movement in February as regards the future of the mission. I learned that Douglas McAdam,[1] a 21-year-old third secretary with some Russian, had been selected to join us in the spring. His wife Susan had worked in the FO on the administration side, which would no doubt bring us some useful know-how. This would be a step towards turning the mission into something more like a real embassy.

There were signs of movement on the Mongolian side on the question of accommodation. I had been shown some flats at the top of a newly built block, but the rooms were impossibly small, the construction was so cramped that there was no possibility of enlargement by knocking down partition walls, the living accommodation and office space would have had to be arranged vertically as in a narrow tower and not horizontally as in a normal apartment, and it was obvious that Mongolian insistence on segregating us from other inhabitants would have posed very uncomfortable access problems. The Mongolian officials and I agreed that it was not a possible option.

However, in February the acting head of the Second Department in the MFA, Tserentsoodol, an able man, told me that the Cubans were finding their house too large, too expensive and too troublesome. If they moved it would be possible to offer us that house. This seemed promising. The house in question was a solid Siberian house, divided inside in a very simple manner with rough but solid timber floors and doorframes and doors of heavy planks more suitable for a stable than a residence. But it had good possibilities for adaptation and transformation.

I asked the Cuban chargé what he had in mind. He confirmed that he wanted to move but said that the alternative accommodation he had been shown was completely unsuitable. I gathered

14. Arrival at Ulan Bator station of the once weekly trans-Mongolia 'express' from Moscow to Peking. Douglas McAdam is holding the bags and a Queen's messenger is winding his camera.

that this was either the flats in a new apartment block that had been shown to me or something similar. There the matter rested for the time being; but the future accommodation of the British Embassy became from then onwards inseparable from the decisions of the Cuban government. In the end the Cubans left, but not until well after my time; the embassy eventually took possession of no. 30 Peace Street in 1969.

From February onwards correspondence began to flow about the appointment of my successor. It was agreed in principle in London that he should be a resident Ambassador and not a Chargé d'Affaires. The question was, should the appointment of a resident Ambassador (which the Mongols wanted) be linked to the question of adequate accommodation (which the British wanted). The pros and cons were debated between London and Donald Hopson in Peking, who would cease to be the non-resident Ambassador at Ulan Bator when a resident ambassador was appointed. In the end it was agreed that the best course would be to appoint a resident ambassador as my successor and to put steady pressure on the Mongolian government to provide suitable accommodation. This way of proceeding succeeded in the end, but not until 1969.

With these changes ahead (a new third secretary to be added to our staff and a resident ambassador to arrive later) I had to apply myself to some administrative questions – more living and office accommodation in the hotel, a second vehicle, presumably a black saloon to match those of the other ambassadors, and a consolidation of our system for obtaining food and other supplies from Hong Kong, Copenhagen and London. These obtruded on my agenda from March onwards.

西藏西藏

Bronwen's husband, Bill, Viscount Astor, died suddenly in Nassau in the Bahamas on 7 March. Ann and I had known that his health had deteriorated in 1965, but we had not appreciated how precarious it was. Ann was much concerned for her parents, whose health was also poor. This would be yet another shock for them on top of the several they had already undergone in the past year.

西藏西藏

Ann to her parents

13 March 1966

I am so sorry not to have been able to be at home with you all just now – not that there would have been anything I could do to relieve the distress you must all be feeling over Bill's death. Reg and I are most terribly sorry.

Alex Thompson, Reg's assistant, heard the news over the radio, but the reception was very bad and we couldn't be sure he had got it right. So I didn't send a message straight away, as I was hoping against hope that there had been some mistake. At least I shall be home again soon after this letter reaches you. I am booked on BE 911 from Moscow on 25 March. I shall be staying for a couple of nights at the St Ermin's Hotel before going to Hampton on the Sunday. I will give you a ring when I arrive. There is always the chance of a delay as the weather is very changeable at the moment.

Thank you, 'Nhad, for having George and William out together. I note that William wrote to you. Presumably George did not. Now that he is at Charterhouse and writing letters is not compulsory, he seems to have given up writing. We have had only one brief letter from him this term. He is going to have to pull his socks up. Jane tells me she was coming to Dunsfold for the weekend. I hope this happened and that you all enjoyed seeing one another.

At the moment we are busy sending advice to the new Third Secretary and his wife who are due to come out here at the end of April. Our staff is growing. We shall be three men and three wives. The Mongols show no signs yet of finding us a building. I am thankful that we shall not be staying beyond July. Life in this hotel gets worse and worse.

I shall be writing to Bron.

Ann to Jane

13 March 1966

I think you may be at Dunsfold today. I wonder if you will be taken to Uncle Bill's funeral at Cliveden. It would be nice if you have been able to represent us there. It was very nice of you to send William a birthday present. I hope he thanked you. It cheers me up a lot that you are all in touch with one another while we are away.

The food is very bad here at present. There is no sort of vegetable now except occasionally cabbage tasting repulsive or salted cucumber. The meat is mostly indescribable and there has been no yoghurt since we got back.

The electricity went off in all the rooms on our side of the corridor last Friday evening at about eight o'clock. There was no one in the hotel who could mend a fuse, so we went to bed by candlelight. In the morning it was still off, so I took my electric kettle and toaster along the corridor to one of those waiting room places and made breakfast there, much to the fascination of any passing Mongol or indeed of any Mongol within a quarter mile, as they all went right out of their way to have a good stare. The electricity is certainly pretty ropey here. Mrs Kolman told me that when they were in the hotel they had a fuse or something in the lift machinery and one morning the lift crashed from the sixth floor down to the ground. You'll never catch me going in that lift.

I think a little man who had been carrying out repairs in the room above caused our fuse. He had been given a deadline and was hammering away into the night just over our heads. Father went up to stop him and he nearly burst into tears, as he said he would not now be able to fulfil his norm. I think that, in spite, he drove a nail through some component and plunged us and the Thompsons into darkness.

Last Saturday there was an outing organized for International Woman's Day – a Soviet idea that has been foisted onto all these communist countries. We (just wives) drove in convoy to Sükhbaatar Way Farm, about 40 kilometres east of UB. We were shown the kindergarten and we all cooed and crooned over 25 wretched looking tots and distributed sweets; and the Chinese and Russians tried to outdo each other giving away picture postcards. Then we had lunch (better than the hotel, starting with cold roast wild hare). After that we were driven to a 'farm' of gers where we admired some baby goats and were given some very second-rate *suutei-tsai* and had our photographs taken. Then we bumped home again.

Women's Day itself, 8 March, was celebrated by all the women sending visiting cards to one another, which was an awful bore. In the evening there was a solemn meeting in the theatre at which delegates from the Soviet Union, Czechoslovakia, Hungary, North Vietnam and the Viet Cong spoke at some length about imperialist aggression. We British did *not* clap. This was followed by a concert that went on far too long – an altogether exhausting business.

Reginald to Jane

14 March 1966

I have written to a Monsieur Malassis, a professor at the French national agricultural school at Rennes, about a possible exchange between you and his daughter Michèle. We shall have to see what comes of it.

Mother will be home a few days after this letter. I hope you all have a good time at no. 79.

At present I have an enormous correspondence, both official and private, to plough through. There does not seem to be much time for getting to know Mongolia. I seem to go out less as time goes on. But I have asked for a visit to Darkhan. No one has yet said that the roads are bad or that it is harvest time. I expect I shall have to batter away for many days yet before I get a reply.

They are probably shy of letting me see all the Soviet soldiers up there.

International Women's Day was hard work for me. Visiting cards poured in for Mother, and I had to write the address on all the cards she returned. All the women were keen to know if we celebrated the day in Britain. I told them that we celebrated Mothering Sunday, but I could not think when it was. They approve of anything to do with mothers of course.

Batsukh is still ill; suffering from hypertension I am told. All that sitting in the hall of the hotel has worn him out. Our temporary chauffeur is a much better driver, but I expect we shall have to have Batsukh back again. Zogsood watches carefully to see what we send him when we send him little parcels.

Reginald to his parents

14 March 1966

Many thanks for the presents you sent me. Ann leaves here on Thursday week and will be in touch with you.

It has become generally warmer, but snow was falling for a time this morning. Snow is a sign of rising temperature. There have been some dust storms and there are few days without wind this year. It is hard to be a Mongol.

西藏西藏

Ann left Ulan Bator on the weekly Aeroflot flight to Moscow and found herself once more travelling in the company of Mongolian/ Soviet bosses. The Soviet Ambassador, L. N. Solovyev, was accompanying a high-ranking Mongolian government delegation to Moscow.

西藏西藏

Ann to Reginald

79 Broad Lane, Hampton, 28 March 1966

I had an easy journey. There was scarcely anyone on the plane besides the government delegation. There was a young German couple and their little girl and one or two unattached Mongols and a Russian couple. The woman was sick as we came down in Irkutsk, so I gave her a couple of Sea-Legs and she perked up a lot.

We found ourselves sharing a breakfast table in Irkutsk (in spite of the late hour we still got tea and hardboiled eggs). Afterwards her husband insisted on sitting next to me for about an hour on the way to Omsk (they got out there and were heading for Novo-sibirsk). We had some stumbling Russian conversation while his wife went into a deep sleep. Solovyev looked slightly askance, I thought, and came over to ask if I was enjoying the journey.

The service on the plane was excellent, and in spite of the cloud or perhaps because of it we were told all about the major cities we were flying over, first in Russian and then in English, which I much enjoyed. It pays to travel with top delegations. In Moscow, exactly on time, Mikoyan met the delegation.

A vice-consul called Thomas met me. We arrived at a VIP ter-minal and there were no customs formalities or entry control, but for the first and only time I was asked for my ticket. At Irkutsk they had not been able to find my name on the passenger list. The Mongols had spelled it in Cyrillic as Kivats, so the Soviet officials had to take me on trust. With all my splendid pieces of paper I had no trouble. The Russians, by the way, left me that nice note from Ambassador Solovyev, so I shall be able to produce it again on my way back.

The Brimelows and Morgans were away, so I stayed with Agnes Wood and was very well looked after. I spent a lazy time. You feel a bit of a burden, but they are terribly nice about it.

The weather in Moscow was horrid, but by Friday afternoon a wind had got up and blew the clouds away. The BEA plane was two hours late as they had come down in Copenhagen to refuel in case they had to turn back because of the weather. This is the form apparently. However, we had a lovely flight back. There were about 25 African men on board. Ghanaians I think. It looked as though they were being sent home, but nobody seemed to know. The sight of London by night in contrast to Moscow would be hard to beat. The pilot took us low down over the city so that you could see the buses going round Nelson's Column – not only sheer beauty of all the lights but a tremendous impression of size and prosperity.

They gave me a rotten room at the St Ermin's. I swapped it for a better one on my second night. Godfrey Davis produced a car and drove to Cliveden on Saturday. Bronwen was in extraordi-narily good form, looking after all the Astor children. I don't see how it can last. From there I drove to Dunsfold. My mother and father seemed remarkably calm and well.

On Sunday I came to Hampton, our diplomatic service tenants having moved out on Saturday. I have never seen the house look so clean. I drove on to Charterhouse and took George out for lunch. He seems well and happy and claims to have written a three-page letter to you. I have asked Travel Section at the FO to arrange my return journey on 9 May.

Reginald to Ann

28 March 1966

Thank you for your cable.

This has been one of our difficult weekends with everything happening at once, including a leak in the Land Rover radiator, cipher telegrams, QMs, and lots of letters to write. Tomorrow I go off to Darkhan. Fortunately the two QMs are very nice, Henry Huth and a new man called Coulson. They are down at the garage mending the radiator. Coulson has been flying Vulcan bombers and things and says he can take a Land Rover in his stride.

I had a letter in the bag saying that Robert Heath Mason,[2] at present a counsellor at Leopoldville (under our old friend John Cotton), will be succeeding me in July. He is said to be a lively man, with experience of Soviet affairs. His wife may write to you. They have three children aged 12 to 14, whom they would need to bring out for the summer holidays. I don't think the appointment is meant to be public knowledge yet.

I was shown over the Cuban house on Saturday – by the Cubans not the Mongols. A good deal could be made of it, but thank goodness it is not we who will have to do the making.

Your contribution to the wives' mag[3] is being much applauded. I am sending you various notes about it, which have arrived here. I have had some entertaining letters from the children, including one from George. William commented that his birthday cake was a bit small; but it lasted two days and went round 26 people.

There are various people for whom we ought to have little presents. ... Could you perhaps buy some? It might be a good idea to give a leaving gift to the second department at the MFA, for example a print of a London scene, the river or Whitehall or Westminster. Tserentsoodol could hang it on his office wall. If you happen to see anything suitable, please buy it.

The English-language teaching expert who is coming under our cultural agreement will arrive while I am away. I have to book a car for Alex to meet him. Everything that happens is so encrusted with accretions of difficulty!

I hope you all have a happy Easter holiday.

Ann to Reginald

30 March 1966

Both William and Jane are now back home and the house is reverting to its natural chaos, which I shall do my best to keep in bounds. I have booked Jane on a plane to Prague on 22 April. Jane has some social engagements with her school friends. Fortunately, the telephone is now automatic, which makes it much easier to deal with these things. On Sunday I shall drop George and William at Dunsfold and then take Jane to join Bron at a memorial service for Bill at Taplow. The number of memorial services is wearing the Astor family out.

西藏西藏

In the last days of March the MFA arranged for me to visit Darkhan and Sükhbaatar, respectively 220 and 340 kilometres north of Ulan Bator. Darkhan was a completely new town, started in 1961, and was intended to become the MPR's industrial base. Lying on the axis of the railway and road running north from Ulan Bator to Sükhbaatar, 20 kilometres from the Soviet border, it was to provide the heart of a dominating economic zone projecting southwards from the Irkutsk region to Ulan Bator and locking the MPR firmly to the USSR. A new coalmine had been built at Sharin Gol about 76 kilometres to the southeast of Darkhan, the two being linked by a new railway. L. I. Brezhnev had visited Sharin Gol and Darkhan in January to inaugurate the operation of the first stage of the newly constructed Darkhan power station, the biggest industrial plant in the country.

What I saw at Darkhan was a huge construction site where up to 10,000 Soviet citizens were at work, many in military labour battalions. There were many Mongolian troops there too, build–ing a brick factory planned and financed by Poland and a cement factory planned and financed by Czechoslovakia. As a minor surprise for me, the Mongolian troops working on the Polish project were commanded by our chauffeur Batsukh's father-in-law.

The Mongolian administrators and engineers were either middle-aged men who had had experience in the relatively small and light industrial enterprises at Ulan Bator or young or very young men and women fresh from university, technical college and school. It was impossible to believe that they could take over at all soon from the skilled and experienced Soviet engineers who were masterminding the project. Foreign aid workers and managers largely occupied the first new residential blocks that had been built in the future town centre. The area where the 20,000 or so Mongolian workers and soldiers lived was a muddy and dishevelled jumble of gers, hutments, wooden cabins and barracks. The Soviet troops appeared to have their own permanent camps outside the town.

Darkhan is in an area of bare hills, markedly colder than Ulan Bator and subject to cold north winds. The whole construction process was kept alive by a massive network of underground pipes carrying steam. I was shown, for example, how all motor transport was left standing, drained, out of doors in night temperatures of –40°C or lower and was brought rapidly into action each morning by the injection of steam directly into the radiators.

I saw little development at Sükhbaatar, although it was obvious that this was going to follow once Darkhan was built. I was able to admire the beautiful setting where the Orkhon River joins the Selenge on its way north to Lake Baikal, the Angara, the Yenisei and the Arctic Ocean.

My visit to Darkhan left me bemused by the contrast, indeed contradiction, between the new Soviet-model Mongolia, which I saw being founded and constructed there on the vertical axis north of UB to Irkutsk and the Mongolian Mongolia of herdsmen on the east-west and southern axes with which I had become familiar in all my other excursions from Ulan Bator. The Mongolian Mongolia did not have the manpower, the educational levels or the material resources to run the Soviet-model Mongolia. The Soviet Union was evidently assuming a very long-term, heavy commitment to the MPR, and the MPR was accepting enduring dependence on the Soviet Union. These considerations must have underlain the turmoil in the Mongolian People's Revolutionary Party, which Tsedenbal had successfully repressed with help from the Soviet leadership in 1965. The only consolation the Chinese could be finding for themselves was their belief that history is very long.

My full report on Darkhan is at the PRO (FO377/187 193) in my dispatch No. 4 of 9 April 1966.

西藏西藏

Ann to Reginald

79 Broad Lane, Hampton, 5 April 1966

[Letter of family news, house news and news of the children.] I think I may have a tenant for the house for at least part of the time until July.

On Saturday morning my father had a heart attack. He is told he must not do anything at all for a month. My mother is deteriorating and is becoming a bit difficult to deal with. I can't think how G copes.

On Sunday I drove to Dunsfold in the morning and then went on to Cliveden for lunch and to Taplow for the memorial service for Bill. A Benedictine monk whom Bron admires gave the address. I did not take to him. He seemed to be playing to the gallery all the time.

My family at the moment are really in a frightful state.

I am thankful that your successor has been nominated. Leopoldville to Ulan Bator! What a life! Perhaps we shall learn before long what is going to happen to us.

Reginald to Ann's father

Ulan Bator, 8 April 1966

I have meant to write to you by every bag since we returned to Ulan Bator, but I find myself taken up each time by all sorts of duties.

Ann has probably told you that my successor is already chosen and is expected to arrive here in the second part of July. I am looking forward fairly keenly to the end of this assignment. It has been an extraordinary experience, but the more I see here the less I like it. Ann and I saw all that is allowed of Mongolian life long ago. I do not enjoy seeing more and more of the underside of communism. And there is no fun in having our private and family life disrupted so much.

I made a trip northwards to the Soviet frontier soon after Ann left. I went to see a new industrial town the Russians are building for the Mongols. It is a Siberian-type operation, creating something out of nothing in the middle of nowhere. The snow was melting and the roads were very muddy. It looked like a forward area in the war in winter. The thousands of Russians seemed to be relieved that it was better than in the deep winter when they had to work in −40°C frosts.

They use high-pressure steam to keep their cement and concrete or bricks and mortar warm until they set. It must be a very expensive way of building, but they say the summer is too short for it to be possible to build in the summer only.

In the far north we ran through some Siberian *taiga* – huge pine forests and then low scrub stretching for hundreds of kilometres. There was the usual excessive eating and drinking in Mongolian tents. It was a fairly serious business as I was alone with the Mongols. I could have done with Ann's help.

Yesterday I detected the first faint green at the bottom of the tussocks of last year's grass. We still have three or four weeks to go before our spring really starts.

Reginald to Ann

8 April 1966

I have at last managed to haul myself clear of the constant pressure of mini-business. I can write this before the bag comes.

It has been a difficult fortnight. My trip to Darkhan was interesting and at the same time boring. Being on tour alone is a bit of a strain.

As soon as I returned to UB things started to go wrong. Our little cooker had a short circuit and blew all the fuses on Friday night. Not realizing that the cooker had caused the failure I switched it on again on Saturday and blew all the fuses again. By then no one competent to mend the main fuses could be found – not until Monday, so that our corridor circuits were on low power all the weekend and kept on failing. We had to have cold breakfasts and go to bed early. I could not trace where the fault was in the cooker. A top electrician from the hotel staff called Altangerel turned up today and has managed to make the stove work again on a provisional basis. For the whole week I have had to make do with the *réchaud* Paul Richer[4] left with us to look after for the French.

We have our English language lecturer[5] here to teach Mongolian teachers how to teach English. He was not shown the post report in London and arrived here completely unequipped. He has not even brought a hat! I have been busy looking after him while he adapts to the place.

Last Monday and Tuesday the restaurant closed for two days to be fumigated. The anti-cockroach poison they used had a terrible smell. All the Mongolian women bound handkerchiefs round their mouths and noses and looked as though they had been having treatment at a Mongolian hospital. We had to make all our own meals just as I found myself reduced to the *réchaud*. I have therefore had the unexpected experience of positively desiring the restaurant to open!

During the week we have had some trouble with telegraph traffic, with the Mongols trying to force us to pay more. I think it is over now, but it was vexatious while it lasted. And all the time I have been trying to catch up with arrears of work. I laugh to myself when I think of Heath Mason writing to me last week and saying he was enthralled to be coming here.

I wonder if you could find time to write to our lecturer John Pride's wife? ... He has no bag privileges and has to depend on the public mail, which is presumably censored.

Donald Hopson is definitely coming on the 23rd. I have asked for a good long journey for him away from UB. I have managed to get him to say that this is the last visit on which he will try to do things and see people. If he comes for two or three days for the National Day in July, it will be very briefly as one of the visiting ambassadorial crowd.

Many people send you their best wishes (communists don't seem to send love), including your good friends Frau Urx and Mrs Kolman.[6] We had the Hungarian National Day on Wednesday, so all the *collègue*s were able to ask me my impressions of Darkhan – all that is except Kolman, who tried to suck up to Sosorbaram by saying loudly how disappointed he was in the reactionary foreign policy of the Wilson government. The Hungarian food and drink were not bad.

I climbed Bogdo Uul this afternoon, my first good outside exercise for a long time.

Ann to Reginald

79 Broad Lane, Hampton, 8 and 11 April 1966

[Letter on family matters including George's fourteenth birthday, tenants for the house, children's activities and Reginald's nephew's wedding at Portsmouth.] I have a letter from Eric Cheyne who tells me that he has met the couple who are due to come out to replace the Thompsons. Their name is Rangecroft and the wife will probably be writing to me. What with the McAdams coming to supper next Wednesday and the other two wives thinking of looking me up, I really feel we are beginning to say goodbye to Mongolia. I must practise being encouraging about the place. Don't worry! I shall be full of calculated optimism.

A journalist from *Reveille* is said to have got through to Ulan Bator on the phone. Is this true? How did she manage it? I would love to telephone you.

Reginald to Ann

Ulan Bator, 11 April 1966

I have managed to get the electric cooker repaired, and the FO has promised a new one in a month or so. I think it would be unwise to rely on the old one for too long.

I hear from the FO that Heath Mason cannot be here before the beginning of August. I shall ask Donald Hopson on 23 April if Peking can send someone to bridge a gap for us. Alan and Janet Donald[7] are coming with the ambassador on the 23rd.

I took a short walk by the airport yesterday. It was cold and very windy, but the signs of spring are beginning to multiply. I am reading *And Quiet Flows the Don*, which the Soviet ambassador gave me. I could do with two or three books if you see any I might like.

Reginald to Jane

22 April 1966

I hope you enjoyed Prague. The Czech ambassador keeps on asking how you are getting on in the golden city. Sometimes I say I have not heard and sometimes I invent little reactions from you.

The spring is definitely here. That is to say there are patches of water with no ice and the hills are an unbroken light brown, just as they were when we went to Kharkhorin last year. When you go outside the door a cold wind snatches at you and you know why there are still a few weeks to go to greenness.

There is a big *subbotnik* campaign going on here. On Friday and Saturday every week between now and June the whole city is to be mobilized to work *subbotniks*, cleaning the place up in honour of the 45th anniversary of the revolution and the Revolutionary Party. The Ministry of Foreign Affairs is completely shut on those days and so are most other ministries and the State Bank. The hotel is beautifully quiet as most of the cleaning women are out shifting rubble. Zogsood is very pi about her contribution to the common weal. Others look a bit fed-up. Batsukh came back to work yesterday and nearly fell ill again when I told him that his first day back would be a *subbotnik*. A group of students from the university is digging a trench across Sükhbaatar Square to lay a new heating line to the opera theatre. Many of the girls are wearing their ordinary everyday *del*s and other clothes, and some of the boys wear blue suits and white shirts. At the end of the day they look terrible, covered all over in dust. I suppose they have no other clothes. Some of them dig with real spades, but some have only children's spades or just iron bars. How lucky that we were not born in a country that is laying the foundations of socialism.

I went fishing on Wednesday. There was nothing to catch. All the fish are still hiding under the ice. But it was good to feel that the winter was over and to see the herds drawing in towards Ulan Bator. We shall probably soon have a shower or two – but I hope not too soon or the flowers will start bursting out before Mother is here to dig up some specimens.

Reginald to Ann

15 April 1966

Today has been the quietest I have spent here for a long time, thanks to *subbotniks*. The Mongol for holiday is 'a completely nice day' as distinct from 'a half-nice day' for a half-holiday. Today has been a holiday.

Yesterday I went for a long climb and walk in the valley to the north where we collected yellow pulsatillas last year and started up a fox. There is a beginning of growth in the larch buds. Little streams have started up here and there and the snow has gone completely from the valleys. All those flowers are getting ready for Kew.

A *Daily Mirror* woman has been bothering us on the phone all the way from London. She was a hard tryer and managed to get through. I suppose there will soon be a column or two of rubbish about us. Have they by any chance asked for a photo of you in a bikini or in a *del*?

The radio and Tass bulletins say it has been snowing heavily in England; perhaps you have wished you were back in sunny Mongolia.

I saw copies of the *Observer* and *Sunday Times* last week and wished that I hadn't. They were full of films and books and plays and music that I would love to have the choice of. One forgets how much one is unaware of here. This is the fourth Friday you have been away. Before the fourth Friday from now you will be back. I hope May will be a quiet month.

19 April 1966

I expect I shall find myself a bit hard pressed with the Ambassador and the Donalds here, so I start writing to you without waiting for the bag to arrive.

I have a bit of a cold and a sore throat, and yesterday evening I went to one of those alcoholic parties in which the diplomatic corps specializes here. It was Mrs Kolman's farewell until June. As a result I feel a bit low today. Zogsood has been washing the net curtains and has rehung them damp, which makes our rooms smell horrid. I spent the morning struggling through the last big analytical dispatch I propose to send from here – on the Academy of Sciences. This evening I feel relatively free and if I feel better tomorrow I shall go fishing. I seem to have spent too much time ministering to others recently, and I shall have to do a good deal more of it next week.

I have just had my arrears of a pay rise: here is a cheque for you.

22 April 1966

It was a lovely day for fishing on Wednesday. You could hear the ice melting. It hissed and crunched as lumps of it squeezed together in the river's narrow open channel. Every now and then there was a loud crack as the ice platforms over most of the river weakened. There were no fish, but that didn't matter. There were duck and geese near the river and a large herd of mares with new foals. You know it is spring in Mongolia not because of things turning green but because of water lying open without ice. The colours of the Mongolian spring are straw and water.

Alex and Grace are taking the bag to Peking on Tuesday. Alex has had toothache this week. I suggested that he should go to the dentist in Peking, but he remembered that one of our visitors had spoken well of the dental clinic here. So I fixed an appointment for him. He came back in a state of shock. The equipment had looked fine, but there was no running water, no anaesthetic and a beefy young woman dentist who drilled straight into the tooth and filled it in five minutes, with another six or seven Mongols hanging around and looking on. I think what disgusted Alex most was that he had to use a communal spittoon that had not been emptied all day. I am afraid I could not help laughing at his long face. Grace laughed too. Our lecturer, John Pride, fulfilling the role of enthusiastic visitor, corrected our perspective for us by telling us tales about the backwardness of English dentistry in rural areas.

Donald Hopson arrives tomorrow with the Donalds. He sent a telegram to London asking for Janet's fare to be paid from official funds because 'Mrs Hibbert and my wife will not be there and we shall probably want a little cooking.' You see how you are missed! Feliks Topolski also arrives tomorrow for three days. I am not particularly enthusiastic about his drawings.

The children will be going back to school when you receive this. I shall write to them at their schools. It is a relief to know that you will soon be back, although it still seems a long way off to me.

24 April 1966

It is wonderful to have so many letters from you at once.

I am sorry about the state into which your family is declining. It seems to be a strong reason for being at home for a while. On this there is good news. I hear from Personnel Department that they are trying to fix up a fellowship for me at Gonville & Caius for a sabbatical year. They will not know until June if all concerned, including the Treasury, will approve it. This is strictly private information. Being at home would be good for the children too.

25 April 1966

It is just on midnight and I have to be up at 6.00 for the train. We have been having an entertaining evening with Topolski, who is a garrulous and amusing old card. Hopson was left a long way behind and probably did not approve. My thoughts are scattered after a trying weekend, but Hopson's visit is not going too badly from my point of view. I think he is finding it a bit frustrating. The

Mongols are showing less and less zeal for making arrangements for non-resident envoys.

Ann to Reginald

79 Broad Lane, Hampton, 25 April 1966

We at last have a fine day after weeks of rain and snow. The painters have been able to start work on the house. Jane left for Prague on Friday. I have agreed with Madame Malassis at Rennes that Jane should go there in September for a fortnight with their daughter.

I hope you can get someone to bridge the gap between your departure and Heath Mason's arrival. She wrote and said that Heath was enthralled by the idea of the post – good luck to them!

27 April 1966

This letter comes to you with the McAdams, I hope. But I gathered yesterday that their visas had not yet come through. We all took to Douglas when they came to supper, an energetic young man, used to taking plenty of exercise in an organized sort of way, and with a sense of humour. Sue evidently knows all about the rules and regulations, which should be useful to you. They are so young that one can't help feeling a little protective towards them.

Reginald to Ann's father

Ulan Bator, 8 May 1966

I shall be very glad to see Ann on Wednesday. I have been overrun with visitors recently, some of whom are good friends of mine. But one grows tired of being nothing but a public servant. Here I am quite literally that and nothing else, at any rate when visitors are around. I find that none of them respects my privacy when I am here alone. When Ann is here, each of us can make a fuss on behalf of the other, but I find it difficult to make a fuss for myself.

Our new assistant and his wife arrived this weekend, very young and very bewildered. Now that we are three households here we seem to be becoming very large. But I wish I did not have the sensation all the time of living with my troop, something the CO of the Fourth Hussars warned us always to avoid.

Reginald to Jane

9 May 1966

Thank you for your postcard from Prague, and I enjoyed your letter, which Mother passed on to me. Tell Jane Bow how grateful we are to her and her family for looking after you.

I have been having a busy time here. The Ambassador came with Mr and Mrs Donald from Peking. The Ambassador was personally exacting, as always. The Donalds were madly enthusiastic about everything, which made me a bit tired. They asked questions all the time. The Mongols were not keen on organizing a trip for the Ambassador. However, in the end they offered a trip to Kharkhorin. We went by the southern route, the one by which we came back to UB when you were with us. We stayed a night at Arvaikheer, the centre of Övörkhangai *aimag*, which you did not see. It was an ordinary *aimag* town, but its museum was very interesting as Övörkhangai is particularly rich in old Turkish, Hunnish and Mongol relics. Then we went on to Khujirt and found that Dr Avimed, the director of the sanatorium has been moved. His successor was an amiable man and we had the usual alcoholic dinner party after a hot sulphur bath. At Kharkhorin there were big changes. The two monks are no longer living there in the monastery, and one can now only look into the temple buildings and not go in. A nasty, dry little man has been made museum director. The first thing he said was that we could not take photographs. I told him that I already had all the photographs I needed, but what about His Excellency, who had come so far to see these treasures of the Mongol genius? Nothing would move him. He said that some American tourists had abused Mongolian hospitality by taking photographs of Erdeni Dzu and using them for commercial purposes (namely selling them to a magazine). It was no use arguing. Altogether it was a depressing experience after our jolly visit last year. The director of the State Farm was the same and gave us his usual long talk about the number of hectares of wheat under cultivation. I did not enjoy the journey as much as our journeys last year. Everything becomes a bit stiff with the Ambassador there.

A big dust storm is blowing, but the summer is nearly here. The mauve pulsatilla are just now coming into flower.

All good wishes for your new term. The end of it will be the end of my term too. Hooray!

15. Gandantegchinlen monastery, at that time the one surviving 'show' monastery in Ulan Bator.

Reginald to his parents

9 May 1966

It has not been very enjoyable doing this job in the last few weeks by myself. But happily Ann will be back on Wednesday.

My new assistant and his wife have arrived, but of course the first effect is to increase and not reduce work. They are very young and will have a lot to learn, but they will have to learn it under my successor.

All the Mongols say that the spring is their nastiest time. It is very dry. We have so far had only one day of rain. More is urgently needed so that the animals can have something to eat in the pastures.

I have been on two journeys this month. Both were strenuous and I doubt if I shall do any more extensive travel here. I find that I know the routines of the Mongolian countryside very well now. A fresh journey adds little new besides scenery, but the enormous emptiness of this country never fails to make an impact every time I move through it.

I feel I am really on the last lap now, but there is plenty to do before I complete it.

Ann to her parents

23 May 1966

Well, here I am back again in the wilderness, but not for long. We have heard by this bag that Reg can leave on 19 July, so I shall be able to bring him back to England with me. We are planning to come home via Peking, Canton (this time by train from Peking) and Hong Kong. A BOAC flight on the 25th should get us to London 24 hours before we have to collect George and William from school.

I think Reg has become rather discouraged by the lack of will on the Mongol side to make any real progress towards cooperation. They just want us to be here so that they can claim that they are open to the West, while wanting us to keep as quiet as possible and rendering us ineffective if necessary. I am a bit sorry for Reg's successor because he is obviously an enthusiast about Mongolia. I am afraid he may be disappointed both as regards the 'romance' of Mongolia and in making much headway in friendship between the two countries.

The spring is late by several weeks, that is to say that scarcely a drop of rain has fallen yet. It is warm, but the grass is still quite brown. This is a serious situation for the Mongols as it means that their animals are very short of fodder. One unpleasant feature of the weather is that we are having constant dust storms. Everything is covered in a thick layer of yellow grit.

I have been to two films since I came back, one at the Soviet embassy of Karl Marx in 1848 (boring, with technicolour bloodshed on barricades), and the other a postwar, badly lit and sickening Hungarian story about an unwanted child. There was also a performance of *Romeo and Juliet* at the Mongolian Youth Theatre – not remotely like Shakespeare. This afternoon I am invited to a Chinese tea party. This means standing for a couple of hours round a table laden with Chinese food (like bamboo shoots), drinking toasts to victory in Vietnam and death to American imperialists.

The British community here is quite large at present – six of us belonging to the embassy, plus two QMs, and the lecturer from Leeds teaching the teachers to teach English. He seems to have worked hard and to have been a success, but he tends to try to launch passionately enthusiastic discussions about serious subjects, which I find tedious. I leave him to Reg, but Reg has been in a dialogue with him for two months, so I should not be too impatient. He leaves on Thursday.

I am off now to the diplomatic shop to buy some milk. Supplies here are as unreliable as ever, but our stock of tinned food and dried milk is better, so life is easier than it was six months or so ago. Reg seems to be very fit. He does his exercises conscientiously every day and can climb any hill within reach without getting out of breath, which is certainly not the case with me. But I am well all the same.

Ann to her father

5 June 1966

We were pleased to hear that you were able to finish your last few days in court in comfort and hope that your farewell party went off successfully and that the Lord Chancellor coughed up the gold watch or whatever it is they do for retiring judges.

We are also in an end-of-term sort of mood. It is difficult to make Reg realize what a short time remains to us here. He is constantly busy and tends to forget the passage of time. At the moment we are getting ready for the Queen's Birthday Party, which we can't have on the proper day but must hold a week later as they are holding a congress of their communist party and it interferes with our dates. Reg has prepared another speech in Mongolian, which he should be able to deliver with even more fluency than last year. And we have just received quite a number of magnums of champagne, so it looks as though it will be a fine farewell occasion for us.

Before we go the Thompsons are being replaced. So the British embassy will have a completely new look in August.

The Mongols have gone crazy over their communist party congress. They expect delegations from 40 different countries. They have done their best to transform the town by making the people plant trees and grass down the edges of all the main streets and paint railings and curb stones. The hotel has been transformed. Extra red carpets have been laid down corridors that never previously had any, potted plants have appeared and special new ashtrays. Copies of the *Daily Worker* or whatever it's now called and *Humanité* and other communist publications have been tastefully laid out on tables on the landings. The cleaning women have all been put into uniform dresses, much to the displeasure of our nice elderly Zogsood who complains that it's all right for the young ones but makes her look too fat.

The only really good thing about it is that they have brought in a cook and maître d'hôtel from Hungary. They are producing Hungarian food that is quite good given the limited materials available here. That is to say we now get chicken *gulya* and risotto and today we had steak and chips – everything smothered in paprika of course, but I believe this is a good source of vitamin C.

The weather is still unseasonably dry here. It is pleasantly warm and sunny, but the grass is still completely brown and I think hundreds of cattle are dying from starvation.

I wonder if the children have been able to visit you in their exeats. I do wish I could ring you up and find out how you all are, instead of having to wait to read it all in a fortnight's time. We shall be here to receive only three more bags. There will be no point in writing to us after the weekend 2/3 July.

Reginald to Jane

6 June 1966

The McAdams are settling in well, but are plagued by a hot water tap that keeps on breaking, so boiling hot water runs out all night, and by the hotel sign, which has been rehabilitated for the party congress and winks into their window (you remember how flimsy the curtains are) red, amber, green and back to red, also all night.

Alex and Grace Thompson have a heavy black ring round 29 June on their calendar – the day they leave. Mr and Mrs Rangecroft arrive to replace them a few days earlier. We are beginning to wonder how to pack all our possessions, and how to do it in time. I am being offered one or two little gilt buddhas on the black market. They are little treasures hidden away from the destruction of the lama monasteries in the 1930s. And the little man in the curio shop downstairs is having a *del* made for me. His reply to my questions is always, 'the day after tomorrow'.

Reginald to his parents

6 June 1966

I hope Jane is paying you for the things she asks you to buy for her. She has an allowance and a bank account and a chequebook. I thought that now she was in the sixth form she was sometimes allowed into Brighton to shop, but perhaps I am wrong.

It will be a tight squeeze to get everything done that needs to be done by 19 July. But there are still various questions to be settled before I can be sure of my timetable.

There is sunshine every day but the Mongols class it as very bad weather. Nothing is growing properly. The wild flowers are coming out in stunted form. The drought is severe and the herds and herdsmen are in a bad way.

The XVth Congress of the Mongolian People's Revolutionary Party is taking place here at present. Our hotel has become a very well guarded citadel for some of the world's important communists. I have not yet found out if there is a delegate from the UK. The attitude among the Mongols is rather like that of a military unit being inspected by a group of generals. The experience of watching it at close quarters is distasteful. The public money being spent to make the show a good one seems limitless. The ordinary Mongols have been made to do an enormous amount of labouring in recent weeks to make Ulan Bator look other than it really is.

9

Party Congress and General Election

The following passage about the preparations for the XVth Party Congress is taken from my, dispatch No. 6 of 16 June (PRO/FCO 371/187193):

西藏西藏

The Congress was a triumph of organization and window-dressing. The preparations for it had occupied the MPR's rulers and people for the previous two months, ever since the end of the winter frosts. The population of Ulan Bator had to work *subbotnik*s or voluntary labour days on Fridays and Saturdays in every week in April and May. For all practical purposes, public business was conducted on the basis of a four-day week during the whole of that period. No business prospered unless it was connected with preparations for the congress.

At first the town was covered with dust and littered with piles of earth and rubble; but as the time of the congress drew near it emerged with a new and pleasing tidiness in its central areas and along its main thoroughfares. The operation was conducted with an admirable economy. Only that which could be seen from the windows of a car received attention; but where attention seemed necessary it was applied radically. Uneven groups of shabby *ger*s (the Mongol tents) were cleared away or fenced in, lampposts and railings were erected, paint was generously applied, trees were planted in hundreds, and flower beds and grass patches were made with earth brought in by lorry from the countryside. The spring this year has been a bad one with prolonged drought, but water has been poured out unsparingly to turn Ulan Bator into a green oasis in a brown steppe. The results have been very effective. The foreign delegates must have been impressed by the town's smart and well-tended appearance. They were kept continuously busy and each had a personal escort who accompanied him everywhere, so that there was no chance of anyone looking backstage behind the scenery.

Virtually the whole staff of the Ministry of Foreign Affairs and many members of the Ministry of Foreign Trade were transferred to work in the offices of the Central Committee during May. They were preparing material of all sorts in foreign languages for the expected visitors. The hotel in which this embassy is housed came increasingly under party control. A deputy chairman of the Council of Ministers made the last dispositions in the hotel before the congress began, and a deputy minister of foreign trade (the hotel belongs to the Bureau for the Service of Foreign Travellers, which belongs to the Ministry of Foreign Trade) took up residence in the hotel as overseer. From the time the foreign delegates arrived we found ourselves in a state of siege, with a detachment of militia continually blowing whistles outside, young men in subfusc from the party and plain-clothed police lounging in the foyer and on every landing, and most of our old acquaintances in the hotel staff reducing their contacts with us to stiff formalities. Carpets were laid where carpets have not been seen before. All the menial staff was dressed in new uniforms. *Unita*, *l'Humanité* and the *Morning Star* were scattered liberally around. Both of the hotel's lifts, but not its clocks, were brought into action. A fleet of some 50 cars was assembled and polished and drilled in convoy driving and mass parking. Two Hungarian cooks and a head waiter were imported, only to be told that they must prepare and serve Mongolian food; happily they have been consoling themselves by serving Hungarian food to the members of the staff of this embassy while members of the Hungarian delegation, faced in their special dining room with exclusively Mongolian food, found themselves forced into an involuntary hunger strike.

My summary conclusion about the congress was that Tsedenbal and his Soviet patrons deserve much credit for their toughness and legerdemain in arranging so orderly a congress and charting the future so clearly for a party that has been in disarray and a country that staggers between deviation and non-fulfilment. But the stabilization of the Mongolian situation is linked with the stabilization of the Soviet Union's leadership in the world communist movement and the successful isolation of China, and these things in turn are linked to the immobility of the CPSU leadership in Moscow. When new tremors begin to run through the communist world, the smart appearances and well-drilled unanimity of the Fifteenth Congress of the MPRP are unlikely to survive. But at present Tsedenbal looks like staying.

西藏西藏

Immediately after the Congress a general election was held to choose members of the Great People's Khural. The organizational anchorman of the party secretariat, Tsagaanlamyn Dügersüren, organized it, and it was indeed an organizational triumph. The following passage is taken from my dispatch No. 7 of 4 July (PRO/FO/371/187 193):

西藏西藏

Thanks to the small size of the Mongolian population the figures published after the election by the central electoral commission provide a model *reductio ad absurdum* of communist election statistics. The total number of registered electors was 558,477. Of these only 14 failed to present themselves at the polls. The number of votes cast for the bloc of the party and independents was 55 fewer than the number of voters presenting themselves at the polls, but the electoral commission claimed that only 27 voters failed to cast positive votes. Perhaps this means that there were 27 adverse votes and 28 abstentions, or vice versa. These figures are remarkable in a country as large, scattered and thinly populated as Mongolia and show Tsagaanlamyn Dügersüren to be one of the world's really great organization men. To arrive at a figure of only 14 stay-at-homes one imagines the natural processes of senility, idiocy, severe illness, death and childbirth standing still at the bidding of the party. Mobile urns are carried round such places as hospitals to collect the votes of the infirm; but one is tempted to suspect that a few dead souls must also have voted for completing the foundations of socialism, unless Shelepin has taught the Mongols some up-to-date way of compiling the election register on election morning. At any rate, 99.99 per cent of the electors voted, and 99.99 per cent of these voted yes. I believe that even the Soviet Union, Mongolia's teacher, is content with 99.98 per cent.

It is perhaps a frivolous detail, but I was telephoned by the head of the Bureau for Servicing the Diplomatic Corps and requested to ensure that I timed a fishing trip in such a way as to enable my driver to vote. The driver counts for all matters except pay and social insurance as an employee of the Ministry of Foreign Affairs. I have been taken aback by the subsequent revelation that it was in my power to make a noticeable difference to the final electoral figures.

The Mongolian leaders lost no time in holding the first meeting of the newly elected Great People's Khural. It met on 1 July in the presence of the diplomatic corps.

Tsagaanlamyn Dügersüren treated it to a long speech on ways and means of improving the role of the Great Khural and its standing commissions and the role of the provincial *khural*s as organs of popular inspiration and popular control in carrying out the country's policies. The choicest sons and daughters of the Mongolian people showed little reaction. The front half of the assembly consisting of dark suited officials (the 49 per cent from the intelligentsia) wrote busily and gossiped among themselves. The back half, consisting mostly of sun- and wind-burned herdsmen and shepherdesses in their bright *del*s and workers in their best suits, medals and bristly haircuts, tried out one another's earphones and scribbling pads and pencils, laughed and talked among themselves and stared and slept.

西藏西藏

On the Queen's Birthday my name was included in the Honours List. I was appointed a Companion of the Order of St Michael and St George (CMG).

西藏西藏

Reginald to his parents
                                                            20 June 1966
Thank you for your telegram about my CMG. I hope you enjoyed the surprise in the newspaper. It is nice of the Queen to give

presents on her birthday. We were told a few days before by telegram.

I am afraid I have no time to write a letter today. I am on the point of going to the airport to meet the French Ambassador[1] who arrives for the first time this afternoon. He is going to find that he too has to live indefinitely in this hotel. As you see, diplomatic life in Ulan Bator is slowly gathering speed.

Reginald to Ann's parents

20 June 1966

Thank you very much for your telegram of congratulations to Ann and me. We enjoyed speculating on who had spotted the surprise in *The Times* first. I had been warned by telegram, but it was reassuring to receive cables from you and my parents and to know that it must have happened as they said. Ann and I opened a bottle of champagne and drank the Queen's health.

No one has ever left here before with our quantity of luggage (no Englishman or westerner, I mean), and we do not know how it will work out. In a country without porters and with unreliable railway staff it is difficult to imagine the problems that may arise. The Mongolian National Day occurs a week before our due date for leaving. It can be relied upon to hold up work in every government department for at least a week. But the curious thing is that everything always works out right in the end in Mongolia. This country will have had the effect of turning me into a fatalist. It certainly encourages feelings of resignation. No wonder Asian religions are religions of escape.

Ann to her parents

20 June 1966

Yes, we are certainly counting the days. At least I am. Reg is more concerned with all the practical problems of getting away. There is the real physical difficulty of packing up without any crates or packing materials and no one to carry it to the station. We are going to try to sell such things as radio, record player, skis, hairdryer, ciné, slide projector and screen. These would pose a difficult packing problem and would probably be damaged. The sales would have to be done through a government department. Such things are either completely unobtainable here or exorbitantly expensive. I hope we shall get a reasonable price.

We have recently been freed from an invasion of communist delegates from some 40 countries. The hotel was rather an unpleasant place to live in while they were here. It was swarming with secret service police. No unauthorized person was allowed in, including Reg's Mongolian teacher (who is head of the Pedagogical Institute), my hairdresser, and even the East German Ambassador's little boy who wanted a haircut. During this time we were treated very politely but kept very much at a distance like people with a contagious disease. The party people seemed to think that we wanted to pry into their deliberations. About 25 cars were parked permanently below our windows and whenever the delegates went anywhere or returned from anything there was a tremendous slamming of doors and revving of engines. Each man had a car, a driver and an accompanying Mongol to himself, no doubt enhancing his already considerable self-esteem.

By Monday their programme in UB had ended and they had all been taken off to visit farms in the country. We were able to hold our postponed Queen's Birthday Party on the Tuesday (14th). Although many of the ambassadors were away with their delegates, junior members of the embassies and plenty of Mongols came. Reg made an impressive little speech in Mongolian and Russian, which went down very well. We had plenty of champagne – half a dozen magnums which looked impressive on the bar among the smaller bottles. All were drunk, besides a dozen bottles of whisky and a good deal of vodka and cognac. They all seemed to be enjoying themselves, except perhaps the Chinese who stood in a corner and looked a little lonely, but proud of it.

The same train that brought the QMs on Saturday also brought the Rangecrofts who are to take the Thompsons' place. They are a nice couple and a good age for UB, he 32 and she 27. We have been lucky that none of the people posted here have been unlikeable. Close proximity for a long period brings out everyone's peculiarities, so we, especially Reg, have had to put up with a few temperamental outbursts – including mine and his of course!

Also on the train from Peking came a Frenchwoman from the French Embassy in Peking who is to act as secretary and interpreter for M. Perruche, the French Ambassador who arrives this afternoon by air from Paris. It will be amusing to have someone from another Western country, but of course the French are now so popular with the communist countries that one can't be sure how friendly they will be with us.

I think Reg is very pleased with his CMG, but it made him suddenly realize that perhaps he had become a member of the Establishment – a bit of a shock. Of course my first thought was, 'What shall I wear at the Palace?'

4 July 1966

First of all I think I should warn you that it now seems most unlikely that Reg will be able to come back with me. London has not managed to keep to the timetable for getting his successor here, and it looks as though Reg will have to stay for another two or three weeks after I leave. I needn't tell you how disappointed we both are. I, of course am furious, but Reg manages to be philosophical about it. He is more sceptical than I am about the FO's management. I don't think he ever really believed that he would get away on the date they originally agreed. Also he has a sense of responsibility towards this post, which I am afraid I find a little difficult to share, except in the sense that it is in effect something that he has constructed. However, there it is. I shall have to come back on my own once more, and the FO will have to pay a bigger bill for airfreight.

We went last weekend on a little fishing expedition, this time to the Kherlen (Kerulen) river eastwards of UB. Having been altogether too dry it has now become very stormy and wet. The change took place last weekend.

We set off at about 9.00 a.m. on Friday and drove through the hills of the Khentei range until lunchtime when we found ourselves on the river bank. We took the young couple, the McAdams, with us and of course Batsukh our driver. We had our lunch and did a little fishing, but we could see the clouds gathering and decided we ought to look for somewhere to pitch our tent.

This is a little tent for two and apart from the Land Rover was the only shelter we had. We found a little copse of trees and got the tent up only just in time. For an hour or so five of us crouched in this little space while the thunder rolled round and lightning flashed and the rain poured down.

When the storm had passed we crawled out and fished, but the fish obviously didn't like the weather either. About seven o'clock we made some supper, which we had to eat standing up as the

ground was so wet. We have a little stove which works on petrol:
it is a great success as it burns in any weather. It began to get dark
at about nine o'clock so we decided to go to bed. By now the sky
seemed so clear that Reg thought he would put up our one and
only camp bed and sleep outside. The McAdams and I crawled
into our sleeping bags in the tent and Batsukh spread out his
bedroll in the back of the Land Rover. About half an hour after
we had all settled down I heard the rain beginning to fall again
and Reg stirring and swearing. Before long he had crawled into the
tent too, so there were four of us lying like sardines head to tail in
a space that would have been cosy for two. Unfortunately he fell
asleep lying on half my sleeping bag, so I was pinned down on one
side by a dead 12-stone weight and quite unable to move hand or
foot. A beetle began crawling up inside my sleeve and what was
worse was that I was pressed up against the side of the tent so that
the rain was seeping through and running down the inside so as to
form a large puddle in which I lay. You can imagine that by 4.30
a.m., as it was beginning to grow light, I had had enough. So we
got up, and the discomfort of the night was almost worth enduring
for the sight of Reg in the middle of Mongolia at five in the
morning spinning for fish in his pyjamas, dressing gown and
Wellington boots.

We spent the morning fishing but caught only two between the
four of us. By lunch we had decided that it would be wise to drive
back to UB. The sky in most directions was navy blue and black.
On the way back we found ourselves in the middle of a terrific
storm. We came up over a pass into a valley that was a sheet of
white, covered in hailstones the size of mothballs and flooded up
to a foot deep. The mountain sides themselves seemed to have
turned to water and great muddy torrents rushed across the track
carrying huge clumps of ice and mud. The poor people in their
gers at the bottom of the valley were almost afloat and it would
need days of hot sunshine to dry them out again. Horses stood
knee deep in water patiently waiting for the storm to pass.

Reg has an enormous pile of work this weekend and he has
received letters and cables from all over the world, which he wants
to acknowledge when he can. People have been very kind.

We have been doing a certain amount of entertainment during
the past fortnight in an effort to take leave of our colleagues – all
rather sticky of course, and nothing to give them except stuff out

of tins. The Frenchman is here now, but de Gaulle's antics have tended to put an official coolness between us, although our personal relationship with him has been entirely amiable. He was a prisoner of the North Koreans for three years with Vivien Holt and Blake, so we are very sorry for him. He is quite deaf. He should have had an easier posting.

10

And the Rains Came Down

Ann to Reginald's parents

4 July 1966

It now seems unlikely that Reg will be able to leave on the date planned. It looks as though it will be impossible for the new man to arrive until the second half of August, in which case Reg will have to stay on for two or three weeks after I leave. I must get back as planned to meet the children from their schools. I am still planning to come via Peking and Hong Kong with the QMs.

Things never seem to go smoothly here. The Thompsons were supposed to leave last Tuesday. We got down to the station at 7.00 a.m., which is when the train is supposed to arrive from Moscow. We were told it would be coming in at 11.00. We had the Hungarian ambassador coming to lunch, so I couldn't go again, but the others all went down – still no train. They were told to ring up after 12.00 as the train was expected at about one o'clock. They decided to have something to eat and were just in the middle of their meal when our chauffeur came rushing in and said the train was already at the station. They all rushed out in complete confusion and arrived at the station to see the rear light of the train disappearing along the track. You can imagine their dismay. It really was ridiculous. One train a week, and they had missed it by a few minutes! However, there was a 'local' train going to the frontier next day, and it was possible to get to Peking that way in 48 hours instead of 36. So they decided to take it. It will not have been very comfortable.

Reg has been so busy with one thing and another that it has been impossible to get out for an afternoon walk recently. My flower collecting has been practically nil this year.

Ann to her father

15 July 1966

I am writing this as you see on my birthday and I must say it has been one of the strangest birthdays of my life and not the most comfortable.

If you have been hearing news of the floods here you will of course have been wondering how we are getting on. Being in the hotel we have been remarkably well looked after. We have had almost first priority after the Soviet, North Vietnam and North Korean delegations who were here for the National Day had to be rescued from the VIP villas across the river by Soviet army helicopters. We have been given every consideration.

The floods happened on Tuesday. The river Tuul burst its banks to the east of the town and flowed right through the industrial area, ruining the power station and cutting through the water supply. Half the population, those living on the south bank, have been cut off as all the bridges are down. Many people's homes, their *ger*s, have been swept away, and about 100 people, including many children left at home by their parents, are said to have been drowned. We have had no electricity for two days but some emergency generators have now been brought into action. We still have no water but are provided with a fairly adequate supply from buckets – floodwater of course. There is a great deal of secrecy about the damage that has been done. I think the Mongols are in a very bad way indeed. They have absolutely no resources to cope with an emergency like this. The Russians are doing what they can to help and they do their best to keep up appearances. But one knows that there is a lot of suffering, and there is a danger to health. As far as we can tell, no sanitary precautions are being taken.

The rail line to Peking has been broken in several places. It will be several weeks before they can repair the damage. I cannot travel that way. I have therefore booked to fly on the Aeroflot plane to Moscow on Thursday 21 July, and shall probably reach London on Saturday 23rd. One great problem is our luggage, which will have to come by airfreight and will cost HMG quite a lot of money I imagine.

The Mongols have asked that Reg's successor, who is to be accredited as Ambassador, should not arrive until a certain amount of order has been restored. They seem to regard Reg as an old

Mongol who can take it. Of course we have no QMs. This letter comes to you by hand of Mrs Cherry Twiss, who has been out here photographing fashion pictures for the colour supplement of the *Sunday Telegraph*. I expect she will have rung you up.

Well, life is certainly full of surprises. I didn't think I could want to leave this place more than I did. But now I find it is possible after all. Reg and I are so much looking forward to seeing you all again.

西藏西藏

The following description of the disastrous deluge and floods that brought ruin to Ulan Bator on the National Day is taken from my dispatch no. 8 of 25 July (PRO/FO/371/187 193).

西藏西藏

Torrential rain had begun on the afternoon of the 9th. It continued throughout the 10th while we laid wreaths of smeared paper flowers on the tombs of Sükhbaatar and Choibalsan and the monument to Mongolia's Soviet liberators. It continued more heavily than ever on the morning of the 11th, the National Day. We learnt afterwards that the Ulan Bator region was receiving about one-third of its annual rainfall in one go, or 98.5 millimetres. Nevertheless, loud and cheerful music blared from the loudspeakers at 6.00 a.m., and the populace began to gather for the parade and demonstration at 9.00 a.m. Visiting members of the diplomatic corps from Moscow and Peking were shocked at the way in which thousands of people without raincoats, including many hundreds of children, were exposed to a thorough drenching and chilling for hours on end. Even the hardened residents began to murmur that it would have been cancelled in Prague or Bucharest or Warsaw. In Ulan Bator it was carried through to the bitter end according to the programme, down to the last roneoed word of the Defence Minister's inaudible speech and the last detail of imitation of the way these things are done in Moscow. In the afternoon the *Naadam* or national games meeting was opened at the central stadium, although it was mostly under water and the wrestlers splashed at every fall. Instead of hurrying the programme, Tsedenbal and his colleagues kept everyone waiting for an hour in the downpour before President Sambu could declare the games open. In the evening there was the usual government reception in Choibalsan's former villa in Great Paradise Valley, south of the river Tuul. It was then that most of us realized how serious the situation was becoming. The river Tuul was obviously dangerously high and our cars had to ford deep floodwaters in spate in the usually dry valley reserved for the top leaders. Most of the resident diplomatic corps thought only of getting back across the bridges before they were swept away. Nevertheless, we had to endure a full round of speeches from the delegations, followed by a somewhat incoherent and long improvisation by Tsedenbal. As the staff of HM Embassy slipped away there were some extra-ordinary scenes of drunkenness among the Mongols and Russians in the lower rooms and some slightly more discreet ones upstairs. This and the pelting rain and rushing water and the start of the scheduled fireworks display created a more demented atmosphere than is usual on diplomatic occasions. We returned safely over the Tuul and Selbe bridges. Two hours later the latter was swept away.

On the morning of the 12th the *Naadam* continued as planned although the rain was still pouring down. We were bidden to return to the stadium at 2.00 p.m. for the finals of the wrestling. When we arrived at 2.00 p.m. the alarm had just been given and people were hurrying from the stadium as floodwater began to pour over the surrounding land. For the next few hours there was a scene of devastation in the southern half of the town. The river Tuul had broken its banks some dozen miles to the east, had taken a shortcut across one of its own great curves, had punched a hole in the road and railway embankment and then flowed into the town along the line of the railway and the minor Selbe River, which normally flows parallel with it through the centre of the town. The whole section of Ulan Bator between the Tuul and the Selbe was scoured by a torrent and inundated. This area contains almost all the capital's industry and many agglomerations of *ger*s (tents) and workers' flats. No one had been warned and no one was ready. Two buses were swept away and went down with all hands. Families and individuals struggled to safety as best they could. As is common in Mongolia many small children were being cared for by older brothers or sisters while both their parents were away at work or at the *Naadam*: there were many casualties among these. By nightfall Sükhbaatar Square and its surroundings were dotted with little groups of refugees in dishevelled misery and the whole town was without water, light or supplies of any sort.

Mongolian troops and soldiers of the Soviet construction battalion had been at the stadium for the games and at the opera house for a concert. These were brought fairly rapidly into rescue operations on the afternoon of the 12th. On the 13th the rain slackened and rescue operations took a more organized form under the direction of a state commission headed by the 1st Deputy Chairman of the Council of Ministers, S. Luvsan. It was, however, impossible to obtain reliable news and everyone had to provide his own news service by going to see for himself. Once the disaster was complete the authorities seemed to cope with it effectively. They had substantial Soviet stiffening. An electricity generating train arrived from Darkhan on the 14th and Soviet specialists brought the town's secondary power station at Tolgoyt back into operation during the night of the 14th. Soviet helicopters arrived and rescued the Soviet government delegation from its secluded hotel in Great Paradise Valley together with a few revellers who had been cut off after the reception on the night of the 11th. The helicopters then set to work ferrying people and supplies between the town and the summer camps beyond the river. A column of riders made a great sweep round to the east via the west and south to pick up refugees who had fled southwards into the hills of Bogdo Uul. But these successes could not diminish the size of the calamity. Ulan Bator was cut off from most of its hinterland and above all from its coalmine at Nalaykha. The coal-mine itself was reported flooded. Many hundreds of 'voluntary' workers are now hurriedly blasting and shovelling a track across the lower spurs of Bogdo Uul on the south side of the river to the one remaining bridge in the west. This should make it possible to fuel the main power station, whose railway spur has been ruined and which normally depends on the railway to Nalaykha, which has been cut by the river. Only when the main power station is back in production can industry be started again.

At the conference to which heads of missions were summoned on 16 July and which I reported in my telegram No. 90 of 18 July, the Czech ambassador extracted a most damaging admission from the deputy head of the State Meteorological Service. When, he asked, did the river Tuul reach its danger level of 160 centimetres?

At 10 a.m. on 11th July came the reply, just at the moment when the Defence Minister was making his speech at the parade in the pouring rain. The Mongolian leaders had carried on with their parade and demonstration and *Naadam* and reception and more *Naadam* and continual speechmaking for 28 hours after the moment at which they should have declared a state of emergency. They allowed the water to reach 311 centimetres, at which level it devastated a large part of their capital, before taking any action to deal with it. The size of the disaster and the loss of life are clearly attributable to them. The eastern European ambassadors are inclined to murmur the word 'irresponsibility'. They naturally cannot admit that the real trouble lay in wrong priorities. This was an example of what can happen when politics are given absolute priority. The National Day celebrations are a major act of pro-party and pro-Soviet dedication and no one short of Tsedenbal could have checked them. Seeing how large a price the Soviet Union now has to pay to help the MPR repair the damage, it is difficult to understand why Efremov and the Soviet delegation did not do something to stop their Nero fiddling on the 11th. It is possible that they too could not contemplate the cancellation of a political event so favourable to themselves. It is of course undesirable for a Praetorian guard to intervene too hurriedly.

I am perhaps being a little too hard on the Mongolian leaders. A *Naadam*, a party and a free drinking bout are things that no Mongol will willingly forego, and there are not many of them these days. The Mongols met the flood with stoicism and absolutely no panic. Cancellation of the *Naadam* might have caused more shock than the flood. There is no framework of local democracy in the MPR through which the people could be roused to a state of disciplined alertness. The system is more suited to letting a crisis arise and then throwing the people in to fight it. The government and people gave a fine example of hard-headed tenacity a week after the flood. The *Naadam* was restarted in another stadium and finally carried through to its conclusion in the presence of big crowds. A cancelled friendship concert with guest artists from eastern Europe was also put on in spite of delays and electricity cuts. On one night the lighting failed halfway through, and after an hour the performers went back to their hotel to bed. An hour and a half later the current was restored and the Mongols fetched the unfortunate eastern Europeans from their beds so that the performance could go on. It ended at 2.00 a.m., and most of the audience was still there. A Mongol does not give up easily, and he does not worry himself thinking about the wastefulness of a hand to mouth existence.

11
Going Home

Ann left UB on the weekly flight to Moscow on 21 July. I stayed until the end of the month. It was sad to leave Mongolia at a moment of disarray in its capital. At the suggestion of HM Ambassador Donald Hopson, at Peking, the British government gave a modest contribution of medical aid to help in the emergency. I was able to communicate this to the Ministry of Foreign Affairs. They appreciated our gesture although their public expression of gratitude was directed almost exclusively towards the Soviet Union.

My departure, also by air to Moscow, was in a low key; but there was a moving moment when I was saying goodbye to friends and staff at the Ulan Bator Hotel. Our elderly chambermaid, Zogsood, pushed forward and pressed into my hands a present wrapped in newspaper. It was a boiled leg of mutton. It was to sustain me on my long journey, she said. It was a final gesture of the generous hospitality that all the members of the embassy had received from all the Mongols with whom we had had dealings from the time of my arrival in 1964. In its simplicity it was also a measure of the gulf dividing the world of the Mongolian steppes I was leaving from the sophisticated urbanized world to which I was returning.

Shortly before we left, Zogsood had obtained exceptional permission from the authorities to invite Ann and me to her flat in one of the apartment blocks for workers. The remarkable feature of it was that its furnishings were arranged much as they would be in a *ger*, and the entertainment offered to us followed the ritual customary in a *ger*. The Mongols had many problems: a problem of identity was not among them.

西藏西藏

16. *Arat* family outside *ger*.

The following passage is taken from a farewell dispatch I sent on the eve of my departure (PRO/FCO/321/187 193, dispatch no. 9 of 26 July):

西藏西藏

The longer I have stayed here, the more I have been impressed by the Mongol people's will to assert itself. The Mongols have almost nothing in their favour, neither climate, nor terrain, nor neighbours, nor numbers, nor culture, nor natural wealth. They nevertheless have hard heads, intense pride and an almost naive faith in their right to a place in the world.

It is easy to spend one's time in Mongolia shaking one's head or laughing or enthusing patronizingly over this infant country's first few shaky steps towards maturity. The fact remains that the Mongols do not see themselves as an infant people.

Whether they support the pro-Soviet Tsedenbal or have devia—tionist, nationalist ideas they are all equally determined to assert Mongolia's sovereign character. It is the feeling that a British and western presence contributes towards this process that makes residence here a worthwhile and sometimes an enjoyable experience.

I have been very lucky to be the first western representative to have the chance of trying systematically to understand and interpret this much-romanticized country by actually living in it. Some first steps towards regular Anglo–Mongolian relations have been taken and I think it will be found that they can be profitably enlarged. HM Embassy is an established and living institution in the mini-mission class, although something still needs to be done to refine the operations of the big machinery of the Diplomatic Service Administration Office to Ulan Bator's small but very precise requirements. Within the narrow limits of their material and ideological possibilities the Mongolian authorities have treated me and the other members of the Mission's staff with courtesy and consideration. Like most adventures, opening up in Ulan Bator has exercised emotions and faculties to the full and has finished by exhausting them. Perhaps I shall find when I am no longer resident at Ulan Bator that I am after all a Mongolphile. It will be easier to remember the Mongols' admirably strong and simple basic qualities when one is no longer dependent on their feckless ways or pinned down by their inhuman system of government.

西藏西藏

Ann and I had considered ourselves to be at the top of the age bracket suitable for service at Ulan Bator. I thought it should be regarded as a post for young men because of the heavy demands it made on physical fitness and versatility, at least while the embassy was housed in the hotel, and also because of its remoteness from normal medical services. Everyone was agreed, however, that there should now be a resident ambassador, and even the most junior ambassadors were drawn from a somewhat older level. Heath Mason was four years older than I was, and his successor, Oliver Kemp, was two years older than that. Unfortunately, both of them had serious health problems while they were at Ulan Bator. Heath Mason had to leave after only a year. Oliver Kemp stayed only for seven months. As a result there were gaps at the head of the post in the second half of 1967, the second half of 1968 and the first months of 1969. The mission was unable to settle down to a more or less steady existence until the middle of 1969, when Roland Carter became the Ambassador and was able to establish himself

in the house at 30 Peace Street, which had at last been acquired as
the embassy's permanent premises.

西藏西藏

Ann and I settled into our house at Hampton with the children. I
soon learnt that the idea of a sabbatical year at Cambridge had
fallen through. I was told that Dr Joseph Needham, who became
master of Gonville & Caius in 1966, had doubted whether a
member of the Diplomatic Service could do adequately scholarly
work in one short year. He was a very distinguished Sinologist,
celebrated for his monumental work on *Science and Civilization in
China*, and he may have felt, as the Chinese did, that Mongolia
had nothing to contribute to Chinese civilization.

The Foreign Office offered me a year at Leeds University
instead, attached to the Department of Chinese Studies, which was
headed by Professor Owen Lattimore, one of the world's rare
Mongolists. Lattimore was a controversial figure. He had been
severely mauled in his own country, the United States, by Senator
McCarthy and the Senate sub-committee on Internal Security (the
McCarran committee), being accused with other members of the
Institute of Pacific Relations of having been an instrument of the
Soviet conspiracy and having contributed to the loss of China to
Mao Tse-tung and the Communist Party of China. In the UK he
was able to pursue academic work peacefully. My own impression
of him was that he was a journalist and traveller at heart rather
than a scholar. His books about Mongolia were exploratory rather
than analytical. His attitude towards me was somewhat similar to
that of the Mongolian government: he was glad to have me there
as a sort of testimonial to his political acceptability, but he seemed
not to want me to do anything at all active. He knew I had critical
views about the policies followed by the Mongolian government
and about the distortions imposed on Mongolia's economy and
society by the Soviet Union's determination to dominate Mongolia
and keep China out. He did not want controversy that might make
him and his department less welcome in Ulan Bator, Moscow and
Peking. He had won financial support from a leading Leeds
industrialist, the head of Montague Burton, for some Mongolian
projects. Some young Mongols had come to Leeds to learn
English. John Pride, who had come to Mongolia to teach the

teachers how to teach English, had come from Leeds. The Chinese
Studies Department at Leeds had become the liveliest cell of pro-
Mongolian activity in the UK. He was happy if I could support
this, but he did not want the propagation of any radical views that
might spoil the image he was building up.

I leased a little flat in Leeds and spent the middle part of most
weeks there in term time, driving back to join Ann at Hampton for
long weekends. My major work at Leeds was a very detailed study
of the Mongolian government's fourth five-year plan for the years
1966–70. This was read with interest by the research and
intelligence branches in Whitehall (it is on file at the PRO, FCO
371, 187201), but Lattimore made no comment on it. It was to a
large extent a chronicle of failure and non-achievement, and this
was not the aspect of Mongolian affairs that interested him. I
delivered a paper in the Department on Mongolia's economic
planning and development. The text of this is attached in the
appendices. Lattimore again received this impassively. The year at
Leeds was in fact an extension of my experience in Mongolia. I
was free to pursue my own investigations and studies but not
encouraged by the local authority to advertise my thoughts and
conclusions.

I enjoyed the company of several engaging and interesting
members of the Chinese Studies staff and of one or two other
departments in the university. It was a new experience for me to
see a university other than Oxford. And it was an opportunity to
get to know Yorkshire. The possibilities of making anything more
of Mongolia rapidly dwindled, and I was glad to return to my
career in the Diplomatic Service in late 1967.

I was then posted to Singapore to the staff of the Political
Adviser to the Commander-in-Chief, Far East, and had no more
contact with Mongolian affairs for several years. Later, in Bonn, in
the 1970s I was invited to give a paper to the Deutsch–
Mongolische Gesellschaft, which was inspired by the prestigious
scholarship of Professor Walther Heissig and studied Mongolia
seriously. Later still, at Bloomington, Indiana, in the United States,
I was able to visit the Graduate School of Uralic and Altaic Studies
at Indiana University, a powerhouse of Mongolian studies and the
base from which the Mongolian Society of the United States issues
its scholarly publications.

Ann and I found our stay in the UK very brief. We had been

abroad since 1957 and were destined to stay abroad until 1975. With me spending much of my time at Leeds, Ann felt that being at home was not very different from being abroad. She was even more disappointed than I was at not having a home posting in London. However, the sabbatical year served to unwind the intensity of our Mongolian experience, and we went off in September 1967 to become acquainted with east and Southeast Asia, Australasia and the Pacific.

Notes

Chapter 1: A New Posting

1. Later Sir David Muirhead, Ambassador at Lima, Lisbon and Brussels.
2. Later Sir Terence Garvey, Ambassador at Moscow and High Commissioner at New Delhi. In Peking he was regarded by the Chinese simply as the British representative for the negotiation of diplomatic relations, or in British diplomatic service terms Chargé d'Affaires. He was accredited as non-resident ambassador at Ulan Bator in 1963 when the UK began diplomatic relations with the MPR.
3. Sir Roderick Barclay had been the principal Private Secretary to Mr Ernest Bevin, a Deputy Under-Secretary of State in the Foreign Office and Ambassador at Copenhagen before taking up his final post at Brussels.
4. Brian Stewart was an old friend from Oxford days. It was indeed he who had introduced Ann and me to each other. He visited Ulan Bator on his homeward journey from a posting in Peking. Most of his career was spent in Malaysia, China and neighbouring countries in east and Southeast Asia.
5. The Mongol narratives or narrations by the friars who travelled to the court of the Great Khan in the thirteenth century are not in print and are difficult to find in bookshops. They provide an easily negotiable bridge with many recognizable features between the present day and the great days of the Mongols eight centuries ago. It was possible for a few western travellers and adventurers to penetrate into Mongolia towards the end of the nineteenth century and in the first three or four decades of the twentieth century. Some Christian missionaries made their way there and have left memoirs recording the difficulties they faced. Inner Mongolia south of the Gobi desert was explored more than Outer Mongolia north of the desert, the latter being largely a field of activity for Russians. Inner Mongolia is part of the Chinese People's Republic and has been inaccessible to westerners since the middle of the twentieth century. Outer Mongolia is now the Mongolian People's Republic and there is a great quantity of Russian research and writing about it. It began to open to western visitors only in the mid-1960s.
6. Later Sir Thomas Brimelow, Permanent Under-Secretary of State at the Foreign and Commonwealth Office, having previously been ambassador at Warsaw. He was generally regarded as the Diplomatic

Service's greatest expert on Soviet affairs. I had served under him for a time in 1956 and 1957 when he was head of the Northern (Soviet) Department in the FCO. In 1964 he was Minister (namely number two) in the Embassy at Moscow.

7. Violet Conolly was for many years the head of the Soviet section of the Foreign Office Research Department. She had an encyclopaedic knowledge of Soviet affairs but never got round to writing an encyclopaedia. Anyone writing about the Soviet Union was wise to show it to her in draft.

8. Later Sir Michael Wilford, Deputy Under-Secretary of State at the FCO and Ambassador at Tokyo.

9. Sir John Nicholls had been Ambassador at Brussels at the beginning of my tour there. Previously he had been Ambassador at Belgrade with Terence Garvey as his number two. Stewart Ross, now in Peking, had been my predecessor as First Secretary (Commercial) at Brussels, but I had not met him there. He did not stay in the service for a full career. He was an amusing man, full of entertaining gossip. Henry Carr had been the Chancery Secretary at Brussels, a man who knew everyone and everything about them and was more or less all things to all men. He did not stay in the service for a full career.

10. The Soviet Ambassador was Leonid Nicolaevich Solovyev, who was appointed in late 1963. He was approachable, courteous and self-assured, always expressing the correct Soviet line but in as reasonable a way as possible. He set a good and sometimes necessary example of dignified, good-humoured behaviour to his communist colleagues and hosts. He kept a strict hand on the large Soviet community in Ulan Bator and everywhere else in the MPR. The Soviet authorities should have been pleased with their representative.

11. The Foreign Minister Dügersüren was appointed in 1963. It seemed that he had not held any high offices previously. He was an amiable and polished performer in his diplomatic role, which is probably what the political leaders wanted of him. It was difficult to judge if he carried as much weight as one or two of his senior subordinates. He had a charming wife who was always very attentive at public functions but would never accept an invitation to the embassy.

12. Yumjagin Tsedenbal's curriculum vitae is reproduced in the Appendix.

13. *Ulaan Baatar* means red warrior or red hero. The original red hero celebrated in the Mongolian People's Republic was Sükhbaatar. His mausoleum, built in 1954 after Choibalsan's death and which he shares with Choibalsan, dominates the main square of Ulan Bator, standing in front of the palace of the Great People's Khural (national assembly). Sükhbaatar was in fact a somewhat insubstantial figure to be a national hero. In the chaotic conditions following the First World War, with fitful attempts by the Chinese to reassert control over

Khalkha Mongolia (which had asserted its independence in 1911 when China was wracked by revolution) and with white Russian and Bolshevik forces fighting and making incursions into the territories of the Buryat and Khalkha Mongols to the south of Lake Baikal, Sükhe, in his late twenties and with an undistinguished background, became the leader of a band of Mongolian revolutionary fighters cooperating with Bolshevik forces in the Russian–Mongolian frontier region. Choibalsan, also in his twenties was doing likewise, and the two combined their efforts. In 1921 they held a conference at Kyakhta (on the Russian side of the frontier) to form a Mongolian People's Party, a provisional government and an army. Later in the year when the Bolshevik forces moved to crush the white Russian forces, which had established themselves in Mongolia, Sükhe and Choibalsan and their Mongolian revolutionaries were swept to Urga, the Mongolian capital. There they set themselves up as a government, requested the Soviet forces to stay, changed the name of their party to the Mongolian People's Revolutionary Party, promoted Sükhe to be Sükhbaatar, and began to rule Outer Mongolia, with China still retaining theoretical suzerainty. Sükhbaatar and others visited Moscow and were honoured by meeting Lenin. Sükhbaatar died in 1923 at the age of 30 before the Mongolian republic could take clear shape. That could not happen until the following year, 1924, after the death of the country's quasi-monarch, Jebtsun Damba Khutuktu, the eighth *Bogdo Gegen* or living Buddha of Urga. Urga became Ulan Bator and Khalkha Mongolia became the Mongolian People's Republic, destined to spend the next two decades being adapted painfully and destructively to a model dictated by the Soviet Union. Khorloin Choibalsan was a more substantial figure than Sükhbaatar. He lived until 1952, surviving the incessant purges, uprisings and repressions that marked the MPR's unsteady march towards socialism. By the time of the Second World War he was indeed the only survivor from the leadership of the Mongolian People's Revolutionary Party in the 1920s and 1930s. After a short spell in Moscow, in 1923 he started his career as a leader of the Revsomols and in 1924 he became the commander-in-chief of the army, a post he retained until he was promoted to Marshal in 1936. On the way up he added to his offices nearly every other government post of importance. His roles in the brutal implementation of collectivization and the destruction of the monasteries in the 1930s and in the resistance to Japanese encroachment from Manchuria during the same period, culminating in Marshal Zhukov's final defeat of the Japanese at Khalkhin-Gol in 1939, contributed greatly to his accumulation of power. By the 1940s he was the dictator, the Stalin, of the MPR. Stalin died in 1953, a year after Choibalsan. The ensuing gradual process of de-Stalinization in the Soviet Union led to a devaluation of Choibalsan in Mongolia. By 1964 he was rarely mentioned in Ulan Bator. His tomb in the mausoleum remained bare when wreaths were heaped round the tomb of Sükhbaatar. Tsedenbal, the current leader of Party and State, had risen to the top under Choibalsan, but this political line of descent was not publicly mentioned. Choibalsan was remembered as a marshal with hardly more reverence attached to him then was attached to marshals of the Soviet Union. And the Mongols of the MPR were left with only the somewhat insubstantial and even mythical figure of Sükhbaatar as their official hero. In private conversation with Mongols at every level and everywhere it became obvious that they did nevertheless have a very clear national hero – Chingis Khan. But Chingis Khan was a forbidden subject. An official attempt had been made in 1962 to celebrate the 800th anniversary of his birth, but this was condemned by Moscow and instantly repressed, to the accompaniment of yet another of the frequent purges in the Mongolian leadership. China meanwhile celebrated the memory of Chingis Khan in the Autonomous Mongolian Region of the Chinese People's Republic (Inner Mongolia); but this can have been small comfort to the Mongols of Inner Mongolia as they found themselves being increasingly hemmed in by a massive immigration of Han Chinese.

14.   Jamsrangiin Sambu was Chairman of the Presidium of the Great Khural and therefore the head of state. He belonged to the generation of Sükhbaatar and Choibalsan, and the merit often ascribed to him was that he had been a member of the first Great Khural in the early 1920s. Given the repeated purges of the 1920s and 1930s there cannot have been many, if any, other survivors. He emerged in the top echelons when he became Ambassador at Moscow in 1937 (until 1946) and to North Korea in 1950 (until 1952), doing two spells as deputy Foreign Minister between and after those appointments. His elevation to the presidency, which brought with it membership of the Politburo, occurred in 1954. He was a fine, upright figure of a man next to his Politburo colleagues, and he lent a certain dignity to state occasions.

15.   Gandantegchinlen monastery was a fragmentary remnant of the huge monastic system with its thousands of lamas that had been utterly destroyed in the late 1920s and 1930s. It was a show piece, indeed a side-show piece, in the Ulan Bator of the 1960s, picturesque but of no practical significance. Religious memories survived silently among the people, but received no public expression except very furtively. In our weeks in the hills and woods near Ulan Bator, Ann and I used to come across *ovos*, votive piles of stones carrying prayer flags and rags with inscriptions and sometimes (in the deep freeze of winter) the head of a favourite horse that had died. These were survivals of shamanism as much as lamaism. No members of the administration or diplomatic

corps were ever to be seen taking walks in the higher hills or woods. When I ventured to mention these *ovos* to one or two of my contacts they expressed incredulity and quickly changed the subject.

Chapter 2: Progress on the Domestic Front

1. Ann's sister Gwyneth and her partner Ron Barry had moved away from London and settled at Chiddingfold. Her younger sister, Bronwen, who had achieved celebrity as a model, particularly for Balmain, had married Viscount Astor and was living at Cliveden. Oliver Van Oss was the headmaster of Charterhouse.

2. Lord Furness was founder chairman of the Anglo-Mongolian Society, which had been formed in 1963. He was also vice-president of the Tibet Society of the UK.

3. *Beasts, Men and Gods* by Ferdinand Ossendowski, published in 1922, gives a vivid picture of conditions in Mongolia in 1920 and 1921. The author wanted to escape from Krasnoyarsk on the Yenisei as the Bolshevik revolution spread into Siberia, and he found himself caught up in a web of travels in western, central and northern Mongolia. The story of his exploits seems exaggerated, but the details he gives of life in Mongolia at that time have the stamp of authenticity. He has three main themes – the shifting, treacherous and murderous relationships throughout the country between the Chinese, the resident Russians, the infiltrating Bolsheviks and the Mongol princes, princelets and high lamas; his contacts with Baron Ungern von Sternberg, the 'white' general from Transbaikalia who had the mad dream of basing an anti-Soviet front on a pan-Mongol union; and his contacts with the last living Buddha, the *Bogdo Gegen*, blind from an alcohol addiction and syphilis and yet supported and cosseted by the high lamas and adulated by the common people. Ossendowski left Urga and made his way to Manchuria very shortly before the Bolshevik forces from the north swept Ungern von Sternberg away and helped Sükhbaatar, Choibalsan and their Mongolian revolutionaries to seize power.

4. Sir Alun Pugh was at this time appointed to be the judge presiding at the West London County Court.

Chapter 3: Ann Settles In

1. President Ayub Khan of Pakistan was on a state visit to China and I happened to witness his departure. Liu Shaoqi was at the time reckoned to be second in status to Mao Tse-tung, but he was subsequently eliminated during the Cultural Revolution. He underwent much ill treatment and died in abject circumstances. Chou En-lai was for many years China's face to the outside world and he managed to survive.

2. This was Eddie Bolland, later Sir Edwin Bolland, who became head of the Far Eastern department in 1965. He was subsequently Ambas-

sador at Sofia and the leader of the British delegation to the negotiations on mutual and balanced force reductions (MBFR) at Vienna.

3. Sir Alun Pugh had been a subaltern in the Prince of Wales's Company of the Welsh Guards at the battle of the Somme.

4. Mrs Fort was the headmistress of Roedean. We found the school a little inflexible in relation to very distant parents such as we were.

5. Dr Hewlett Johnson was famous at the time as the Red Dean of Canterbury, an unfailing fellow traveller of the Soviet Union.

6. The Great Khural, bearing its ancient Mongol name, had much the same function in the MPR as the Supreme Soviet had in the Soviet Union. It met for only a few days a year and applauded the government's pronouncements. Insofar as the Politburo of the Mongolian People's Revolutionary Party and the Council of Ministers needed the formal sanction of state organs, this was provided by the Executive Committee of the Great Khural, under the chairmanship of President Sambu, which was available with its rubber stamp throughout the year.

7. The battle of Khalkhin-Gol put an end to a long period of military pressure by the Japanese from Manchuria on the eastern borders of the MPR. The Soviet Union built a railway line from Borzya on the Trans-Siberian Railway to Choybalsan in the easternmost *aimag* of the MPR, and a narrow-gauge line from Choybalsan to Tamsag Bulag in the MPR's easternmost salient. These constructions served an obviously military purpose. The Soviet communications with Transbaikalia and the maritime provinces running through a bottleneck to the south of Lake Baikal make a forward defence in Mongolia imperative.

8. Later Sir Donald Hopson, Ambassador at Caracas and Buenos Aires.

Chapter 5: Family Separation

1. Sir Geoffrey Harrison had been Ambassador at Rio de Janeiro and Tehran and a Deputy Under Secretary of State in the Foreign Office. The Brooke case was a *cause célèbre* at the time. It concerned a young British man who had been arrested and imprisoned by the Soviet authorities for distributing literature that was allegedly subversive.

2. Father Bill Masters had been the embassy chaplain in Vienna when we were there in 1952–54. He had baptized our son William at Hampton parish church in 1957. My father and an aunt, who, as staunch Anglo-Catholics saw him from time to time at the church of St Alban the Martyr at Holborn, also knew him. He was welcome as an old friend, but his visit filled me with trepidation because of his unsteady state and need for a watchful eye on him.

3. Randle Darwall-Smith was one of the joint heads of St Wilfrid's Preparatory School at Seaford, to which we sent both George and William.
4. Anthony Blishen was at a later date Chargé d'Affaires at Ulan Bator during an ambassadorial interregnum.
5. Mrs Chabbaria was a British Honduran, mother of one of the local security guards at the Legation in Guatemala, whom we engaged as nanny for William when he was one to two years old and who turned out to be the best and certainly the most patient nanny we ever had.
6. Bora was the number two at the Yugoslav embassy.
7. Aunt M was Miss Stenning, Jane's housemistress at Roedean.

Chapter 6: Yak Hair for the Cavalry
1. Douglas Carruthers's accounts of his stalking of *ovis ammon* in the Altai Mountains in his *Unknown Mongolia* (1913, 2 vols) are a classic of their genre.
2. Hilary King had been Ambassador at Conakry. I had shared an office with him when we were both junior secretaries in Chancery in Vienna, he dealing with Quadripartite occupation matters and I with Austrian internal affairs. We found ourselves working closely together again in the 1970s when he was Consul-General in Hamburg and I was minister at the Bonn Embassy. Meanwhile he was appointed to Warsaw and not to Mongolia.
3. Later Sir John Morgan, ambassador at Seoul and Mexico. John Boyd became Political Adviser to the Governor of Hong Kong and, as Sir John Boyd, Ambassador at Tokyo and Master of Churchill College, Cambridge.

Chapter 7: A Spell in England and Back to Ulan Bator
1. Later Lord MacLehose of Beoch, after serving as Ambassador at Saigon and Copenhagen and then as Governor of Hong Kong.
2. Anthony Elliot was an old acquaintance. He was later Ambassador at Helsinki where he played an important part in the preparatory work for the Helsinki Final Act (CSCE). He then became Ambassador at Tel Aviv where he unfortunately drowned in 1976.
3. St David's Day, 1 March.

Chapter 8: Upgrading the Mission
1. Douglas McAdam did another term in Ulan Bator in 1978. He was appointed Ambassador to Kazakhstan and Kyrgizstan in 1996.
2. The posting to Mongolia was to serve Heath Mason ill. He was enthusiastic about it, but his health broke down there and of course first-class medical attention was far away. He stayed for only a year,

and he died shortly after returning to the UK. He had been serving as Counsellor at Leopoldville under John Cotton, later Sir John Cotton, under whom I had served at Brussels where he was the Commercial Counsellor.

3. Ann had written an amusing article about our experiences for the magazine of the Diplomatic Wives Association.

4. Paul Richer was a charming Frenchman who came to Ulan Bator to carry out a reconnaissance in preparation for the arrival of a French Ambassador. He was very good company during his short stay.

5. John Pride came from Leeds University as an expert in teaching English as a foreign language. He was sponsored by the British Council and worked at the Central Pedagogical Institute at Ulan Bator. He had a bit of a shock when he found that the only English texts available to his pupils for translation into Mongolian were English translations of Brezhnev's speeches. He did a good pioneering job in uphill circumstances. Leeds University and the British Council have made a great contribution to the spread of knowledge of English in the MPR, Russian having previously enjoyed a virtual monopoly in the foreign language field.

6. Mrs Urx was the wife of the Czech Ambassador and Mrs Kolman the wife of our Yugoslav colleague.

7. Later Sir Alan Donald, Ambassador at Djakarta and Peking.

Chapter 9: Party Congress and General Election

1. The new, and first, French ambassador, Monsieur Perruche, had been a prisoner of the North Koreans during the Korean war and had endured much physical hardship there. I thought it was unkind to post him to Ulan Bator with the task of opening a mission there. He found a way of easing his task by residing in the Ulan Bator hotel for only about half the year and retreating to his home in the Loire valley for the other half. His secretary soon contracted hepatitis, as Ann had done, but she refused to submit herself to treatment in a Mongolian hospital and instead undertook an arduous journey to Peking, from which sadly she did not recover. I felt that my French colleague ought to announce his arrival to Paris by addressing a dispatch to President de Gaulle himself on the following lines: 'As the successor of the last French Ambassador to the capital of the Mongols, the friar William of Rubruck, envoy of St Louis in the thirteenth century, I have the honour to address my first dispatch to you, the successor of St Louis.' My French colleague did not think I could be serious.

Appendix
Economic Planning and Development

Below is the text of a paper on the Mongolian People's Republic that Reginald Hibbert delivered at Leeds University in 1967.

西藏西藏

The Mongolian People's Republic is only a part, the northern central part, of the historic Mongol lands. There is of course a wider Mongolian question, and this wider question comes up, at least by implication, as soon as Sino–Mongolian relations are mentioned. But I shall not be talking about the wider question, or about the Mongols as a people. My theme concerns the Mongolian People's Republic as an independent sovereign state.

I think it is prudent to assume a considerable degree of ignorance about the Mongolian People's Republic, even in this distinguished audience. At the risk of boring those who are already widely read about central Asia east of the Pamirs, the Tien Shan and the Altai, I must first establish a groundwork of simple facts about the country of the Khalkha Mongols, which is now known as the MPR.

Geography
Mongolia (like the rest of the central Asian plateau) has a highly distinct set of geographical features. Essentially, this springs from the fact that it is a very old piece of dry land. It has been exposed as dry land for about ten times longer than Britain, and the whole area has been lifted to very high levels by successive geological upheavals. As a result it is a mountain country, but with its

mountain systems far gone in erosion and decay. Its profile is not one of jagged peaks, steep rock faces and deep, narrow ravines and gorges, but of rounded, crumbling crests and long curving contours enclosing broad, gravelly valleys.

As it has been lifted up, so it has become progressively drier. Outer mountain walls cut off the whole of central Asia from the monsoons of Oceanic Asia. Powerful winds blow across Mongolia, mostly from the northwest, but they are dry winds. And this has had the odd effect over tens of millions of years of making China the beneficiary of Mongolia's erosion. On most days in spring you can see and feel the prevailing north–west winds slowly rubbing out Mongolia and carrying its dust via the Gobi as a free gift of topsoil to the toiling millions of China. It is a form of unrequited technical assistance on a scale of geological time.

Rainfall
We need to take a closer look at the problem of Mongolia's dryness. The rainfall is erratic and varies widely from year to year – but not from a little to a lot, rather from almost none to a barely adequate amount. Only a few areas in the extreme north of the MPR receive more than 300 millimetres of rain in a good year. Down south in the Gobi provinces there are less than 100 millimetres a year. Nearly all this precipitation is concentrated in the short months of summer, and often it falls in sudden storms of devastating ferocity. However, Mongolia can count itself lucky that the short rainy season and the short summer coincide. If it were otherwise, Mongolia would be a complete desert.

Climate and temperature
Ferocity is the main characteristic of the Mongolian climate. It has an extreme continental character, with wide and rapid fluctuations of temperature every day. In mid-winter the temperature can drop to −50°C. At midsummer in the Gobi it can rise to over 40°C. The mean annual temperature is round about, and usually a little below, 0°C. There is little snow cover in winter, but this intensifies the effects of the frost, and permafrost conditions are to be found as far south as Ulan Bator. The number of days in the year on which the thermometer falls below freezing point varies from 200 in the south to 260 in the north. At the same time, substantially more than 200 days a year are brilliantly sunny. This combination

of sunshine and frost produces a brilliant sparkling atmosphere, which greatly enhances the natural beauty of the country. But such beauty forms a treacherous and hostile environment for people. Perhaps its most treacherous feature is that the northern region of maximum rainfall is also the region of maximum frost. This coincidence goes far to balance out the other, happier coincidence of the rainy season and summer I mentioned a few minutes ago.

Plant life

I have dwelled on the climate because of its most important consequence, which is that the period of plant growth in the MPR is limited to about 100 days, from late May to the end of August, even in the most favoured places and in the most favourable years. If you go to Mongolia in summer you have an illusion of richness – glorious pastures of apparently limitless extent, millions of wild flowers, the whole country knee-deep in grass and, in the north, great tracts of virgin forest. But, in fact, the flora of Mongolia is poor and of little variety compared with that of Siberia or China, or even that of eastern Kazakhstan. It is this that has dictated to the Mongols their way of life from the earliest times. It is this that has made them pastoral nomads. And, as pastoral nomads, their wealth and capacity to develop have been determined not by the richness of the summer pastures but by the numbers of cattle it is possible to keep alive in the winter, namely by the number of places that are not too exposed, not too likely to have snow, and that are endowed with a good growth of grass in summer that stands as dry, uncut hay for the animals to graze in the winter.

Already perhaps you can discern the starting point from which I shall begin to talk about Mongolia's economic development. But before I do that, there are two topics that need to be examined.

Communications

The first is communications. There is only one town of any size in the MPR – Ulan Bator, the capital. There are 18 provinces or *aimag*s. In the last 30 years each of these has acquired a small, settled administrative centre. There are no roads between the centres or linking them with the capital, only well-worn tracks. But this is one of the few instances in which Mongolia's geography and climate are favourable. The gradients are not prohibitive and the ground is mostly hard, so that truck transport is reliable, though hard on the trucks and their crews. Within provincial boundaries, camel, ox, yak and horse transport still play key roles. The Trans-Mongolian Railway from Transbaikalia to China has become of relatively little use. From the point of view of internal development, it runs the wrong way, north–south instead of east–west. It has become a victim of the Sino–Soviet dispute. The Ulan Bator to Naushki section is, however, of vital importance as the MPR's lifeline to the USSR and, through the USSR, to the world beyond. The Trans-Mongolian Railway constitutes the only exit to China for trade and passenger traffic. It is now little used. By contrast there are four busy and important routes linking the MPR with the Soviet Union. These are, from west to east:

(a) a motor road ending at a trade depot in the extreme north of Bayan Ölgiy province, linking western Mongolia through Kosh-Agach and Biisx with Barnaul on the Turksib railway;
(b) a route leading from a trade depot at Khatgal on Lake Khövsgöl across the lake by tug and barge and then by motor road from Turda to Irkutsk. This route serves the whole of Mongolia's middle west;
(c) the railway and motor road leading from the capital, Ulan Bator, to Ulan Ude in Soviet Buryatia and thence by the Trans-Siberian Railway to Irkutsk.
(d) a railway and motor road leading from trade depots at Choybalsan in the eastern province to Borzya and Chita on the Trans-Siberian Railway.

In addition to the truck services and railway there is a small but frequent air service to all parts of the country. Like the country-wide network of telephone and radio services, this largely facilitates the highly centralized administration of the country.

The only other point that needs to be made under the communications heading relates to the great strategic importance of the eastern part of the MPR. The nature of this importance emerges if you draw a line on a map between Irkutsk and the Gulf of Liaotung. You will see that the eastern part of the MPR would constitute the shortest line of approach for anyone from the north-west who wished to cut the communications between the great industrial region of Manchuria and China proper. It would also provide the shortest line of approach for anyone from the southeast who wished to sever the Soviet Union's communications with the Soviet Far East at the highly vulnerable bottleneck south of Lake Baikal. Eastern Mongolia became a *place d'armes* in the 1930s and again in 1945 precisely because of these strategic considerations. They have permanent value. Perhaps the most significant monument to Soviet interest in the MPR is the metre-gauge railway that runs from Choybalsan to the Tamsag Bulag salient. It was the building of the broad-gauge railway to Choybalsan and of this narrow-gauge railway further southeast-wards that put the seal on Japanese miscalculations in the 1930s and 1940s. The railway is still there today. It cannot be said to exist for economic reasons.

Population

We can now come to the most important single fact about the MPR – its tiny population, its acute shortage of manpower for any and every purpose. The MPR is as big as western Europe and Britain put together. In that vast space, measuring just over one and a half million square kilometres, there is a population roughly equal to that of Glasgow or Birmingham, 1,100,000 inhabitants. The average population density is 0.7 per square kilometre. But as one-quarter of the population lives in Ulan Bator, average density outside the capital is 0.5 per square kilometre. Another quarter of the population lives in the provincial and district centres. The net rate of population increase is high, over 30 per 1000, but of course the first effect of this is to cause half the population to consist of children and to cause the women to spend a large part of their lives being pregnant. Taking all these considerations into account there is one able-bodied adult man to every eight or nine square kilometres in the Mongolian countryside, and the proportion is of course worse in the southern, Gobi areas.

The only country that I have been able to find with a density comparable to that of the MPR is the Falkland Islands (0.5 per square mile). The Trucial States have 3 per square mile, Botswana 2.5 per square mile and South West Africa 1 per square mile. The nearest figures from well-to-do countries come from Canada and Australia (respectively five and four per square mile). But neither Canada nor Australia has 700 million Chinese on its southern border.

In quality, the labour force is only a little less deficient than it is in numbers. The progress from almost total illiteracy to almost total literacy in 45 years is probably the MPR's finest achievement; but to this day the great majority of Mongolian children receive only four years of schooling from the age of eight to the age of twelve. Universal seven-year schooling was to have been achieved by 1965, but has slipped back into the targets for 1970. Higher education has advanced in recent years relatively faster than middle school education. Mongolia has become one of those countries where it is easier to find a cellist for a symphony orchestra than a plumber capable of mending a tap. The shortage of engineers and trained technicians is a great handicap to economic growth. As a university audience you will perhaps be able to savour the situation if I tell you that in 1964 only five Mongols held doctorates. However, some 170 were at that time in the grade of Kandidat, so that a rapid expansion at the top of the academic pyramid is assured. The crucial problem is in the middle school grades.

History

There is no need to say much about the history of the Mongol people. I shall confine myself to noting the situation that existed in 1921 when the MPR's independence was established by a handful of Mongolian revolutionaries supported and sustained by the Red Army. At that time the Khalkha Mongols, living in this hard and forbidding but wildly beautiful country, were well over 90 per cent illiterate in their own language, riddled with disease, especially syphilis and plague, and not more than 700,000 in number. They had no state apparatus worthy of the name, no national institutions except the Lama church, no trained officials, no fund of wealth except their herds. Their natural, pastoral–nomad economy, in which they fed, clothed and housed themselves with the products of their five traditional animals, had been disrupted by the impact of the world market operating through Chinese and to a lesser extent Russian traders towards the end of the nineteenth and the beginning of the twentieth century. The MPR in 1921 was a sort of half-administered and wholly undeveloped frontier region, much impoverished and damaged by the marching and countermarching of armed bands from Siberia and China. It existed in a political vacuum under the loose and arbitrary control of numerous territorial princes and nobles; and it was debarred from any fruitful contact with modern scientific or political thought by the institutionalized shamanism of the lama church, which held the economic and social life of the country in a picturesque but, in twentieth-century terms, hopeless paralysis.

Before the October Revolution occurred in Russia, the imperial tsarist government had for long been at grips with a Mongolian problem. In essence, the problem was to prevent Outer Mongolia becoming a danger to Siberia. There were many Russian merchants, orientalists and others who were keen for various reasons for Russians to get into Mongolia; but the principal interest of the Russian government was to keep the Chinese from colonizing it and garrisoning it in such a way as to pose a threat to Siberia and specifically to Irkutsk. One factor that seems to have had a sobering effect on tsarist officials was their realization that control over Outer Mongolia would not only be embarrassing internationally but also unprofitable economically.

The events that occurred in and around Mongolia between the October Revolution in 1917 and the Mongolian Revolution in 1921 brought about an apparently accidental and unthought-out change in Russia's attitude to the Mongolian problem. The Chinese in their weakness, failed to assert themselves effectively, and Outer Mongolia was simply swept up into the Russian civil war. In a sense it is possible to say that the Soviet Union, as heir to all the Russias, found itself landed with a country that Russia had not really wanted. Of course, with their usual genius for assimilating practical experience with ideology, Lenin and his colleagues and the Comintern soon managed to make it look as though they had a clear idea of Mongolia's requirements. But I think the truth is that they had not given much thought to anything quite like Mongolia before, and they did not at first have any firm formula for dealing with it. Here, as in other aspects of the revolution, improvisation was the decisive factor.

Economic development

At first, in the early years after the revolution, there was no serious economic development. The first priority was to hold the ground gained for the revolution. This was done by setting up a system of soviets as a foundation for what has come to be known as a regime of people's democracy. Even this elementary stage took four years to accomplish under the conditions that existed in

Mongolia. By mid-1920 the MPR had acquired the barest machinery of economic sovereignty – a customs service, a state bank and a national currency.

In 1924 at the third Congress of the Mongolian People's Party, which at that time became officially the Mongolian People's Revolutionary Party, a decision of fundamental importance for the country's future economic development was taken. It was formally decided that the MPR should follow a non-capitalist line of development, and that it should try to proceed straight to socialism from feudalism. I should perhaps say in parenthesis that this decision was a revolutionary one, recognized as such at the time and revered as such to the present day. It was reached with the help of much revolutionary violence.

Now, I do not think anyone knew what the formula about proceeding straight to socialism from feudalism meant in practical terms when it was agreed upon in 1924. Ideologically, Lenin and the Comintern could not be expected to tell the Mongols that what they really needed was a strong dose of capitalism, even if this were true. In practice, the Russians seem to have been more concerned about China than Mongolia. The Soviet government, like the tsarist government before it, has never wanted to have Mongolia as an irredentist issue between itself and China. The reason for this is simple. The ultimate fate of the revolution in China, and the possibilities of fruitful Sino–Soviet cooperation were, and are to this day, far more important than possession of Mongolia could ever be. It was therefore important to reach a position that would permit withdrawal of the Red Army from Mongolia, while at the same time keeping out the Chinese. Now the Chinese at that time were conveniently capitalist. Mongolia's revolutionary self-committal to the process of proceeding straight to socialism from feudalism provided, from the Soviet point of view, an ideal formula for dealing with them. It authorized the squeezing out and exclusion of all capitalists, namely of all Chinese, without any need to identify them in the national sense; and it tied Mongolia's fate firmly to that of the Soviet regime without making it necessary for the Soviet Union to offend in international law against Mongolian sovereignty.

What did the move straight from feudalism to socialism mean in practice to the Mongols? Unhappily, in the first place, it led straight to disaster. In the latter part of the 1920s and the begin-

ning of the 1930s the MPR tried rapidly and without any preliminary economic construction to confiscate the herds of the rich, set
up collective farms, abolish private trade, create a state trade monopoly and break the power of the church. By 1932 the country
was in an uproar with armed insurrection in many areas. This
could be put down only with Soviet help. The MPRP had to
change its line and did so by pinning responsibility for the disaster
on what they called a left-wing deviation, but without identifying
any prominent left-wing deviationists. No doubt the roughness of
the methods used was a reflection of the roughness of the methods
being used in forced collectivization in the Soviet Union by Stalin
and his colleagues; but both the policy and its failure were largely
determined by the specific conditions of Mongolia.

The failure of 1932 meant that the MPR was faced by a long
haul in order to reach the goal of socialism; and in the next two or
three years the first practical steps towards genuine economic
growth were taken in the country. In 1933, 1934 and 1935 the
MPR acquired its first modern industries in the shape of a wool-
washing plant at Khatgal and the basic workshops of an industrial
combine to process animal products and manufacture textiles and
footwear at Ulan Bator. The Ulan Bator power station was
founded at the same time and this was followed in 1937 by a
narrow-gauge railway – Mongolia's first railway line – to bring
coal to the power station from the mine at Nalaykha. All of this
was on a very small scale. In 1935 the total number of workers in
industry was just over 2000. Even this small-scale development
was completely dependent on Soviet aid. The Soviet Union was
having a first taste of the cost of the responsibilities it had undertaken in moving the frontier between things Russian and things
Chinese southwards to the Gobi desert.

It seems fairly clear that the Soviet Union had not at this time
prepared a blueprint for Mongolian development. Even if a blueprint had existed, it is doubtful whether the Soviet Union of the
1930s could have shouldered the burden of carrying it out. In any
case the activities of the Japanese in Manchukuo and China thrust
any question of economic development firmly into the background.

From January 1935 onwards the primary concern of the Soviet
and Mongolian governments was military. This state of affairs
lasted until September 1945, a period of ten years. In 1936 a

fraction under 50 per cent of all Mongolian state budget revenues were spent on defence. By 1938 over 50 per cent of all state budget revenues was being spent on defence. Obviously, a miserably poor state with defence expenditures of this sort had no reserves for economic development. It must be remembered too that this was the period of the great purges in the Soviet Union. The purges spread to the MPR also; and, in addition, the late 1930s saw the final destruction of the lama church in Mongolia and the total elimination of the 'black and yellow feudals'.

However, the MPR did derive some economic profit from these years. This took the form mostly of improved communications. The railway to Choybalsan (Solovyevsk to Bayan Tümen) was built between 1937 and 1939. Its construction, as I suggested earlier, was the key to the Khalkhin-Gol campaign. The roads to Ulan Bator and Choybalsan were built by 1941. During the war against Germany it was obviously impossible for the Soviet Union to do much for the MPR. On the contrary, it was the MPR that had to do what it could for the Soviet Union. But the Soviet Union helped with one or two small projects that could contribute to the Soviet war effort. It provided equipment for a meat processing plant at Ulan Bator and small dairy stations throughout the country.

There are two detailed aspects of Soviet aid dating back to about 1937 that deserve to be mentioned. The first is aid in the training of Mongolian cadres. In 1937 there were 859 Mongols studying in educational establishments of various sorts in the Soviet Union. In 1938 there were again more than 800. In 1939 there were 383 Mongols in higher educational establishments alone in the Soviet Union. In 1941, there were 451. And in that year the Mongolian State University was set up at Ulan Bator with extensive Soviet help, initially with three faculties – medicine, zoo technology and teacher training. This very important aid in the cadre sector seems to suggest that, towards the end of the 1930s, with the completion of the people's democratic stage of the transition to socialist society, the infrastructure for economic development was at last being prepared seriously. But the process of developing it was delayed by the war.

The second aspect of Soviet aid dating back to 1937 also points in the same direction. In 1937 and 1938, 24 machine hay-cutting stations were set up with a considerable quantity of Soviet machinery and Soviet specialists. This seems to have been the first attempt to tackle one of the fundamental and chronic weaknesses of Mongolian animal husbandry, the lack of winter fodder. Perhaps we can see in this a first attempt to construct before collectivizing, instead, as previously, of trying to collectivize before constructing. But the war cancelled any follow-up to the hay-cutting project that may have been intended.

I think we can now move straight on to 1948, the year of the first Mongolian five-year plan. But first I should like to say one more word about cadres. What I want to say is best illustrated by the career of Yumjagin Tsedenbal, now the General Secretary and Chairman of the Council of Ministers of the MPR. His curriculum vitae is as follows:

西藏西藏

Born in 1916 of a western Mongolian minority nationality, he went to school in a tent near Khovd and received higher education in economics (presumably in Moscow).

In 1931, at the age of 15, he entered the Revsomols, and began his career as a schoolteacher.

In 1939, aged 23, he joined the Communist Party and became Deputy Minister of Finance, being swiftly promoted to Minister of Finance and Chairman of the State Bank.

In 1940, at the age of 24, he became a member of the CC and immediately thereafter a member of the Politburo and General Secretary of the Party. Then, during the 1945 campaign against Japan, at the age of 29, he was a Lieutenant General, Deputy to the Commander in Chief and Chief of the political division of the army.

From the age of 30 he was Deputy Prime Minister and Chairman of the Planning Commission.

In 1952, at the age of 36, he became Chairman of the Council of Ministers.

He celebrated his fiftieth birthday last year (1966).

西藏西藏

This curriculum vitae is fairly typical. Tsedenbal belongs to the first generation that is 100 per cent revolutionary. It is important to bear in mind that the construction of socialism and economic growth would have been impossible without men like Tsedenbal and such men were not ready until the 1940s.

The MPR's first five-year plan covering the years 1948 to 1952 described its objectives in words that have appeared at the beginning of every subsequent five-year plan. It stated that the aim was comprehensive development of the country's productive capabilities on the basis of maximal use of internal resources. I imagine (but have not checked the point) that this is a formula hallowed by Soviet usage. Its use in the Mongolian context has a certain pathos and irony. The fact is that, because of the absolute lack of manpower reserves, the MPR was incapable of increasing significantly the exploitation of any of its natural resources in such a way as to permit a comprehensive rise in national output.

Nevertheless, the plan set fantastically high targets. The total head of cattle was to increase by half to 31 million animals. This was to be achieved by cutting hay to provide winter fodder, by digging wells to make larger areas of pasture available, by constructing cattle shelters and by improving veterinary work. There were to be relatively greater increases in camels and goats than in sheep and cows.

The detailed measures proposed show that the Mongolian leaders understood very well what was required to improve the country's animal husbandry. What is astonishing is their apparent belief that clear diagnosis of physical ills would lead naturally to overcoming them. The hard facts are that the MPR has never had 31 million animals and does not have them to this day; that by far the biggest increases both relative and absolute since 1948 have been in sheep and cows and not in goats and camels; and that every five-year plan from then until now has had to repeat the same lucid diagnosis of ills and shortcomings in the animal husbandry sector without ever being able to propound a sound programme for eliminating them. The extreme harshness of the natural conditions and the desperate shortage of labour made and still make it virtually impossible to achieve any serious advance in animal husbandry without heavy capital investment based on foreign aid.

Apart from animal husbandry, the first five-year plan called for a 97 per cent increase in gross output from industry. This high target is all the more extraordinary because little capital investment in new industry was promised. Even if the exploitation of the

MPR's internal resources could have reached an ideal maximum, the amount of capital that could have been accumulated for investment in new industry would have been small. In practice, nothing like a 97 per cent increase in output was achieved. Instead of reaching 370 million tugriks, gross industrial output reached only 190 millions. Here, as in animal husbandry, the means of giving a strong upward impulse to productive capacities were almost totally lacking.

In the second five-year plan, for the period 1953–57, the hard lessons of the first plan were shown to have been to some extent absorbed. The total cattle target was brought down to 27.5 million and gross industrial output was to increase by no more than 46 per cent. Once again the targets proved to be too high. The cattle figure of 27.5 million, like the earlier target of 31 million, has also never been reached even to the present day. But still, the lower figure was a move towards recognition of the realities of the immense difficulties facing the MPR.

The real impulse towards economic development in Mongolia was by now coming from a direction quite outside the Plan. Between 1947 and 1949 the Soviet Union built the railway from Naushki to Ulan Bator, initially as a Soviet–Mongolian joint stock company. In 1949 a joint stock company for mining non-ferrous and rare metals was set up – Sovmonogmetal.

In the same year the Soviet Union received a concession for oil extraction and refining and set up a Soviet trust, Mongolneft, which began production at Dzüünbayan in the following year.

Between 1948 and 1952 the industrial combine at Ulan Bator was partially reconstructed and enlarged with Soviet help; and electricity was introduced into the provinces for the first time with the setting up of small power stations in 13 *aimag* centres. But these developments were of small importance compared with the railway, the mining and the oil. The Soviet Union had at last reached a stage in its own development at which it could begin to take the development of Mongolia seriously. But at this time the Soviet aid was not very relevant to Mongolia's needs as indicated by the plan. It was more relevant to the Soviet Union's interests. These were, of course, the last years of Stalin.

To give perspective to the end of my story, I must emphasize at this point the odd paradox by which in the late 1940s and early 1950s economic expansion that was planned did not occur, while the economic expansion that occurred was not planned. The reason for the paradox is that the Mongolian plans really were, as claimed in their preambles, predicated on the maximal utilization of internal resources, and these (as I have already said) were almost non-existent. The Soviet Union was beginning to stir itself to help Mongolia with a little economic expansion, but Soviet economic policy does not seem to have been tied in at all with Mongolian planning or even with a broad Soviet plan of what Mongolia ought to be or to become. When, in December 1947, Tsedenbal delivered the report to the XIth Party Congress on the directives for the first five-year plan, he did not once mention the project that was to outclass all others in the five-year period, namely the building of the railway from Naushki to Ulan Bator. Yet the preliminary negotiations for the building of the railway must already have been in hand when Tsedenbal made his speech, and the railway was opened in 1949. This divorce between planning and reality has been characteristic of Mongolian economic development to the present day, although there has been much improved coordination between Mongolian planning and foreign aid since 1960, and more specifically since 1962, when Mongolia became a full member of the CMEA or Comecon. But it is important to grasp the fact that Mongolian planning starts, quite rightly, with animal husbandry, while foreign aid starts, quite inevitably, with industrialization; and the two have never yet met satisfactorily or, if they have met, it is only very recently, within the framework of the current fourth Five-Year Plan. I am therefore not contradicting myself if I speak of constant planning failures and constant economic advance. The contradiction is resolved by the fact that the important advance has never yet occurred in the area in which, from a strictly Mongolian point of view, it ought to occur, in animal husbandry.

After digressing into these generalizations I must return to the early 1950s. At this time the rise of the Chinese People's Republic, followed by the deaths of Choibalsan in Mongolia and Stalin in the Soviet Union, rapidly transformed the situation. In 1950 China set up a diplomatic mission at Ulan Bator, the second country after the Soviet Union to do so. In December 1952 an agreement for economic and cultural cooperation between the MPR and the CPR was concluded, and construction of the railway from Ulan Bator to Tsining was begun (opened in December 1955). China extended credits and gifts to the MPR to an eventual total of 465 million roubles. In 1965 an agreement was reached for the MPR to hire Chinese contract labour to help with the work of economic con-struction. China's influence began to be felt indirectly and directly. For example, China began to socialize its agriculture and build up industry with Soviet help. Even more importantly, the Chinese in 1954 and 1956 extracted vital concessions from Khrushchev and Mikoyan, for example over Port Arthur, over the relinquishment of the Soviet shares in joint stock companies, over credits and over the number of industrial construction projects. All these Chinese successes were rapidly reflected in Soviet–Mongolian relations.

From 1952 onwards the volume and variety of Soviet aid to the MPR grew very rapidly. It is impossible to list the detailed projects in this paper. The most important new developments were that the Soviet Union began to help with the task of making Ulan Bator a respectable and solid capital city instead of an agglomeration of felt tents; that in 1957 it completed the transfer to the MPR of all its own direct holdings in Mongolia and all its shares in the joint-stock companies, simultaneously wiping out the MPR's remaining indebtedness from similar transactions in the past; that it built numerous new factories in Ulan Bator and began to turn the town into a respectable little industrial centre with a sound fuel and power base; and finally that it began to give substantial aid for the first time to Mongolian farming. A Mongolian publication in praise of Soviet friendship claims that between 1948 and 1960 the Soviet Union extended to the MPR credits totalling 1400 million roubles; gave the MPR free of charge installations valued at 400 million roubles; and freed the MPR of debts totalling 110 million roubles – all this for a population of fewer than one million.

It must be remembered that, during all this time, the herds of Mongolia were un-collectivized. The MPR was a country of small, private owners. Under the second five-year plan efforts were made to move in the direction of collectivization, but in 1954, for example, only 15,400 people in the whole country, or 1.5 per cent of the population, belonged to cooperatives. The trouble was that the plan called for growth, while the gradual moves in the direction of collectivization discouraged growth. In the end, despite juggling with the animal husbandry tax and the system of compulsory deliveries of animal products, the MPR finished up with the worst of both worlds, very little growth and hardly any collectivization. And, of course, the absence of both meant that there was no significant accumulation of capital for investment in new productive resources.

At this point, a curious development took place, the significance of which is even now, I think, obscure. The background is as follows. Early in 1958 the Mongolian leaders inaugurated a full-scale collectivization drive. When progress proved still to be sluggish, there was a shake-up in the leadership that brought Tsedenbal back to the first Party secretaryship from which he had been removed after Stalin's death. This produced quick results.

By the end of 1959 collectivization was complete and the new collectives were sorted out into large units under new and strict model regulations. All this was normal. The curious development was that the Soviet Union began to pour economic and technical aid into the Mongolian countryside, but it was predominantly aid for a Virgin Lands campaign and not aid for animal husbandry. The situation was made even more curious by the fact that the primary aim was always stated to be the rapid advance of animal husbandry, and the new organs charged with using what turned out to be predominantly *agricultural* machinery were called *animal husbandry* machine stations. The operation might have fitted the nomenclature used if the main product of the Virgin Lands campaign had been animal fodder, but it was not. The main product was wheat, of which the Mongols are not big consumers. From the beginning of the 1960s the MPR became an exporter of wheat. The quantities involved are, in world market terms, very small, but the effort required to produce them is great. We have the odd spectacle of a country that is only marginally suitable for agriculture, and even then only for agriculture on the basis of irrigation, and that is desperately short of manpower even for the primitive sort of animal husbandry it has hitherto practised, putting capital investment into and therefore attracting manpower and other resources to the marginal agricultural activity and letting the main and fundamental activity of animal husbandry become the residual sufferer. And this just at the moment when the herds had been collectivized and were therefore ready, both theoretically and practically, for expansion and improvement under centralized control and scientific leadership.

One thing can be said with certainty – the Virgin Lands campaign was not a logical development of Mongolian planning. One wonders if it was perhaps chiefly due to Khrushchev's well-known liking for Virgin Lands campaigns, though this hardly seems a sufficient reason for so radical an innovation of doubtful economic value. Of course the Russians themselves have a long history of mismanagement of animal husbandry dating back to the days of collectivization. They are trained to measure farming primarily in terms of grain output. Also, the Soviet Union has been desperately short of grain, so much so that it may have been anxious to have even the MPR's marginal production to set off against, say, Cuba's marginal requirements. The one advantage I can see for the MPR in the virgin lands campaign is that it has facilitated the process settling the nomads and has provided a *raison d'être* for the great state farms that were formed in the northern river valleys in the late 1950s and. early 1960s. These farms provide a solid rural foundation for the MPR's future industrial heartland. If this is the real purpose behind the virgin lands campaign, we can only hope that the economic and agricultural bases of the campaign are better than I have been suggesting.

All this discussion of the virgin lands campaign has taken us away from the main theme. The collectivization drive and the start of the virgin lands campaign were catered for by a special three-year plan of their own from 1958 to 1960. The main series of five-year plans was resumed with the third five-year plan in 1961. We are now very near the present day, and the details of Mongolian economic development become complicated. I must therefore confine myself to a broad, summary presentation of them.

The essence of the third five-year plan was a bold, by conventional standards, perhaps foolhardy, programme of industrial development, backed by massive Soviet aid and small but politically important aid contributions from eastern Europe. The key project was the construction of the first stage of a completely new industrial town in the empty steppe at Darkhan; and this was successfully carried through by what can be described only as sheer Soviet determination and driving power. There are some 10,000 Soviet citizens working at Darkhan, many of them in construction battalions of the Soviet army The backbone of the project is a big new coal mine supplying the MPR's biggest power station, which feeds current into a grid running from Sükhbaatar to Ulan Bator. This axis from Sükhbaatar to Ulan Bator, served by the power grid, the road and the railway and within easy reach of the Trans-Siberian Railway, is to be the future industrial heartland of the country. You can see how it and the grain growing state farms will eventually knit together.

For the present however, building Darkhan creates rather than solves problems. Above all it diverts resources of every sort from what is supposed to be the key sector of the economy, animal husbandry. And, of course, it does so in addition to the diversions of resources caused by the virgin lands campaign, the growth of Ulan Bator and the provincial centres, and the rapid development of health, educational and other social and cultural services. If we recall the population statistics, it is obvious that there are not enough hands to do every urgent job. The job that is lagging worst of all is undoubtedly the one that is always said to be the most important – animal husbandry.

At this point it is perhaps fair to make two comments about Soviet development aid. First, it was very slow in materializing for the MPR. Second, when it did materialize, it did so on a relatively huge scale and it was apparently inspired by concepts that differ radically from those underlying modern Western aid to under-developed countries. The Soviet aim seems to be, not to develop the existing Mongolia, but to create a quite new Mongolia, a Mongolia that cannot possibly be viable for twenty years or more, a Mongolia that will be unable to survive during that time without heavy external help, but at the same time a Mongolia that in theory will be a remarkably vigorous concern when it is finally in a position to fend for itself.

Now, of course, I am assuming here that the Soviet Union has a clear concept and knows what it is doing. I used to be intrigued in Ulan Bator by the confidence with which the Chinese Ambassador and his staff used to indicate to me that the Soviet Union did *not* know what it was doing. The Chinese have taken some hard knocks and have dealt some shrewd blows in Mongolia in recent years. The key events are the cessation of transit traffic on the Trans-Mongolian Railway after 1960, and the departure of the Chinese contract workers, some 10,000 or so, in 1964. Both of these events seem to have grown out of the deepening Sino–Soviet quarrel, with neither side being wholly responsible for either of them. The cost to Mongolia of these happenings has been severe. You can judge this from the fact that a Soviet source estimates Mongolia's income from the railway to have constituted 9.6 per cent of the gross national product and 8.3 per cent of national income in 1959. As regards the contract workers, it must be remembered that about one-sixth of the national budget is spent on construction, and yet in 1964 the MPR was virtually without a building industry and had to improvise one in the most unfavourable circumstances imaginable. It may be that the Chinese are confident that the Soviet effort in Mongolia cannot be sustained in the teeth of all the adverse factors I mentioned earlier. They are patient people and may be prepared to wait a decade or so for the Soviet policy to crack and fail. But of course they, the Chinese, may underestimate their opponent, just as the Japanese underestimated him in the 1930s in the events leading up to the battle of Khalkhin-Gol. It is interesting to see that up to last year the Chinese were keeping up their aid programme to the MPR, sending about 4000 Chinese a year to do important construction jobs in Ulan Bator on the basis of the unexpired Chinese aid credits. They obviously attached importance to keeping a foot in the door, ungratefully though the Mongols treated them. It is too soon to know whether the 4000 Chinese will return to Ulan Bator to continue their work this spring.

The MPR stands now at the start of the second year of its fourth five-year plan. This new plan contains an interesting shift of emphasis compared with the last. My theme so far has been that the five-year plans have paid lip service to the primacy of animal husbandry without disposing of resources heavy enough to improve it, while external factors, working through the medium of foreign aid, have produced situations damaging to animal husbandry. This continued to be true in the third five-year plan from 1961 to 1965. The concentration of effort on Darkhan, on Ulan Bator and on harvesting grain in the state farms of the north diverted resources from animal husbandry; and animal husbandry, the key sector, stagnated. During the third five-year plan gross farm production increased by only 20 per cent, and most of this would have been in wheat, while gross industrial production increased by 65 per cent. Only 16 per cent of all capital expenditure went to the farms and again most of this must have gone into wheat growing, while some 30 per cent of total capital invested went to industry. Under the fourth five-year plan the farms are promised a bigger share of the country's resources. Indeed, farming is to receive more investment funds than industry (30 per cent of the whole). If this promise is properly implemented it should mark the beginning of a new deal for Mongolia's herds. As a sort of pledge of the seriousness of this new look, important quantities of Soviet aid funds have been earmarked for the farms, and specifically for animal husbandry. However, there is an insoluble problem of manpower to be overcome. There are between 100 and 200 animals per active herdsman or herdswoman in Mongolia. This sort of proportion obviously demands highly skilled, highly trained, highly mechanized farm hands. Such people simply will not be available in the MPR before the 1980s or 1990s.

I have not given you detailed up-to-date figures of aid, budget, investment values or production, though I can produce a full range of figures if required. More surprisingly, perhaps, I have not so far mentioned trade or the MPR's foreign trade balance and pattern. The fact is that the MPR conducts three-quarters of its trade with the Soviet Union and has a chronic trade deficit. Mongolian export earnings run at about 70 million roubles a year, which is less than annual receipts in foreign aid. In Mongolia's present circumstances trade is subordinate to aid. The trouble with Mongolia's export earnings is that they derive overwhelmingly from the sale of animal products, and the output of animal husbandry is, as we have seen, stagnant.

Perhaps I can finish by pointing out a series of paradoxes with which the study of Mongolia's economy presents us:

(1) a country whose economy is essentially pastoral has been lavishing resources on everything except its herds;
(2) China, the one country with the manpower resources to help solve Mongolia's crippling manpower shortage, is debarred from helping;
(3) the MPR has a highly-centralized planned economy, but foreign aid and not the Mongolian planners determine almost everything that happens in and to the economy;
(4) as a result of its support for Mongolian independence in 1921, the Soviet Union has assumed an unlimited obligation to pay the piper in Mongolia, but the Chinese People's Republic, by its mere presence, plays a big part in calling the tune;
(5) Mongolia, one of the smallest and most elementary economies in the world, has turned out to be one of the biggest open-ended commitments ever to be faced by an aid-giving country.

The existence of these paradoxes shows that there are enough variables in the Mongolian situation to guarantee an interesting future in central Asia.

The key to each of the paradoxes is, of course, political and I am not here today to talk about political matters. Internally, there have been several crises in the Mongolian Party in recent years and the turnover of leading cadres has been very high for a country so short of talent. I have little doubt that the internal political difficulties have their roots in the economic situation I have been describing. I hope that some of the considerations I have advanced about Mongolia's economic development will throw light on these and other fundamental political questions that are everyone's concern.

Index

2nd Hospital, 104, 105

Academy of Sciences, 191
Acland Hospital, 111
Adapazari, 9
Aeroflot, 5, 69, 75, 108, 132, 180, 210
Afghanistan/Afghan, 113, 162, 173
Africa, 92
Albania, 92, 159
Aleksandrov Red Army Song and Dance Ensemble, 28
Algiers, 100
Alonso, Alicia, 47
Altai, 124, 228, 231
Altai Mountains, 148, 228
Altangerel (electrician), 187
Amsterdam, 139
Amur River, 130
Andrasfi, Mrs, 145
Andropov, Y. V., 169
Angara River, 127, 184
Anglo-Mongolian Society, 226
Anning, Chadwick & Kiver, 150
Arakan coast, 167
Arctic Ocean, 83, 127, 184
Ariavalo temple, 80
Arkhangai *aimag*, 118, 124
Arkhangelski Sobor, 30
Army & Navy Stores, 63
Arvaikheer, 124, 193
Ashkhabad, 8

Astor, Bronwen, 52, 85, 95–6, 101, 108, 133, 177–8, 182–3, 185, 226
Astor, Viscount William Waldorf, 52, 85, 133, 177–8, 183, 185
Athens, 72
Australasia, 221
Australia, 43, 236
Auxiliary Territorial Service, 13, 31, 92
Aviemore, 7
Avimed, Dr, 194
Ayub Khan, Mohammad, 72, 227

Badarch, Mr, 104
Bahamas, 177
Baikal, Lake, 7, 9, 15, 56, 83, 119, 127, 129, 184, 224, 227, 235
Bangkok, 166, 168
Barcelona, 104
Barclay, Sir Roderick, 2
Barnaul, 234
Barry, Ron, 42, 94
Batsukh (chauffeur), 18, 20, 25, 41, 47, 59, 112, 147, 173, 180, 184, 189, 206
Bawden, Charles, 7
Bayan Ölgiy, 125, 234
Bayan Tümen, 240
Bayankhongor, 124
BEA, 54, 75, 133, 181
Beatles, 27, 42, 50, 133, 155
Beijing; *see under* Peking
Belgrade, 223

Beoch, 228
Berlin, 92
Bevin, Ernest, 222
Biisx, 234
Birmingham, 235
Black Country, 9
Blackheath, 4
Blake, George, 208
Blishen, Anthony, 140, 145, 147, 149–50, 152, 228
Blishen, Sarah, 140, 145–7, 149–50, 152–3
Bloomington, 220
Blues and Royals, 143, 144
Board of Trade, 165
Boer War, 173
Bogdo Gegen, 29, 36, 226
Bogdo Ula, 29, 75
Bogdo Uul Mountain, 90, 99, 130, 140, 153, 157, 188, 213
Bolland, Sir Edwin, 227
Bolsheviks, 226
Bolshoi, 8, 15
Bonn, 220, 228
Bora, Mr, 140, 228
Borzya, 227, 234
Bosphorous, 11
Botswana, 235
Bow, Jane, 193
Boxer Rising, 72
Boyd, John, 158, 228
Brezhnev, Leonid I., 168, 184, 229
Brighton, 7, 11, 73, 74, 139, 198
Brimelow, Jean, 10, 54, 102, 108, 132–3, 181
Brimelow, Thomas, 8, 10, 54, 74, 108, 132–3, 181, 223
Britain, 1, 100–1, 115, 129, 134–5, 146, 173, 180, 231, 235; see also England; UK
British Council, 134–5, 165, 229
Broad Lane, 20, 107, 132, 137–8, 153, 155, 181
Brooke case, 132

Brora, 42
Brussels, 2–4, 222–3, 229
Bucharest, 211
Buenos Aires, 227
Bulgan, 116–20, 122–3, 129, 148
Bulgaria(n), 26, 57, 62, 144, 159, 173
Buratiya, 7
Bureau for Servicing the Diplomatic Corps, 104, 203
Bureau for the Service of Foreign Travellers, 201
Burma, 167; Burmese, 76

Calcutta, 167
Cambodia, 113
Cambridge, 7, 219, 228
Canada, 236
Canterbury, 227
Canton, 166–8, 195
capitalism, 161, 168, 238
Caracas, 227
Carpine, Friar Giovanni Del Piano Di, 159
Carr, Henry, 12, 223
Carruthers, Douglas, 147, 228
Carter, Roland, 219
Castro, Fidel, 47
Caxton Hall, 4
Central *aimag*, 118
Central Committee, 48, 58, 104, 161, 169, 201
Central Pedagogical Institute, 229
Ceylon, 43, 45, 113
Chabbaria, Mrs, 140, 228
Chapman Andrews, Roy, 91
Charterhouse, 85, 111, 139, 154, 178, 182, 226
Chekhov, Anton, 15
Cheyne, Eric, 7–8, 10–11, 14, 17, 24, 27–8, 32, 34–7, 39, 42, 48, 50, 52, 57–8, 62, 64, 98–9, 110, 153, 188
Chiang Kai-shek, 1

Chicago, 133
Chiddingfold, 42
Chimiddorj, Mr, 135
China, 1, 9, 11, 13–16, 68, 72–3,
    130, 140, 144, 154, 159, 162,
    164, 166, 168–9, 202, 219, 222,
    224–5, 227, 232–5, 237–8, 240,
    245, 251; Chinese, 1, 5, 10–14,
    16, 23, 35, 44, 52, 56, 61, 64,
    68, 70–73, 76, 91, 101, 117,
    119–20, 142, 144, 147, 153,
    158–9, 166, 168, 173, 179,
    185, 196, 205, 219, 222, 224,
    226
Chingis Khan, 82, 225
Chita, 234
Choibalsan, Khorloin, 30, 102,
    211–12, 223, 225–6, 245
Chou En-lai, 72, 227
Choybalsan, 227, 234–5, 240
Churchill College, 228
Cliveden, 7, 41–2, 52, 82, 95–6,
    108, 178, 182, 185
CMEA, 244
collectivization, 224, 239,
    246–7
Commonwealth, 113, 166, 223
communism, 61, 87–8, 161–2,
    186
Conakry, 228
Conolly, Violet, 8, 223
Copenhagen, 5, 7, 60, 65, 177,
    181, 222, 228
Cotton, John, 182, 229
Coulson, Mr, 182
Council of Ministers, 100–1, 201,
    213, 227, 241–2
Cox & Kings, 50, 108, 133
CPSU, 202
Crowe, Ambassador, 89
CSCE, 229
Cuba/Cubans, 24, 27, 34, 44, 47,
    156, 175–6, 182, 247
Cultural Revolution, 227

Czechoslovakia, 42, 117, 135,
    156, 159, 179, 184; Czech(s), 5,
    26–7, 58, 189, 214, 229

Dalandzadgad, 148
Dambaravchaa (chauffeur), 173
Darkhan, 180, 182–5, 187–8, 213,
    248, 250
Darwall-Smith, Randle, 139, 228
de Gaulle, Charles, 208, 230
Delhi, 167
Denmark, 58
Deutsch–Mongolische
    Gesellschaft, 220
Devon, 66
Diplomatic Wives Association,
    229
Djakarta, 229
Dominican Republic, 87
Donald, Alan, 189–91, 193, 229
Donald, Janet, 189, 190–1, 193
Dügersüren, Mangalyn, 18, 223
Dügersüren, Tsagaanlamyn, 202
Dunsfold, 94, 102, 139, 173, 178,
    182, 183, 185
Dzamyn Ude, 13
Dzüünbayan, 243

Efremov, Comrade, 214
Eg River, 127, 128
Elephant & Castle, 133
Elliot, Anthony, 166, 228
England, 2, 45, 66, 94, 106, 112,
    118, 128, 140, 153, 168, 190,
    195; see also Britain; UK
Erdeni Dzu museum, 80, 83, 90,
    194
Erlien, 13
Everest, Mount, 166

Falkland Islands, 235
feudalism, 161, 238–9
First World War, 1, 224
Forbidden City, 10, 16, 68, 72

Foreign Office, 2, 5, 14, 17, 20, 27, 35–6, 41, 49, 51, 54, 63, 73, 75, 84, 92, 99, 102, 115, 134–5, 146, 149, 153, 156, 165, 175, 182, 188, 202, 206
Fort, Mrs, 78, 108, 227
Fortnum & Mason, 157
Fourth Hussars, 193
Furness, Lord, 44, 150, 154–7, 226

Gaidosh, Chargé d'Affaires, 136
Gandantegchinlen monastery, 80–1, 225
Garvey, Rosemary, 9, 12, 36, 49, 62, 66, 76, 78, 146
Garvey, Terence, 1, 3, 5, 9, 12, 35, 37, 43, 49–50, 52, 61–2, 68, 76, 78, 146, 154, 165, 222–3
German Democratic Republic (GDR), 92, 159; Germany, 12, 88, 91, 240
Ghana, 139
Glasgow, 162, 235
Gobi, 9, 29, 59, 68, 83, 89, 91, 95, 130, 145, 148–9, 151–2, 222, 232, 235, 239
Gobi Altai, 124
Godalming, 94
Godfrey Davis, 133, 182
Gogol, Nikolay, 161
Golders Green, 54
Gombojav, Damdini, 100, 101
Gombojav, High Lama, 80
Gonville & Caius, 192, 219
Graduate School of Uralic and Altaic Studies, 220
Great National Khural (Parliament), 42, 87, 102, 203, 225, 227
Great Paradise Valley, 212–13
Great People's Khural, 30, 100, 202–3, 224

Great Wall of China, 9–11, 15, 72, 73
Green, Mr, 150, 154
Gromyko, A. A., 169
Guatemala, 228
GUM, 54
Gurvan Saikhan Uul, 148

Hamburg, 228
Hampstead, 66, 94, 133, 173
Hampton, 41, 84–5, 108, 110, 132–3, 137–8, 153, 155–6, 165, 174, 177, 181–2, 219–20, 228
Harrison, Mr (housemaster), 139
Harrison, Sir Geoffrey, 132, 227
Haslund, Henning, 6, 158
Heath Mason, Robert, 182, 187–8, 192, 218, 229
Hedin, Sven, 6, 158
Heissig, Walther, 220
Helsinki, 134, 228
Hibbert, Alan, 74, 146
Hibbert, Ann, 52, 76, 141, 191, 193–4
Hibbert, Christopher, 134
Hibbert, George, 2, 4, 16, 27, 42, 46, 63, 73–5, 78, 82, 85, 90, 108, 111–12, 133, 139–40, 154, 156, 178, 182–3, 195, 228
Hibbert, Jane, 2–4, 16, 18, 27, 73–5, 78, 80, 85, 95, 108, 111, 132, 134, 139, 156, 178, 183, 192, 198
Hibbert, Margaret, 74
Hibbert, Mr and Mrs Alfred, 74, 95, 170
Hibbert, William, 2–4, 16, 27, 63, 73–4, 78, 85, 90, 108, 111, 114, 139–40, 154, 156, 168, 173, 178, 183, 195, 228
Hibbert family, 146
Himalayas, 167
Hitchens, Ivon, 132
Hitler Youth, 88

Holborn, 228
Holt, Vivien, 208
Holy Mountain, 66
Hong Kong, 12, 20, 26–8, 36,
    40–1, 50, 52, 60, 62, 64–6, 69,
    89, 93, 99, 135, 145, 150, 152,
    154, 166, 168, 177, 195, 209,
    228; Hong Kong Island, 166
Hong Kong New Territories, 166
Hopson, Danièle, 146, 148, 150–1
Hopson, Donald, 102, 140, 145–6,
    148, 150, 154, 156, 176, 187,
    189, 191–2, 216
Horse Guards, 144
Hotel Altai, 160
Household Cavalry, 143
Hungarian State Circus, 26
Hungary, 6, 140, 144, 159, 179,
    197; Hungarian(s), 26–7, 44, 50,
    58, 61, 67, 76, 79, 142, 144,
    146, 188, 196–7, 201, 209
Huth, Henry, 182

Ikh Uul, 120, 122–3
India, 33, 113
Indiana University, 220
Innocent IV, Pope, 6, 159
Institute of Pacific Relations,
    219
International Women's Day, 180
Intourist, 9, 14, 18
Inverness, 115
Iran, 113
Irkutsk, 5, 9, 15, 56, 69, 75, 78,
    91, 96, 112, 125, 133–4,
    136–8, 140, 181, 183, 185,
    234, 237
Irrawaddy, 168
Italy, 92

Japan, 113–14, 241; Japanese,
    87–8, 114, 162, 224, 227, 235,
    240, 249
Javkhlant, 124

John o'Groats, 1
John of Plano Carpini, Friar, 6
Johnson, Hewlett, 81, 227

Kadar, Janos, 140, 142, 144
Kalgan, 130
Karakorum, 25, 82, 87
Kazakh, 38, 125; Kazakhstan,
    229, 233
Kemp, Oliver, 218
Kerulen River, 130, 206
Kew Gardens, 86, 90, 190
Khalkhin-Gol, 88, 225, 227, 240,
    249
Khangai Mountains, 124, 126
Kharkhorin, 6, 80, 82, 84, 91,
    159, 189, 193
Kharkov, 13, 105–6
Khatgal, 124–7, 234, 239
Khentei range, 206
Khovd, 124, 241
Khövsgöl, 116, 122–3
Khövsgöl aimag, 120–1, 126
Khövsgöl, Lake, 115, 124, 127–8,
    234
Khrushchev, Nikita Sergeyevich,
    160, 245, 247
Khubilai Khan, 83
Khujirt, 83, 90, 135, 194
Khural of Workers' Deputies, 117,
    120, 122
Khutuktu, Jebtsun Damba, 224
King, Hilary, 156, 228
King, Margaret, 156
Kolman, Hela, 85, 156, 178, 188,
    191, 229
Kolman, Stane, 88, 144, 156,
    188
Korean war, 229
Kosh-Agach, 234
Kowloon, 166
Krasnoyarsk, 226
Kremlin, 8, 30–1, 54
Kyakhta, 224

Kyrgizstan, 229

La Paz, 97
lama church, 80, 16–2, 236, 240
lamaism, 36
Landreth, Mr, 141
Lattimore, Owen, 7, 10, 38, 219, 220
Lawrie, Mrs, 42
Leeds, 7, 101, 196, 219–21
Leeds University, 7, 101, 219, 229, 231
Lenin, Vladimir Ilyich, 30, 88, 90, 237–8, 224; Leninism, 140, 161
Leningrad, 26, 36
Leopoldville, 182, 185, 229
Lessing, Ferdinand D., 50
Liaotung, Gulf of, 234
Lincoln's Inn Fields, 146
Lindgren-Utsi, Dr Ethel John, 7, 38
Liu Shaoqi, 72, 227
Loire, River, 229
London, 1, 3–5, 7, 15, 23–7, 37, 41, 44, 47, 49–50, 52, 58–60, 74–6, 89, 94–6, 103, 108, 113, 115, 132–3, 135, 139, 146, 149–50, 152–4, 156–9, 165, 171, 174, 176–7, 181, 183, 187, 190–1, 195, 206, 210, 221
London University, 7
Lord, Mrs Oswald, 91
Lovell, Sir Bernard, 173
Luvsan, S., 213

McAdam, Douglas, 175, 188, 193, 198, 206, 229
McAdam, Susan, 175, 188, 193, 198, 206
McCarran, Pat, 219
McCarthy, Joseph, 219
Maclean, Fitzroy, 133
MacLehose, Murray, 165, 228
Malaga, 3

Malassis, Madame, 192
Malassis, Michèle, 179
Malassis, Monsieur, 179
Malaysia, 222
Malinovsky, Marshal, 169
Manchester, 54
Manchu, 29
Manchukuo, 240
Manchuria, 224, 226–7, 235
Manchus, 162
Mandalgov, 148, 152
Mao Tse-tung, 159, 219, 227
Marx, Karl, 88, 196
Masters, Father Bill, 134, 136–7, 140–1, 228
MBFR, 227
Medvei, Dr, 137
Menon, Mrs, 113
Mexico, 228
Middle Gobi, 148
Mikoyan, Anastas Ivanovich, 181, 245
Ming tombs, 10–12, 71–2
Ministry of Agriculture, 120
Ministry of Foreign Affairs, 18, 27, 29, 37–8, 40, 47, 57, 64, 75–6, 101, 104, 115–16, 121, 143, 145, 163, 171, 173, 175, 183, 189, 201, 203, 216
Ministry of Foreign Trade, 201
Molotov, Vyacheslav Mikhailovich, 160
Mongolian Airlines, 75, 91, 136
Mongolian National Day, 93, 109, 204
Mongolian People's Revolutionary Party, 100, 122, 161, 185, 189, 199, 202, 224, 227, 238
Mongolian Pioneer Corps, 88, 91
Mongolian Society, 221
Mongolian State University, 240
Mongolian Youth Theatre, 196
Mongolneft, 243
Montague Burton, 220

Morgan, Fionn, 158, 181
Morgan, John, 158, 181, 228
Mörön, 119–21, 123–4, 129
Moscow, 5, 7–8, 10, 15–16, 18,
    27, 30, 37, 41, 49, 54–5, 59–60,
    65–6, 69, 73, 75, 77, 85–7, 95,
    102–4, 108–9, 111, 132–4,
    136–7, 140, 149–50, 158, 161,
    169, 176–7, 180–1, 202,
    209–11, 216, 219, 222–5, 241
Moskva River, 8
Muirhead, David, 1, 2
Murray, Colonel, 20
Museum of the Living Buddha, 36

Naadam, 109, 211–12, 214
Nalaikh, 37
Nalaykha, 213, 239
Namsraidorj (escort), 148
Nassau, 177
Naushki, 234, 243–4
Nazi, 91
Needham, Joseph, 219
Nepal, 113
New Delhi, 166, 167, 222
New York, 28
New Zealand, 113
Nicholls, Sir John, 12
Nikolaev, Andriyan, 99
North Korea, 159, 225; North
    Korean(s), 44, 208, 210, 229
North Vietnam, 210; see also
    Vietnam
Novosibirsk, 55, 181
Nukht, 140

October Revolution, 18, 153–5,
    237
OCTU, 92
Omak, 5, 132
Omsk, 8, 55, 69, 78, 85, 181
Onon River, 130
Orkhon River, 83, 117, 119,
    184

Ossendowski, Ferdinand, 226
Ostermann-Petersen, 5, 41
Övörkhangai, 91, 124, 193
Oxford, 14, 20, 94, 111, 220, 222

Pacific, 219, 221
Pakistan, 113, 227
Pamirs, 231
Paris, 70, 206, 230
Pasternak, Boris, 24
Patricia (Jane's friend), 139
Peace Street, 21, 29, 59, 176, 219
Pearl River, 167, 168
Pedagogical Institute, 22, 205
Pei-hai, 72
Peking, 2–5, 8–12, 14–15, 25–6,
    28, 35, 37, 41, 49–50, 52, 58,
    62, 65–74, 76, 78, 89, 96–7,
    103–4, 109, 135, 140–1, 151,
    154, 158–9, 166–8, 176, 189,
    191, 193, 195, 206, 209–11,
    216, 219, 222–3, 229–30
Peninsula Hotel, 166
Perruche, Monsieur, 206, 229
Philip, Prince, 89
Philippines, 139
Piccadilly Circus, 88
Pilgrims Lane, 8, 50, 95, 96
Planning Commission, 242
Poland, 12, 159, 184; Poles, 26–7,
    54, 58; Polish, 12, 44, 142,
    144–5, 147, 160, 184
Politburo, 58, 225
Port Arthur, 245
Prague, 173, 183, 189, 192–3,
    211
Pride, John, 187, 191, 220, 229
Prince of Wales's Company, 227
Pugh, Gwyneth, 42, 72, 75, 94,
    96, 102, 139, 185
Pugh, Lady, 3, 53, 71, 73–5, 78,
    85, 107, 138, 156
Pugh, Sir Alun, 71, 74–5, 94–5,
    102, 108, 178, 226–7

Purev, Dologrin, 14, 115, 119–20, 122, 125–9

Queen's Messengers, 4, 16, 20, 25, 27–8, 36, 43, 48, 50, 52, 58–9, 61, 65, 73–5, 78, 89, 110, 113, 115, 134–5, 153–4, 167, 182, 196, 205, 209, 211

Rangecroft, Mr and Mrs, 188, 198
Rangoon, 76, 166, 168
Red Army, 1, 88, 122, 236, 238
Reform Club, 25, 48
Rennes, 179, 192
Revsomols, 224, 241
Richer, Paul, 187, 229
Rio de Janeiro, 227
Roedean, 78, 85, 139, 227, 228
Romania, 159; Romanian, 61, 152
Rome, 72, 167
Ross, Stewart, 12, 223
Royal Free Hospital, 137
Rumeli Hisar, 11
Russia, 88, 237; see also Soviet Union; USSR
Russo–Japanese war, 162

Sahara, 171
Saigon, 228
Saikhan somon, 118
St Antony's College (Oxford), 156
St Ermin's Hotel, 4, 132–3, 177, 182
St Francis of Assisi, 6, 159
St Louis of France, 6, 159
St Wilfrid's, 85, 154, 228
Samarkand, 133
Sambu, Jamsrangiin, 30, 212, 225, 227
Sangino, 150
Saunderites, 111, 139
Sayan Mountains, 15
Scandinavia, 109
Schouten, Ronny, 145

Scotland, 1
Scott Polar Research Institute, 7
Seaford, 7, 11, 73, 228
Second World War, 224
Selbe River, 212
Selenge aimag, 118
Selenge River, 119–21, 123, 127, 129, 184
Selfridges, 66
Seoul, 228
Shakespeare, William, 24, 170, 196
Shamanism, 7, 36, 161
Sharin Gol, 43, 184
Shelepin, A. N., 58, 169, 203
Sheremetyevo, 7
Sherlock, Professor Sheila, 137
Siberia, 9, 15, 55, 130, 226, 233, 237
Singapore, 43, 220
Smith, Mr and Mrs Harold, 96–8, 148
socialism, 18, 92, 127, 161, 189, 203, 224, 238–9, 242
Sodnomdorji, Mr, 136, 142
Sofia, 227
Solovyev, Leonid Nicolaevich, 180, 181, 223
Solovyevsk, 240
Somme, 227
Sosorbaram, Deputy Foreign Minister, 188
South Gobi, 147, 148
South West Africa, 235
Soviet Buryatia, 234
Soviet Union, 1, 7, 9–10, 12–14, 18, 24, 28, 30, 34, 42, 47, 49, 54, 57–8, 64, 87–8, 91, 99, 101, 107, 114, 116, 118, 122–7, 130, 137, 145, 155–6, 159–60, 162–4, 169, 173, 179–84, 186, 189, 196, 201, 203, 210–11, 213–14, 216–17, 219, 223–4, 227, 234–5, 237, 239–40,

243–7, 249–51; see also Russia; USSR
Spain, 3, 27, 145
Speaight, Richard, 135
Stalin, Joseph, 159, 225, 239, 244–6; Stalinist, 159
State Bank, 25, 144, 189, 241
State Meteorological Service, 214
Stenning, Miss (Aunt M), 141, 228
Stewart, Brian, 5, 222
Stockholm, 7, 8, 134, 156, 158
Sudets, Marshal, 169
Sukhbaatar, 126, 127
Sükhbaatar, 183, 184, 226, 248
Sükhbaatar, Damdin, 29, 30, 87, 91, 102, 211, 223
Sükhbaatar Square, 29, 45, 160, 189, 213
Sükhbaatar Way Farm, 37, 179
Summer Palace, 72
Sverdlovsk, 9
Switzerland, 56, 62, 114
Sylvester, Victor, 26

Tallinn, 41
Tamsag Bulag, 227, 235
Taplow, 183, 185
Tashkent, 8
Tass, 190
Tehran, 227
Tel Aviv, 229
Temple of Heaven, 72
Terelj, 135, 171
Tereshkova, Valentina, 99
Thailand, 113
Thomas, Vice-Consul, 181
Thompson, Alex, 99, 102–3, 109, 135–6, 144–6, 150, 152–5, 158, 177, 179, 183, 188, 191, 197–8, 205, 209
Thompson, Grace, 99, 103, 109, 135–6, 145–6, 150, 152–5, 157, 179, 188, 191, 197–8, 205, 209
Thorez, Maurice, 8

Thresher & Glenny, 51
Tibet Society, 226
Tien Shan, 231
Tientsin, 12, 41
Titoists, 144
Tokyo, 69, 223, 228
Tolgoyt, 213
Topolski, Feliks, 192
Torgut Mongols, 124
Transbaikalia, 162, 226–7, 234
Trans-Mongolian Railway, 234, 249
Trans-Siberian Railway, 5, 95, 227, 234, 248
Trucial States, 235
Tsaatan, 127
Tsedenbal, Yumjagin, 27, 31, 32, 48, 91, 92, 147, 168, 169, 185, 201, 202, 212, 214, 217, 223, 225, 241, 242, 244, 246
Tserentsoodol, Mr, 175, 183
Tsetserleg, 25, 124
Tsining, 13, 245
Tul River, 56, 77, 83, 117, 129, 210
Turda, 234
Turkey, 2, 11, 30, 56, 102; Turks, 173
Turksib railway, 234
Turta, 125, 126
Tuul River, 212, 214
Tuvin, 125
Twiss, Cherry, 211

UK, 1, 24, 50, 59, 113, 163, 199, 219, 221–2, 226; see also Britain; England
Ukraine Hotel, 10
Ulan Bator, 1, 3–10, 12–16, 18, 20–2, 25–6, 28–9, 32–3, 35, 37, 40–2, 46, 49, 53, 56, 59, 62, 64, 67–73, 75, 77–8, 82–6, 89–90, 97–101, 106, 108, 111, 115–17, 119, 124, 126–7, 129–30, 132,

134–7, 140–1, 145, 149–50,
152–4, 156–60, 162–6, 168–71,
176–7, 179–80, 183–8, 190,
193, 195, 199–201, 204–7,
211–13, 216, 218–19, 222–3,
225, 228–9, 232–5, 239–40,
243–5, 248–50
Ulan Bator Hotel, 5, 216
Ulan Ude, 234
Ulus, 9
United Nations, 1, 28, 113
United States, 1, 133, 219, 220
Universal Aunts, 73
Urals, 9
Urga, 6, 36, 224, 226
Urx, Mrs, 188, 229
US Air Force, 168
USSR, 183; see also Russia; Soviet
    Union
Uzbekistan, 8

Valley of the Kings, 12
Van Oss, Oliver, 42, 139, 226
Victoria, 4
Vienna, 227, 228
Viet Cong, 179
Vietnam, 63, 81, 87, 179, 196; see
    also North Vietnam
virgin lands campaign, 246–8
von Sternberg, Baron Ungern, 226
Voronov, G., 169

Walker, Gordon, 18
Warsaw, 211, 223, 228
Washington, 1
Watson (William's schoolfriend),
    139

Welsh Guards, 227
West, Mr, 135
Western Hills, 72
Western Samoa, 113
Westminster, 132, 183
Westminster Abbey, 133
Whitehall, 183, 220
Wildlife Preservation Trust, 89
Wilford, Joan, 10, 12
Wilford, Michael, 9, 10, 154, 223
Willerding, Herr, 92
William of Rubruck (Willem van
    Ruysbroeck), 6, 159, 230
Wilson, Harold, 174, 188
Windsor, 92
Wood, Agnes, 132, 181
Worcester College, 5

Yellow River, 130
Yenisei River, 83, 127, 129, 184,
    226
Yondon, Mr, 91
Yorkshire, 220
Young Farmers' Club, 140
Yugoslav(s), 28, 42, 57, 58, 85,
    86, 88, 95, 144, 229
Yugoslavia, 43

Zavkhan, 124
Zavkhan aimag, 126
Zhukov, Marshal Georgi, 225
Zhuulchin (Mongolian travel
    agency), 14, 18, 91, 95
Zogsood (chambermaid), 40, 90,
    142, 150, 173, 180, 189, 191,
    197, 216